# GLOBAL GOVERNANCE
# and INTERNATIONAL LAW

—Some Global and Regional Issues—

revised edition

# GLOBAL GOVERNANCE and INTERNATIONAL LAW

## Some Global and Regional Issues

Boo Chan Kim

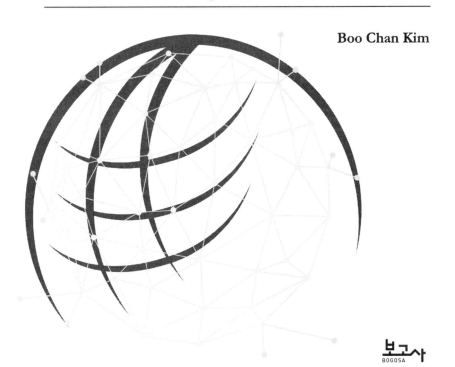

보고사
BOGOSA

# PREFACE

## (of the revised edition)

Both international society and international law have constantly evolved and have undergone vital changes from their inception. The evolution of international law responds to changing conditions and needs in international society. Therefore the structure of international law has changed in order to respond to changing structure of international society. From the beginning up to now, international society has been transformed into international community as a whole which is consisted of not only states but also diverse non-state entities including individuals.

Nowadays, states and non-state entities such as IGOs, NGOs and individuals are expected to move to active collaboration and cooperation on the global basis. We know that the once homogeneous community of states, whose sovereignty lay at the very heart of the system, has given way to a much wider community of diverse actors and interests. In the legal perspective, international community means an international legal community. It is evident that international law has performed crucial role in the formation and evolution of international legal community.

To review the changing structure and paradigm shift in international law, some problematic issues such as reconceptualization of sovereignty, the international rule of law, the humanization of international law, the constitutionalisation of international law, and strengthening of global governance, are to be examined in general. It is admitted that the new paradigm of international law such as community–based approach or human–centred paradigm is needed for international legal scholarship to explain the changing structure of international law and promote the newly needed community interests and values in the international legal system.

It is admitted that the need and justification for paradigm shift lies in that we are no longer justified or satisfied in explaining the structures and theories of international law in view of older traditional paradigm based on Westphalian system. Indeed, there have been persistent competitions between the older paradigm and the newer paradigm. As of now, the shift from the older paradigm to the newer paradigm is not at all full–fledged, so the successful process of paradigm shift in international law remains to be seen.

Therefore, it is urgent for the international legal scholars to reform the structure of international law and develop new paradigm in international law in order to respond to the need of the international community.

After the publication of *Global Governance and International Law*(the first edition), I visited Soka University Law School in Japan as a Visiting Professor and once again Cornell University Law School as a Visiting Scholar in 2017 to study and make special lectures on international rule of law and global governance. And after the first edition, I have published two Articles in English, one of them is "Protection of the Sea Lanes in the Jeju Waters and the Maritime Cooperation in Northeast Asia(co-authered by Prof. Seokoo Lee, Professor at Inha University Law School) in *Navigating Straits: Challenges for International Law*(David D. Caron and Nilufer Oral eds., Brill/Nijhoff, 2014)" and the other is "The Changing Structure and Paradigm Shift in International Law" in *The Korean Journal of International Law*(Vol.63, No.4, 2018). The revised edition of this book contains the two Articles mentioned above and partly modified and supplemented some of the remaining Chapters. Especially, I would like to thank Prof. Lee, co-author and Publishers Brill/Nijhoff for the permission to reprint the Article mentioned above.

I will retire from Jeju National University(JNU) Law School at the end of this coming August. Therefore, this book is very meaningful in celebration of my retirement. I'm deeply grateful to JNU and JNU Law School which I have served for about 35 years and also to Bogosabooks for the publication of this revised edition. And, I thank Dr. Song, Seo Soon for her assistance. Lastly, I would like to express my deep thanks and indebtedness to my lovely family, wife Won Bok, and two sons, Jae Seok and Yoon Seok.

*Boo Chan Kim*

in August 2020

# PREFACE

(of the first edition)

These days, political, social, and economic processes operate predominantly at a global level, and the international society has been transformed into world community due to processes of globalization. Globalization requires global governance. As the 'Commission on Global Governance' put it in *Our Global Neighborhood*: "Governance is the sum of the many ways individual and institutions, public and private, manage their common affairs. It is a continuing process through which conflict or diverse interests may be accommodated and cooperative action may be taken."

At the global level, governance has been viewed primarily as intergovernmental relationships focusing on the acts of States and intergovernmental organizations(IGOs), but it must now be understood as also involving non-governmental organizations (NGOs), and other actors of civil society. For the promotion of international peace and security, global common welfare, and human rights, there must be an agreed global framework for actions and policies to be carried out at global level. A effective strategy for global governance is therefore required.

We should strive to subject the rule of arbitrary power—conomic, political, or military to the rule of law within global society. During the 20th century, international society had been undergoing a thorough change, which results in a need for a new world order, establishing liberal and democratic systems and great concern for the international rule of law for global governance. The establishment of global governance on the basis of the international rule of law is recognized to be absolutely necessary, both to ensure the protection of human rights and to promote the common values and welfare in world community.

Since I began to research and teach courses on International Law and Legal Philosophy at Jeju National University in 1985, I had opportunity twice to visit USA as a Visiting Scholar; first at Washington University in St. Louis(Wash U) Law School from 1996 to 1997 and next time at Cornell University Law School in 2005. Then, the subject matter of my research is as to connection between the General Theory of International Law and the Philosophy of Law, that is "the Reinforcement of International Rule of Law for Global Governance."

After I returned from Wash U, I visited Budapest, Hungary in 1999 to present the paper, "the International Rule of Law and the UN Reform" at the 19th Biennial Conference hosted by the World Jurist Association(WJA), and visited Oslo, Norway in 2000 to present the paper, "The Evolution of Concept of Global Governance and Institutions Up to the End of the 20th Century ― focusing on the Role and Reform of the UN ―" at the 13th Annual Conference of the Academic Council on the UN System (ACUNS).

I wrote several papers in English on "Global Governance and

International Law": the first is "New Trends in International Law and the Common Heritage of Mankind in *the Korean Journal of International Law*(Vol.40, No.1, 1995) published by the Korean Society of International Law, and after returning from Wash U, I wrote: "The United Nations and the International Rule of Law" in *the Korean Yearbook of International Law*(Vol.1, 1997) published by International Law Association(ILA) Korean Branch; "The System for Dispute Settlement in the Law of the Sea and Korean Perspective" in *the Korean Yearbook of International Law*(Vol.2, 1998); "Global Governance and the International Rule of Law in *the Korean Journal of International Law*(Vol.45, No.2, 2000); "Global Governance and International Non–Governmental Organizations" in *the Korean International Law Review*(Vol.20, 2004) published by the Korean International Law Review Association.

After returning from Cornell University, successively I wrote the paper, "The International Rule of Law and Universal Jurisdiction" with Prof. Seung Jin Oh(then, JSD Candidate at Cornell Univ. Law School) in *the Korean Journal of International Law* (Vol.51, No.1, 2006), and "Political Rights of Koreans in Japan at a Local Level" in *International Legal Issues in Korea–Japan Relations* published by the Northeast Asian History Foundation in 2008.

Fortunately, this time, I has an opportunity to revise and combine the papers as mentioned above into one Volume, *Global Governance and International Law — Some Global and Regional*

*Issues* — under the auspices of Jeju National University(JNU) Law School. This book doesn't have a comprehensive but limited contents and scope of the issue relating to global governance and international law because it is based on the contents of the papers mentioned above.

Relating to the publication of this book, first, I'd like to give thanks to JNU Law School for its financial support and my colleague Professors and Staffs for their great concern. I also owe a profound debt to Bogosabooks for making this book possible. Further, I specially thank Dr. Song, Seo Soon for her much assistance, and lastly I wish to express my deep indebtedness to my lovely family.

*Boo Chan Kim*
In February, 2011

# Contents

## CHAPTER 1

Introduction: the Significance of Global Governance

## CHAPTER 2

Global Governance and the International Rule of Law

# CHAPTER 3

## Global Governance and Paradigm Shift in International Law

# CHAPTER 4

## Global Governance and the United Nations

# CHAPTER 5

## Global Governance and Non-Governmental Organizations

# CHAPTER 6

## Global Governance and  Universal Jurisdiction

# CHAPTER 7

## Global Governance and the Common Heritage of Mankind

# CHAPTER 8

## Global Governance and the Dispute Settlement System

# CHAPTER 9

## Global Governance and  Human Rights

# CHAPTER 10

## Global Governance and  Maritime Cooperation

# CHAPTER 1

# Introduction:
# the Significance of Global Governance

## I. Introduction

For a long time many philosophers, jurists, and statesmen have persistently advocated and searched for the rule of law in the society of States.[1] Nowadays, the argument that States may be bound by the rules of international law to which they have not consented is increasingly supported by the radical changes in international system that were made in response to the promotion of common values and welfare.

From the creation of the United Nations(UN) after the Second World War to the present, multilateralism[2] has gained credibility,

---

1 William L. Tung, *International Law in an Organizing World*(Thomas Y. Crowell Company, 1968), p.xi.

2 Multilateralism involves policy coordination through the development of persistent and connected sets of rules, formal and informal, that prescribe behavioral roles, constrain activity, and shape expectations among three or more States with respect to an issue or issue area. See

which is founded on international dialogue, mutual tolerance and respect, consensus building, accommodation of interests and values, and mutual understanding. Multilateralism has become increasingly more acceptable to not only States and inter—governmental organizations(IGOs), but also non—State actors such as non—governmental organizations(NGOs),[3] which have a growing influence on the international stage.[4] The post—Cold War era was

A. LeRoy Bennett & James K. Oliver, *International Organizations — Principles and Issues —*, 7th ed.(Prentice Hall, 2002), p.16.

3  Cambridge University's professor D. W. Bowett advocated the traditional paradigm of organizational classification by using a 'functional' approach. International organizations thereby (1) are public or private, (2) are administrative or political, (3) are global or regional, and (4) possess or do not possess supranational power. The initial public versus private distinction refers to the establishment of 'public' organizations by a group of States. States often enter into written treaties to inaugurate international trade or communications associations which then implement the joint decisions of the State representatives. Private international organizations are typically established by non—State entities(individuals or corporations) relying on non—governmental representatives to execute the mission of the particular organization — hence, the term 'Non—Governmental Organization' or 'NGO.' This latter type of international organization is not created by a treaty between sovereign States. And UN Economic and Social Council(ECOSOC) Resolution 288(x) of 1950 provided that every "international organization that is not created by means of international governmental agreements(treaties) shall be considered as a non—governmental international organization." IGO thus refers to international governmental organization, while INGO refers to an international non—governmental organization. See William R. Slomanson, *Fundamental Perspectives on International Law*, 3rd. ed. (Wadsworth/Thomson Learning, 2000), pp.115—116. Hereinafter I would like to use 'INGOs' together with 'NGOs' in the sense of international organizations.

4  Mihaly Simai, *The Future of Global Governance*(United States Institute of Peace Press, 1994), p.xi.

heralded by expectations for a new world order relying on multilateralism, international law, and international organizations.

And new issues and changes towards more democratic and free international society have occurred since the end of the Cold War. These issues no longer divide easily into security or economic and environmental issues, domestic or international issues, public or private sector issues; rather they are, in both theory and practice, multifaceted including elements of areas once thought to be independent of each other.

A broad, dynamic complex process of interactive decision-making that is constantly evolving and responding to changing circumstances develops rapidly at the international level. It must build partnerships that enable global actors to pool information, knowledge, and capacities and to develop joint policies and practices on issues of common concern.

A new language or term has now emerged to address today's issues and interactions like 'globalization,' 'global governance,' 'global civil society,' 'transnational civil society' or 'world (global) community.'[5] These terms describe a global arena in which individuals and organizations other than sovereign States come together and engage in activities separate from those pursued by

---

5  Charlotte Ku and Thomas G. Weiss eds., *Toward Understanding Global Governance, Academic Council on the United Nations(ACUNS) Reports and Papers, 1998 No.2*(ACUNS, 1998), p, ix; Akira Iriye, *Global Community — The Role of International Organizations in the Making of the Contemporary World*(University of California Press, 2002), p.7.

national governments. That is why terms such as 'global civil society' and 'transnational civil society' have gained in popularity.[6]

The rule of law has been the ethical cornerstone of every society; respect for it is at least as essential to the global neighbourhood as to the national one. Global governance without law would be a contradiction in terms. Its primacy is a precondition of effective global governance.[7] Therefore, global governance and the international rule of law[8] should be regarded as a basic principle of law and politics in global civil society or world community[9] is no different in most respects than domestic civil society, because a society controlled by human persons desires a system of predetermined generalized rules of behavior

---

6 Akira Iriye, *ibid.*; As for the origins of global community, see *ibid.*, pp.9–36.

7 The Commission on Global Governance, *Our Global Neighborhood*(Oxford University Press, 1995), p.67.

8 The international rule of law means the rule of law in international society or affairs. Hereinafter, I use the term, 'international rule of law,' as equivalent to 'the rule of law in international society.' See Arthur Larson, *The International Rule of Law*(Institute for International Order, 1961), p.3; Hans Köchler, *Democracy and the International Rule of Law* (Springer–Verlag, 1995).

9 Many claim that the very term 'community' denotes something more than 'society,' and indicates a more closely knit group. Peaceful, friendly relations characteristic of a 'community' are lacking in many areas of the world and it may therefore be more appropriate to speak of an international 'society,' saving the word 'community' for the unrealistic optimists who shut their eyes to reality. Such semantic arguments may be exaggerated and in the common language of international lawyers the term 'society' and 'community' may be synonymous. See Ingrid Detter De Lupis, *The Concept of International Law*(Norstedts Verlag, 1987), p.35.

upon which its subjects can rely in their every day affairs.[10]

The establishment of the international rule of law and global governance is recognized to be absolutely necessary, both to ensure the protection of human rights and provide a firm basis for international peace, as well as economic and social co-operation. International organizations, both governmental and non-governmental, continued to grow in number and scope during the last two decades towards global civil society. The study of international organizations, therefore, may be viewed as one way of examining the phenomenon known as globalization and global governance.

In this study, I would like to begin with an attempt to make clear the concept of global governance and review the relations between global governance and the international rule of law, and continue to review the way in which their role can be promoted in global civil society, specially relating the actors for global governance, equitable distribution of natural resources, strengthening of dispute settlement system, protection of human rights.

It is admitted that although the role of non-governmental actors should not be underestimated in the 21st century, the United Nations among the international organizations must continue to play a central role in global governance or global civil society. With its universality, it is the only forum where the

---

10  Jonathan I. Charney, "The Role of IGOs in Global Governance," Charlotte Ku and Thomas G. Weiss eds., *op. cit.*, pp.55–56.

governments of the world come together on an equal footing and on a regular basis to try to resolve the world's most pressing problems.

But it is also true that over the years, the intergovernmental organizations(IGOs) including the UN and non-governmental organizations including both international NGOs and domestic NGOs have made vital contributions together to international communications and cooperation in a variety of areas including international peace and security, and human rights, especially after the Cold War era. They continue to provide a framework for collaboration that is indispensable for global progress and governance.[11]

# II. The Concept of Global Governance

## 1. Globalization and Global Governance

These days, social and economic processes operate predominantly at a global level, and the world is changing due to process of globalization.[12] Globalization can be defined as the

---

11   The Commission on Global Governance, *op. cit.,* pp.2-6.

12   The term 'globalization' has been used primarily to describe some key aspects of the recent transformation of world economic activity. But several other aspects and activities have also been globalized. See The Commission on Global Governance, *op. cit.,* p.10; But, indeed the concept of 'globalization' has generated a huge, intensively contested, and

"denationalization of the clusters of political, economic, and social activities" that undermine the ability of the sovereign State to control activities on its territory, due to the growing need to find solutions for global problems on an international level.[13] Globalization is being facilitated by the end of Cold War and the decline of communism, the integration of world markets, the advent of multinational corporations and the revolutionary development of information technology.[14]

The processes of globalization have required more negotiations and decisions among States that affect domestic policy and legislation.[15] By globalization, the world has become more integrated. The human rights violations in a country caused by

---

unresolved definition debate among students, observers, and practitioners of world affairs. See A. LeRoy Bennett & James K. Oliver, *op. cit.*, p.13.

13 Karsten Nowrot, "Legal Consequences of Globalization: The Status of Non-Government Organizations under International Law," *Indiana Journal of Global Legal Studies*, Vol.6, Spring, 1999, p.586.

14 Herbert V. Morais, "The Globalization of Human Rights law and the Role of International Financial Institutions in Promoting Human Right," *George Washington Int'l Law Review(A Festschrift Honoring Professor Louis B. Sohn)*, Vol.33, 2000, pp.71, 77. But, there is other view that "system of large-scale international trade and co-operation can be traced back many centuries, beginning in Europe and Asia and extending to Africa and New World. Global governance, however, with its treaties and other formal arrangements among governments can be said to have begun in 1814 with Congress of Vienna, which sought to stabilize Europe in the post-Napoleonic period, with a balance among the great powers."(Joseph A. Camilleri *et al.*, *Reimagining the Future: towards democratic governance*(the Department of Politics, La Trobe University, 2000), p.1.

15 K. Nowrot, *op. cit.*, p.589.

internal conflicts such as civil wars can affect directly to the international community. States actively interact with each other in an international system. They have sufficient impact on their decisions to act as parts of a whole community. Sovereign States now lie at the intersection of a vast array of international regimes and organizations that have been established to manage whole areas of transnational activity and collective policy problems.[16]

Since the 1980s, the concept of governance has increasingly been employed to describe policy-making in the national, regional, and global arenas. But, definitions and uses of governance are as varied as the issues and levels of analysis to the concept is applied. As the concept of governance has increasingly been used for the analysis of not only national but also regional and global policy-making, its range of meanings has also expanded.[17] The application of the term governance to the global level has particularly increased since the early 1990s.

---

[16] David Held, "Democracy and Globalization," *Global Governance*, Vol.3, No.3, 1997, pp.252-253.

[17] Elke Krahmann, "National, Regional, and Global Governance: One Phenomenon or Many?" *Global Governance*, Vol.9, No.3, 2003, pp.323-324; As governments of sovereign States have recognized the limitations to their resources and capabilities in dealing with global issues, globalization has also contributed to the formation of networks among governments, international organizations, and nongovernmental organizations(NGOs) that engage in global governance. Thus, like national and regional governance, the rise of global governance arrangements seems to have been fostered in part by the processes of globalization and in part by national governments themselves through their adoption of neoliberal ideas that have encouraged greater use of private actors. See *ibid.*, p.330.

The more globalization expands, the more the necessity for governance at global level is necessary. Governance at global level is called 'global governance.' Global governance is political and legal management at the global level of a given area of human existence in the absence of global (world) government.[18] It is just a 'global governance' because there is no World State that can impose its rules and values on sovereign States.

Now, the concept of global governance is typically used to describe the increasingly regulated character of transnational and international relations.[19] The necessity of global governance is increasingly supported by the worldwide processes of globalization.

As the 21st century dawns, there is a desperate need for more useful knowledge about global governance. For international peace and common welfare, there must be an agreed global framework for actions and policies to be carried out at the global level. A multifaceted strategy for global governance is required. And it will require the articulation of a collaborative ethos based on the principles of consultation, transparency, and accountability. It will seek peace and welfare for all people, and improve the capacity for the peaceful resolution of disputes. And it will strive to subject the rule of arbitrary power to the rule of law within global civil society.[20]

---

18  William H. Meyer & Boyka Stefanova, "Human Rights, the UN Global Compact and Global Governance," *Cornell Int'l Law Journal*, Vol.34, 2001, pp.501, 515.

19  Elke Krahmann, *op. cit.*, p.329.

The desire to rule the world orderly has been a part of the human experience throughout the human history, though, a world government capable of controlling States has never been evolved. Nonetheless considerable governance underlies the current order among States, facilitates absorption of the rapid changes at work in the world, and gives direction to the challenges posed by interstate conflicts, environmental pollution, currency crises, and the many other problems to which an ever expanding global interdependence give rise.

Nation—States find themselves less able to deal with the array of issues that face them. States and their people find they can do so only by working together with others. An aspect of this change is the growth of global civil society. These changes call for reforms in the modes of international cooperation — the institutions and processes of global governance.[21] We can, therefore, define 'global governance' as efforts to bring more orderly and reliable responses to social and political issues that go beyond capacities of States to address individually.

From this perspective 'the Commission on Global Governance'[22]

---

20  The Commission on Global Governance, *op. cit.*, p.5.

21  *Ibid.*, pp.xiii—xiv.

22  The Commission on Global Governance, established in 1992 was an independent commission, meaning that it was not created by a resolution of the UN General Assembly. It operated officially as a non-governmental organization(NGO) but, as a practical matter, it was an instrument of the United Nations. It received the formal endorsement of UN Secretary—General, and funding from the UN Development Programme(UNDP).

pointed that;

> "Governance is the sum of the many ways individuals and institutions, public and private, manage their common affairs. It is a continuing process through which conflicting or diverse interests may be accommodated and co-operative action may be taken ⋯ At the global level, governance has been viewed primarily as intergovernmental relationships, but, it must now be understood as also involving non-governmental organizations(NGOs), citizens' movements, multinational corporations, and the global capital market."[23]

## 2. Difference between 'Global Governance' and 'World Government'

As mentioned above, it is usually said that globalization does not require 'world government,' but may require just 'global governance.' It must be noted that 'governance' is not synonymous with 'government.' Both refer to purposive behaviour, to goal-oriented activities, to systems of rule; but government suggests activities that are backed by formal authority, by police powers to ensure the implementation of duly constituted policies, whereas governance refers to activities backed by shared goals that may or may not derive from legal and formally prescribed responsibilities and that do not necessarily rely on police powers

---

23  The Commission on Global Governance, *op. cit.*, pp.2-3.

to overcome defiance and attain compliance.

Governance is a more encompassing phenomenon than government. It embraces governmental institutions, but it also subsumes
informal or non-governmental mechanism whereby those persons
and organizations within its purview move ahead, satisfy their
needs, and fulfill their wants.[24] The new uses of governance
commonly refer to the fragmentation of political authority among
governmental and nongovernmental actors at the national,
regional, and global levels. They pose governance against government, which is understood as the centralization of authority
within the State.[25]

In terms of general definition, 'governance' can thus be understood
as the structures and processes that enable governmental and
nongovernmental actors to coordinate their interdependent needs
and interests through the making and implementation of policies
in the absence of a unifying political authority. Conversely,
'government' is defined as policy-making arrangements and
processes that centralize political authority within the State and
its agencies.[26]

In anarchy, there is not any element of governance. Outcomes
of conflicts are determined by the relative power positions of the

---

24   James N. Rosenau and Ernst-Otto Czempiel eds., *Glovernance Without
     Government: Order and Change in World Politics*(Cambridge University
     Press, 1995), p.4.

25   Elke Krahmann, *op. cit.*, p.331.

26   *Ibid.*

actors, that is, 'power politics' rather than by the application of law or some other regulatory devices by a legitimate authority, that is, 'rule of law.'[27] Yet, as in domestic realm, the possibility of coercion may also be in the background of compliance. A system of governance must have some capacity to enforce decisions in the case of non-compliance, but it cannot rely solely on coercion or violence.[28]

Thus, it is possible to conceive of 'governance without government' — of regulatory mechanism in a sphere of activity which function effectively even though they are not endowed with formal authority.[29] We should bear in mind that governance among sovereign and equal States is bound to be a 'governance without government.'

---

27  James N. Rosenau and Ernst-Otto Czempiel, *op. cit.*, p.30. But Ernst-Otto Czempiel understands 'governance' to mean the capacity to get things done without the legal competence to command that they be done. Where governments, in the Eastonian sense, can distribute values authoritatively, governance can distribute them in a way which is not authoritative but equally effective. Governments exercise rule, governance uses power. From this point of view, he says that the international system is a system of governance. See *ibid.*, p.250.

28  *Ibid.*, p.44.

29  *Ibid.*, p.5.

# Ⅲ. Conclusion

Yet, it may be true that there can be no authoritative system of global governance until most international legal subjects and other international entities have a common political will or *opino juris communitatis*. And, indeed, the weakness in the international legal and political system today are largely a reflection of weakness in the decentralized structure of the international society.

But, it is also true that the organizational element(*i.e.*, governance) is one of the most significant features of contemporary international or world community. The international or world community has at least the beginnings of a potentially effective legal system to support global governance other than world government. The United Nations, among lots of IGOs relating to the international rule of law and global governance can most effectively promote the law-making process, encourage law observance and enforce the law. As we noticed above, especially, the end of the Cold War gave new visibility to the United Nations and raised hopes for a more effective international legal order.

Since the end of the Cold War, international society has been undergoing a thorough change, which results in a need for a new world order, establishing liberal and democratic systems and great concern for the international rule of law and global governance for social, economic and humanitarian needs, as well as human rights.

The establishment of global governance on the basis of inter-national law is recognized to be absolutely necessary, both to ensure the protection of the human rights and to promote the common values and welfare in world community. The world community and many actors including civil society members face, therefore, unprecedented demands and opportunities towards the new century and Millennium.

Among them, not only the United Nations itself and its member States but also other members of world civil society must strive to ensure that the world community of the future is characterized by 'law' and 'governance,' not by 'lawlessness' and 'anarchy.'

Global governance is not an event; it is a process. It is a process that has been underway for years. Common vision for the future and substantial political will on the part of international actors such as states, international organizations, as well as individuals is, therefore, indispensable requirement for progress in this direction.

# CHAPTER 2

# Global Governance and
# the International Rule of Law

## I. International Society as a Legal Community

There are some scholars who are inclined to use the term
'anarchy' to designate a society of sovereign States. From this
perspective, anarchy necessarily exists when there is no supreme
or centralized authority to order the State how to act at the
international level. They usually explain the essence of the
'anarchic' international system by the fact that there is no actor
with legitimate authority and coercion to tell a State what to do,
and each State tends to go its own separate way without regard
for common principles, norms, rules, and procedures.[30]

But, from the inception of the modern international society,
States have never always carried out their mutual intercourse or

---

30  *Ibid.*, p.7; Elisabeth Zoller, "Institutional Aspects of International
     Governance," *Indiana Journal of Global Legal Studies*, Vol.3, 1995, p.121.

relationship in an anarchic manner without any regard for common principles or rules. In the society of States, the members conceive themselves to be bound by a common set of rules in their relations with one another, and share in the working of common institutions due to international law and organizations. If we accept that there is an international society it follows that there must exist an international legal order, for *ubi societas ibi jus.*[31]

When we refer to the 'order' of international society, we necessarily imply that there is a kind of 'governance' or 'rule of law' in international society and this society is at least 'governed' in the loose sense of the term.[32] This organizational element(i.e., governance) is one of the most significant features of contemporary international society. Besides States, most of the international organizations have their own legal personality; they are able to act through their own organs, the activities of which are imputed to the organization as a subject of international law. The recognition of individual as not only an object, but also an international legal subject is a historical event of primary importance.[33] As the world shrinks through developments of

---

[31]   Ingrid Detter De Lupis, *op. cit.*, p.35.

[32]   James N. Rosenau and Ernst–Otto Czempiel eds., *op. cit.*, p.30; Elisabeth Zoller, *op. cit.*, pp.121–123. One asserts that we can not use the term 'world government,' but 'global governance' in order to characterize the international society today. If 'government' denotes the formal exercise of power by established institutions, 'governance' denotes cooperative problem–solving by a changing and often uncertain cast. See Anne–Marie Slaughter, "The Real New World Order," *Foreign Affairs*, Vol.76, No.5, 1997, p.184.

transportation and technology, and recognition of common interests and concerns, so does the distance between the inter- national law and non—State actors.[34]

International society, like other societies, has needed to develop rules to govern behaviour among its members, and judicial machinery for interpreting and applying the rules. In this regard, some scholars once argued that international law was not law in the true sense, as there was no international police force to enforce it, no sanctions if it were disobeyed, and no international legislature.[35] On further examination, however, we can find the Constitution of international society as a higher law[36] and other rules of international law which are the basis of international society as a legal community and basically regulates the life and

---

33  P. K. Menon, "The International Personality of Individuals in Inter- national Law: A Broadening of the Traditional Doctrine." *Journal of Transnational Law and Policy,* Vol.1, 1992, pp.151—182.

34  Ronald A. Brand, "The Role of International Law in the Twenty—First Century: External Sovereignty and International Law," *Fordham International Law Journal,* Vol.18, 1995, p.1695.

35  The Commission on Global Governance, *op. cit.,* p.304; Anthony D'Amato, "Is International Law Really 'Law'?" *Northwestern University Law Review,* Vol.79, 1984, pp.1293—1314.

36  For example, a norm that is *jus cogens* cannot limited or derogated from by agreement between states in their relations with each other. See Rosalyn Higgins, *Problems & Process*(Oxford university Press, 1995), pp.21—22; Humphrey indicates that in a large sense the Charter of the United Nations provides "the constitutional framework of international law today." And it is argued that the UN Charter proclaims fundamental principles of law for the world community. See Blaine Sloan, "The United Nations Charter as a Constitution," *Pace Yearbook of International Law,* Vol.1, 1989, pp.61—62.

acts of the members of the society. International law transformed an international society affected by the 'power politics' into a world community governed by law, that is, a legal community.[37]

# II. The Significance of the International Rule of Law

## 1. The Concept of the Rule of Law

Why is it necessary to define the concept of the rule of law? There are two reasons: The first is obviously that we must be clear at the outset about the study on the matter of the rule of law; The second is that it is necessary to spell out the ingredients of the rule of law, partly in order to demonstrate that it is a genuine and real juristic principle and not merely a vague political aspiration or ideology.[38] The rule of law is a convenient term to summarize a combination of ideals and practical legal experience concerning which there is over a wide part of the world, although in embryonic and to some extent inarticulate form, a consensus of opinion among the legal profession.

Two ideals underlie the concept of the rule of law. In the first

---

37 Hermann Mosler, *The International Society As a Legal Community* (Sijthoff & Noordhoff, 1980), pp.11–16.

38 Geoffrey de Q. Walker, *The Rule of Law* (Melbourne University Press, 1988), p.7.

place, it implies without regard to the content of the law, that all power in the State should be derived from and exercised in accordance with the law. Secondly, it assumes that the law itself is based on respect for the supreme value of human dignity. Traditionally, the concept of the rule of law has seemed to mean the principle of rule(government) of the *Rechtsstaat* or supremacy of law. In its origin, the concept of *Rechtsstaat* was formed in German jurisprudence, by which it was once asserted that every rule of government could be justified, as long as it was exercised only on the basis of law. It did not matter whether the content of law was democratic or not. In a word, in the first place, the rule of law implies without regard to the content of the law that all power in the State should be derived from and exercised according to law.[39]

But, nowadays it is usually admitted that the rule of law is essential to the modern democratic society. It cements our community and protects our liberty and rights. It is one of barometers that distinguish civilization from anarchy.[40] Since Dicey articulated the rule of law as a 'feature' of the political institutions of England,[41] the rule of law has become the

---

39   Franz Neumann, *The Rule of Law*(Berg Publishers, 1986), pp.179–180. And cf. Stanley L. Paulson, "Neumann's Rule of Law," *Diritto E Cultura*, 1/92, Edizioni Scientifiche Italiane, pp.209–216.

40   Sandra Day O'Connor, "Vindicating the Rule of Law: Balancing Competing Demands for Justice," Norman Dorsen & Prosser Gifford. eds., *Democracy and the Rule of Law*(CQ Press, 2001), p.31.

41   Michael Neumann, *The Rule of Law*(Ashgate Pub. Ltd., 2002), p.1.

cornerstone of democracy.

He states that the rule of law means: ( i ) no man is punishable or can be lawfully made to suffer in body or goods except for a distinct breach of law established in the ordinary legal manner before ordinary courts of the land, (ii) no man is above the law and every man, whatever his rank or condition, is subject to the ordinary law of the realm and amenable to the jurisdiction of the ordinary tribunals, and (iii) the constitution is the result of the ordinary law of the land.[42]

The rule of law by Dicey means "the absolute supremacy or predominance of regular law as opposed to the influence of arbitrary power"[43] and "it excludes the existence of arbitrariness, of prerogative, or even of wide discretionary authority on the part of the government."[44] It secures the equality before the law.[45]

Hayek goes further. He says that the rule of law means:

"[G]overnment in all its actions is bound by rules fixed and announced beforehand rules which make it possible to foresee with fair certainty how the authority will use its coercive powers in given circumstances, and to plan one's individual

---

42  John Phillip Reid, *Rule of Law*(Northern Illinois University Press, 2004), pp.8−9.

43  *Ibid.*

44  *Ibid.*

45  *Ibid.*; Berta Esperanza Hernandez−Truyol, "Panel v. Human Rights Commitments in the America: From the Global to the Local the Rule of Law and Human Right," *Florida Journal of Int'l Law*, Vol.16, 2004, pp.167−168.

affairs on the basis of this knowledge."[46]

On the other hand, Rawls argues that the rule of law is simply the conception of formal justice applied to a legal order or system. He says that "the legal order is a system of public rules addressed to rational persons, we can account for the precepts of justice associated with the rule of law."[47] According to him, the rule of law is achieved by a coercive order of public rules addressed to rational persons for the purpose of regulating their conduct and the framework for social cooperation.[48]

The basic idea of the rule of law mentioned above produces many specific principles. In order for the rule of law to be established, for example, all laws should be prospective and clear.[49] Laws must be general and feasible.[50] The law–making process should be open, stable and clear.[51] Further, the judiciary branch must be independent.[52] The rule of law presumes that the people understand what is required of them. The rules should have the character of commands or instructions to the ruled.

---

46  Friedrich A. Hayek, *The Road to Serfdom*(University of Chicago Press, 1944), p.54.

47  M. Neumann, *op. cit.,* p.7.

48  *Ibid.*

49  Joseph Raz, "The Rule of Law and its Virtue," Robert L. Cunningham ed., *Liberty and the Rule of Law*(Texas A & M University Press, 1979), pp.7–12.

50  M. Neumann, *op. cit.,* pp.30–31.

51  J. Raz, *op. cit.,* p.8.

52  *Ibid.*

Bruce Broomhall states:

"[T]he rule of law is an idea that aims to legitimate the internal sovereignty of the State in its claim to an exclusive right to law—making, adjudication, and enforcement within its territory, and as such has a key role in the constitutional order of the modern State; it fulfills this role through ensuring the separation of powers, legal controls on the use of power, and the application of laws possessing at least minimal formal qualities."[53]

The rule of law is contrasted to arbitrary rule and tells us how to act, and prepares punishments in the event that we refuse to obey it.[54] The rule of law also secures human dignity. Human dignity is respected by "treating humans as persons capable of planning and plotting their future."[55] The rule of law enhances human dignity by allowing a person's autonomy and control over his life and future.[56]

As mentioned above, over the years, the concept of the rule of law has been developed into the concept of 'the supremacy of law' or 'the predominance of Parliament' for the protection of individual freedom and fundamental rights specially under the

---

[53] B. Broomhall, *International Justice and the International Criminal Court*(Oxford University Press, 2003), p.53.

[54] M. Neumann, *op. cit.,* p.26.

[55] J. Raz, *op. cit.,* p.14.

[56] *Ibid.*

constitutionalism in England. And in Germany also, the concept of *Rechtsstaat* has been changed into the principle of limitation of State(government) power for the protection of human rights. In both cases, 'the content' of law has the primary role in the concept of the rule of law.

In this perspective, now, it is asserted that the rule of law means the principle of realizing the individual freedom, equality, and other fundamental rights for the human dignity and under the Constitution in domestic level.[57] Therefore, the rule of law requires every State to restrict its governmental power and abide by its law which is made for the protection of human rights. The rule of law has stood as a constitutional barrier between the governor and the governed, between power and people.[58]

Generally, from the constitutional perspective, many scholars usually explain that the rule of law means the principle that restriction of individual rights or the imposition of duties on individuals should be exercised on the basis of the law, the purpose of the rule of law, lies in the protection and promotion of basic freedom and fundamental rights of individuals, and its constitutional meaning is the 'principle of separation of powers.'

---

[57] For the 'minimum conditions' of a juridical system in which fundamental rights and human dignity are respected and 'basic requirements' of representative government under the rule of law, see International Commission of Jurists, *The Rule of Law and Human Rights — Principles and Definitions —* (Geneva, 1966), pp.5-8.

[58] Allan C. Hutchinson & Patrick Monahan eds., *The Rule of Law — Ideal or Ideology —* (Carswell, 1987), p.100.

From the philosophical perspective, on the other hand, the concept of the rule of law means the 'rule of reason(*ratio*), not of men.'[59]

I think that it is the appropriate meaning of the rule of law, moreover, the constitutional meaning of the rule of law can be reconciled with the philosophical meaning of the rule of law on condition that it aims to protect or preserve the fundamental human rights which are to be derived from the reason or the human nature, prohibiting the arbitrary rule of men or power. That is, the ideal of 'the rule of law, not of men' calls upon us to strive to ensure that law itself, not the wishes of powerful men will rule(govern) us.

According to this traditional ideal, government must be by 'just and positive laws,' not by 'absolute arbitrary power.' It is, therefore, necessary to note that the concept of the rule of law is based on the values of a free or open society, which means a society that recognizes the supreme value of human personality and conceives of all social institutions, and in particular the State, as the servants rather than the masters of the people.[60]

The International Commission of Jurists has held a number of international meetings, which have contributed decisively to the analysis and elaboration of the concept of the rule of law in

---

59  Ian Shapiro ed., *The Rule of Law*(New York University Press, 1994), p.64, 65, 122, 149, pp.328–330.

60  Robert D. Bryant, *A World Rule of Law, A Way to Peace*(R & E Research Associates, Inc., 1977), p.6.

accordance with the needs of contemporary society. In 1959, Delhi Conference of the International Commission of Jurists undertook to draw a clear picture of what the rule of law means. It conceived the rule of law as:

"the principles, institutions and procedures, not always identical, but broadly similar, which the experience and traditions of lawyers in different countries of the world, often having themselves varying political structures and economic backgrounds, have shown to be important to protect the individual from arbitrary government and to enable him to enjoy the dignity of men."[61]

## 2. The Concept of 'the International Rule of Law'

### 1) Is 'the international Rule of Law' Possible?

What, if anything, is meant by term such as 'the international rule of law'? Is international system or international community governed or should be governed by the rule of law as is in national legal system?

In a democratic State, people recognize and accept their community's rules because they find common interest and the benefits of a governance system. They actively participate in the rule-making process and this active participation of rule-

---

61  *Ibid.*, p.6.

making process reinforce the rule of law in a State.[62]

Some scholars argue that States are the only actors in the international realm and struggle with each other for survival. They also argue that States think and act in terms of interest defined as power to maximize their relative power over other States to maintain their position in the international system.[63]

World society or community, compared with nation–States, lacks centralized governance or sovereignty and power to enforce its rules. States in the international system, however, regard legal rules as a legitimizing source and they base their actions according to the legal rules. At international level, States can participate in the international rule–making process especially through the UN, by concluding and ratifying conventions or treaties, and form customary international law by their consistent practice. States mostly accept international rule as governing their behavior toward other States or international community.

Louis Henkin says that

"almost all nations observe almost all principles of international law and almost all of their obligations almost all of the time."[64]

---

62   The Commission on Global Governance, *Issues in Global Governance: Papers written for the Commission on Global Governance*(Kluwer Law International, 1995), p.221.

63   K. Nowrot, *op. cit.*, pp.579, 600.

64   L. Henkin, *How Nations Behave: Law and Foreign Policy,* 2nd ed. (Columbia University Press, 1979), p.47.

States accept international rules because they find the common interests and benefits of an international governance system, in which international rule of law plays an important role. In this respect, the international or world society have been transformed into a legal community.[65] The international community could and should be governed by rule of law. Therefore, the concept of the rule of law is not unique in the national legal system.

Further, the traditional notion that States are the only actors at international level is no longer maintained. This trend is, in part, due to the growing role of non-State actors such as intergovernmental organizations(IGOs) and non-governmental organizations(NGOs). NGOs as well as IGOs are now playing an important role in strengthening the international rule of law.

As globalization progresses, political, economic and social activities of States, IGOs and NGOs impact other international actors in many aspects. Especially many former nationally-oriented NGOs "have had to transnationalize to keep their status as pressure groups on the international as well as the domestic decision making level."[66]

NGOs cover almost every area of international concern. First, NGOs take part in the international decision-making process.[67] They propose new international conventions and participate in the negotiation and drafting of treaties.[68] They often serve as member

---

65  Hermann Mosler, *op. cit.*, pp.11–16.
66  K. Nowrot, *op. cit.*, p.586.
67  *Ibid.*, p.589.

of government representatives and participate in international conferences concerning various areas.[69] By doing so, they contribute to the progressive development of international law. Second, NGOs actively participate in the enforcement of international law. They investigate and let the world know of violations of international law committed by States.[70] This tactic is, in fact, very important and effective to make States comply with international law, especially concerning international human rights.

As mentioned above, it is established today that one important ideal of modern legal systems is described by the phrase 'the rule of law.'[71] The ideal of the rule of law is rather historical, though, appeals to the rule of law remain powerful in this 21st century. As the Commission on Global Governance put it;

"The rule of law has been a critical civilizing influence in every free and democratic society. It distinguishes a democratic from a tyrannical society; it secures liberty and justice against

---

68 For example, NGOs played an important role in the negotiation of ⌜the Convention on International Trade in Endangered Species⌟, ⌜the World Heritage Convention⌟, and ⌜the Convention on Biological Diversity⌟. They also played an initiative role over the prohibition of anti personnel mines. See *ibid.*

69 *Ibid.*, p.593.

70 *Ibid.*, p.596.

71 As to the concept of the rule of law and the international rule of law, see Boo Chan Kim(hereinafter also 'Kim, B. C.'), "The United Nations and the International Rule of Law," *Korean Yearbook of International Law,* Vol.1, 1997, pp.81-84.

repression; it elevates equality above dominion; it empowers the weak against the unjust claims of the strong. Its restraints, no less than the moral precepts it asserts, are essential to the well-being of a society, both collectively and to individuals within it. Respect for the rule of law is thus a basic neighbourhood value. And one that is certainly needed in the emerging global neighbourhood."[72]

But in its origin, the concept of the rule of law was developed in reference to the modern State; it concerns the internal operations of a State, not the relations among States. Therefore, although the ideal of the rule of law clearly has application to the realization of rule-based association in the society of States, this application is indirect and complex. And even when the courts hold government to the rule of law, the rule of international law is not guaranteed.

Indeed, the reluctance of sovereign States to conduct themselves according to the rule of law in their relations with one another is a main problem. This reluctance is illustrated by the advocacy by many States of dispute settlement provisions in multilateral treaties according to which compulsory arbitration or judicial settlement is to be replaced by what is referred to as 'free choice of means,' which has evidently been taken by some States to mean free choice in their settlement of international disputes.

They, thus, assert that international law exists in the absence

---

72 The Commission on Global Governance, *supra* note 7, p.303.

of institutions for securing the rule of law in the strict sense.[73] This is, however, simply a lack of information and basis upon the subject.[74] There are much developments in international society that results in significant change in the concept of international law. The law including international law can not exist without compliance. But compliance is not always secured through coercion. Indeed, 'compliance without coercion' indicates legitimate authority.

A system of governance in international society, that is, 'global governance' must have some capacity to enforce decisions in the case of non-compliance, but it cannot rely solely on coercion or force.[75] No longer is State conduct immune from international scrutiny, or even from sanction. Mechanisms are being created through which 'sovereign' conduct is held accountable to international law.

If the role of the sovereign is to provide international peace and promote human rights on world-wide basis, and strengthening the international rule of law and global governance results in increased peace and human welfare, then the role of the sovereign must be to strengthen the international rule of law and global governance.[76] It seems evident that 'the rule of law' is to

---

73 Terry Nardin, *Law, Morality, and the Relations of States*(Princeton University Press, 1983), pp.183–185.

74 Schuyler W. Jackson, "The Rule of Law Among Nations," H. Malcolm MacDonald *et al.* eds., *The Rule of Law*(Southern Methodist University Press, 1961), *p. 71.*

75 James N. Rosenau and Ernst–Otto Czempiel eds., *op. cit.*, p.44.

'government' in every sovereign State what 'the international rule of law' is to 'global governance' in international society or world community. In short, global governance is doing internationally what governments of civilized nations do at home.[77]

## 2) the Objective and Meaning of the International Rule of Law

At the Heads of State Meeting of the UN Security Council on January 30, 1992, world leaders impressively called for observing the rule of law in the conduct of international relations and for strict adherence to the law of the UN Charter. In their respective pronouncements, the Heads of States took up a widespread sentiment among States and governments that the rule of law and law enforcement ought to be given priority in international relations, particularly in the field of international human rights protection.[78]

The International Commission of Jurists has contributed decisively to the analysis and elaboration of the concept of the rule of law in accordance with the needs of contemporary international society. The Commission further referred to the 'international(world) rule of law' as having the primary objective

---

76  Ronald, A. Brand, *op. cit.*, pp.1695–1697.

77  A. LeRoy Bennett & James K. Oliver, *op. cit.*, p.16; Finkelstein, "What is Global Governance?" *Global Governance*, Vol.1, 1995, p.369.

78  Jost Delbruck, "A More Effective International Law or a New 'World Law'? — Some of the Development of International Law in a Changing International System," *Indiana Law Journal,* Vol.68, 1993, p.706.

as follows;

"To strengthen the body, the machinery, the acceptance, and the sanctions of international law so that law will increasingly come to occupy the place in international affairs that it does in the domestic affairs of civilized nations."[79]

It would seem that this definition is based on the 'institutional' approach and the 'values' approach of the concept of rule of law.[80] The concept of rule of law means that in every human society on both domestic and international level, the principle of governing

---

79   *Ibid.*

80   One could define 'the rule of law' in terms of the values which that institution is designed to serve, such as human dignity or individual fulfillment through the full development of one's capacities; or in terms of the several principles whereby those institutions are to be safeguarded, such as the rule that a legal basis must be shown for every government action interfering with the rights of the citizen; or in terms of the parliaments and the police who are responsible for doing the safeguarding, in their own distinctive ways; or finally, in terms of the procedures which those institutions use for that purpose, such as public hearings, jury trial, *habeas corpus* and the like. There is some overlapping between all four of these approaches, especially between the principles, institutions, and procedures approaches. Thus I would like to reduce the number of possible classifications to only two — the 'values' approach and the 'institutional' approach which also incorporates the principles and procedures whose function it is to maintain the rule of law. We can readily distinguish two main contested views: a primarily instrumental(institutional) approach and a more substantive(values) approach. The institutional version holds that the rule of law is a prerequisite for any efficacious legal order. The substantive version, on the other hand, holds that the rule of law embodies tenets of a particular political morality. Geoffrey de Q. Walker, *op. cit.*, pp.7–12.

society which is to be reconciled with the reasonable human nature only could be justified.

Further, at the UN World Summit in 2005, member States unanimously recognized the need for "universal adherence to and implementation of the rule of law at both the national and international levels" and reaffirmed their commitment to "an international order based on the rule of law and international law."[81]

Chesterman's pointing out that there are three possible meanings and it is helpful to distinguish between them is helpful to understand what the 'international rule of law' exactly means. The three meanings are: ( i ) the 'international rule of law' may be understood as the application of 'rule of law' principles to relations between States and other subjects of international law; (ii) the 'international rule of law' could privilege 'international law' over national law, establishing, for example, the primacy of human rights covenants over domestic legal arrangements; (iii) a 'global rule of law' might denote the emergence of a normative regime that touches individuals directly without formal mediation through existing national institutions.[82]

---

81  Simon Chesterman, "An International Rule of Law?," *American Journal of Comparative Law*, Vol.56, 2008, p.332.

82  "The first sense is how 'the rule of law' is typically understood in this context here and as it will be applied. The second may be relevant to certain regional organizations, notably the European Union, but such regimes are exceptional and , with the aggregation of power, resembles State-like institutions rather than international organizations in the strict sense of the word. The third approach accurately reflects the rise

## III. Conclusion

The international rule of law demands: ( i ) international
society should be ruled by not only the active role of the States
and IGOs but also the wide participation of NGOs on the basis
of established international law; (ii) all the subjects and actors
should rely on law as opposed to arbitrary power in international
relations; (iii) international conflicts and disputes should be
settled peacefully and justifiably by the international law and
internationally agreed methods for settling international disputes
rather than power or forcible means; (iv) the realization that law
can and should be used as an instrumentality for the cooperative
international furtherance of social aims, in such fashion as to
preserve the values of freedom and human dignity for
individuals.[83]

The international rule of law, therefore, could be, or rather
should be applied and realized for the protection of human rights,
as well as promotion of human welfare, as the aim and objective
of the international law and organizations should be to protect

of quasi–administrative regimes that fall outside traditional domestic
and international legal categories, but remains at an early stage of
development. It is possible that justice will one day be sought through
global law, but at the present time it is most likely to be pursued through
the global organization of well–ordered States." See *ibid.*, pp.355–356.

[83] William W. Bishop, "The International Rule of Law," *Michigan Law
Review*, Vol.59, 1961, p.553; Brian Z. Tamanaha, *On the Rule of Law:
History, Politics, Theory*(Cambridge University Press, 2004), pp.127–
136.

or promote the international peace and human rights.[84] In this global civil society the crucial role that the new actors such as NGOs play in the management of global affairs requires a reassessment of the relationship between the UN and its family of organizations and the growing world-wide array of organized non-State activity.[85]

Therefore, we should be concerned with the international rule of law as the basis of global governance, and the role of international law and institutions relating to global governance focusing on the NGOs as well as IGOs operation,[86] to achieve human rights, development, and peace in the global level.

---

84  The post-World II era has been the start of international protection of human rights. Especially, the UN Charter obligates member states to promote universal respect for human rights and not to discriminate on the basis of race, sex, language, or religion in implementing human rights obligations. Based on this broad obligation, the international community has extensively codified classical human rights for the protection of individual fundamental rights and freedoms. In addition, the international community has codified economic, social, and cultural rights directed at improving the economic, social, and cultural conditions of the individual to make the enjoyment of fundamental rights and freedoms more meaningful. More recently, the international community has attempted to define and codify group rings and rights of peoples, so-called 'third-generation rights.' These 'rights' or standards of achievement are intended to enhance the political, economic, social, and cultural self-determination and development of peoples to ensure the full and equitable participation of all nations, rich or poor, in the international community of states. Jost Delbruck, *op. cit.*, p.712.

85  The Commission on Global Governance, *op. cit.*, p.253.

86  Richard A. Falk, "The United Nations and the Rule of Law," *Transnational Law & Contemporary Problems*, Vol.4, 1994, pp.612-613.

# CHAPTER 3

# Global Governance and
# Paradigm Shift in International Law

## I. Introduction

Similar to international society, international law has constantly evolved and has undergone vital changes from its inception. Accordingly, the evolution of international law responds to changing conditions and needs in international society. It is clear that a static or statist vision of the structure and function of the international legal system would be ignorant of this changing conditions.[87] As is often the case, a changing world needs a new paradigm.

From the beginning up to the late 19th century, international society had been consisted of states which had sovereignty. State sovereignty has been regarded as the basis of international

---

[87] Joel P. Trachtman, *The Future of International Law — Global Government* —(Cambridge: Cambridge University Press, 2013), p.1.

society and international law. In this regard, only states had been regarded as the subjects of international law. The classical sources of international law depended on the interaction and consent of states primarily in the form of treaties and customary law. Central concepts of international law such as sovereignty, territorial integrity, diplomatic relations, non-intervention all relied on the exclusive or dominant role of the states.

However, during the 20th century, especially after the establishment of the United Nations or rather, after the end of the Cold War and much more in the 21st century, other entities than states, *i.e.*, non-state actors such as intergovernmental organizations(IGOs), nongovernmental organizations(NGOs) and individuals have been appeared in the international arena and expected to move to active collaboration and cooperation on the global basis among them and with states.

The development or evolution of international society and international law is often described by the technique 'ascending periodization.' Ascending periodization of international law means the cutting the history of international law in two or more periods and giving the most recent period the most favourable label.[88] The international legal discourse offers many examples of the use of the ascending periodization technique. The distinction between classical and modern(contemporary) international law is a

---

[88] Tilmann Altwicker and Oliver Diggelmann, "How is Progress Constructed in International Legal Scholarship?," *The European Journal of International Law*, Vol.25, No.2, p.432.

typical illustrative example.[89] Some scholars use the technique of old/new dichotomy which Anne-Marie Slaughter employs in her work, *A New World Order*.[90] Slaughter suggests a periodization of international law — the time axis is cut into the eras of the old and the new model — and conveys the progress message by the labelling of the periods.[91] Another author employing the old/new dichotomy is Philip Allot. According to him, 'old international law' means the mode of modest self-limitation, whereas 'new international law' means the law of universal legislation.[92] Whereas, Antonio Cassese suggests that it is helpful to think of international law having evolved over four major periods.[93]

It seems that the doctrine of subjects lies at the center of periodization of the international law, making traditional inter-

---

89 *Ibid.*, p.433.

90 Anne-Marie Slaughter, *A New World Order*(Princeton and Oxford: Princeton University Press, 2009)

91 Tilmann Altwicker and Oliver Diggelmann, *op. cit.*, pp.433-434.

92 Philip Allot, "The Emerging Universal Legal System," *International Law Forum du Droit International*, Vol.3, 2001, p.16.

93 According to Antonio Cassese, in tracing the historical evolution of the world community, it is useful to divide it into various stages. It may prove helpful for a better understanding of some major turning points. The evolution of the international community can be roughly divided into four major stages: (1) from its gradual emergence(16th — early 17th century) to the First World War; (2) from the establishment of the League of Nations to the end of the Second World War(1919-1945); (3) from the establishment of the United Nations(UN) to the end of the Cold War(1945-1989); (4) the present period(A. Cassese, *International Law*, 2nd ed.(Oxford: Oxford University Press, 2005), p.22).

national legal scholarship diffident about the repercussions that a structural change in the international society might have on the paradigm of international law. Indeed, the traditional doctrine of subjects is no longer able to offer a satisfactory explanation of the legal complexities of contemporary international society. We know that the once homogeneous community of states, whose sovereignty lay at the very heart of the system, has given way to a much wider community of diverse actors and interests.

History demonstrates that the single most significant development in international law is the dramatic shift in the status of individuals from a mere 'object' to a 'subject' of international law[94] in addition to the IGOs. Especially, the protection of internationally recognized human rights is by all accounts a revolutionary change in international law.

In this sense, international society has been transformed into an international community of human beings rather than international community of states.[95] It is the existence of an

---

94 V. P. Nanda, "International Law in the Twenty-first Century," in Nandasiri Jasentuliyana ed., *Perspectives on International Law*(London · The Hague · Boston: Kluwer Law International, 1995). p.83.

95 Menno T. Kamminga, "Final Report on the Impact of International Human Rights Law on General International Law," in Menno T. Kamminga & Martin Scheinen, eds., *The Impact of Human Rights Law on General International Law*(Oxford: Oxford University Press, 2009), p.21; 'International society' and 'international community' are inter-changeably synonyms and often interchangeably used, but it is useful to distinguish between the two. Both call for a degree of cohesion and interdependence among the actors associating in some sort of group affiliation. The difference in degree between the two, however, is great.

international community of all individuals, and the capacity of international law to serve the interests of this community, that grounds international law's promise of universalism.[96] In the legal perspective, international community means an international legal community.[97] It is evident that international law has performed crucial role in the formation and evolution of international legal community.

This chapter aims to examine the changing structure of international legal order and elucidate the paradigm shift in international law. To this, the meaning of paradigm and the significance of paradigm shift in international law are to be reviewed first, and then some problematic issues such as reconceptualization of sovereignty, the international rule of law, the humanization of international law, the constitutionalisation of international law, and strengthening of global governance will be discussed.[98]

---

A community has more solidarity, so the identity and loyalty to the group are strong. A society. in contrast, is always busy adjusting significant differences among a loose association of actors. It is possible to think of a society evolving into a community, or a community deteriorating into a society(Conway W. Henderson, *Understanding International Law*(Chichester: John Willey & Sons, 2010), p.8).

96  Benedict Kingsbury and Megan Donaldson, "From Bilateralism to Publicness in International Law," in Ulrich Fastenrath, Rudolf Geiger, Daniel-Erasmus Khan, Andreas Paulus, Sabine von Schorlemer, Christoph Vedder, eds., *From Bilateralism to Community Interest: Essays in Honour of Judge Bruno Simma*(Oxford: Oxford University Press, 2011), pp.79-89.

97  Hermann Mosler, *The International Society as a Legal Community*(Alphen aan Rijn and Germantown: Sijthoff & Noordhoff, 1980).

Although all of these issues are needed to be explained respectively in detail, in this paper they will be treated in general only to the extent of their relations to the paradigm shift and interconnectedness among themselves in international law.

---

**98** There are few papers in domestic area which deal with the issue of paradigm shift in international law in earnest. However, refer to the following papers for more details of these problematic issues: Boo Chan Kim, "Global Governance and the International Rule of Law," *The Korean Journal of International Law*, Vol.45, No.2, 2000, pp.1–17; Tae–Hyun Choi, "An Analysis on the Nature and Function of the International Rule of Law," *Dong–A Law Review*, No.43, 2009, pp.391–425; Sung Won Kim, "A Review on the Constitutionalization of International Law," *The Korean Journal of International Law*, Vol.58, No.4, 2013, pp.73–102; Byungchun So, "Some Thoughts on Discourse of Sovereignty in International Law," *The Korean Journal of International Law*, Vol.58, No.4, 2013, pp.133–162; Boo Chan Kim, "An Introduction to the Study on the Humanization of International Law: Focusing on its Background and Trend," *The Korean Journal of International Law*, Vol.59, No.4, 2014, pp.41–79; Seok–hyun Kim, "*Erga omnes* Character of the Obligations of Human Rights Protection in International Law," *The Korean Journal of International Law*, Vol.59, No.4, 2014, pp.81–115; Boo Chan Kim, "The Evolution of International Community and the Role of the United Nations," *Ajou Law Review*, Vol.10, No.2, 2016, pp.227–258; Boo Chan Kim, *Special Lectures on International Law*, revised edition(Bogosa, 2018), pp.72–88.

# II. Paradigm Shift in International Law

## 1. The Meaning of Paradigm and Paradigm Shift

In his 1962 book, *The Structure of Scientific Revolutions*, Thomas Kuhn described the history of scientific development and has attracted considerable attention through his depiction of the structure of scientific revolutions. Kuhn describes the scientific revolution by the attractive term, 'paradigm' which means "universally recognized scientific achievements that for a time provide model problems and solutions to a community of practitioners."[99] In addition, Kuhn described the structure of that development as revolutionary in nature, occurring at that point in time "in which an older paradigm is replaced in whole or in part by an incompatible one." The impetus or motive for this paradigm shift is malfunction that an existing paradigm has ceased to function adequately in the exploration of an aspect of nature to which that paradigm itself had previously led the way ···. The sense of malfunction that can lead to crisis is prerequisite to revolution."[100]

According to Kuhn, when, in the developments of a natural science, an individual or group first produces a synthesis able to attract most of the next generation's practitioners, the older

---

99  Thomas Kuhn, *The Structure of Scientific Revolutions*, 2nd. ed.(Chicago: University of Chicago Press, 1970), p.viii.

100  *Ibid*, p.92.

schools gradually disappear. In part their disappearance is caused by their members' conversion to the new paradigm. But, there are always some people who cling to one or another of the older views, and they are simply read out of the profession, which thereafter ignores their work. Therefore, the new paradigm implies a new and more rigid definition of the field.[101]

## 2. Significance of Paradigm Shift in International Law

When Kuhn wrote *The Structure*, few people encountered it. But, soon it became trendy, and nowadays, paradigm, along with its companion paradigm shift, is embarrassingly everywhere.[102] Although Kuhn has been critical of facile extrapolation of his ideas about paradigm to the discourse of social sciences,[103] he himself analogized his conception of the theory and operation of scientific revolutions to political revolutions, drawing out parallels in genesis, form and function between the two.[104] The

---

101 Thomas Kuhn, *The Structure of Scientific Revolutions with An Introductory Essay by Ian Hacking*, 50th Anniversary Edition(Chicago and London: The University of Chicago Press, 2012), p. xix.

102 *Ibid.*, p.19.

103 Richard Falk, *Revitalizing International Law*(Ames: Iowa State University Press, 1989), p.9.

104 P. Glen, "Paradigm Shifts in International Justice and the Duty to Protect: in Search of an Action Principle," *University of Botswana Law Journal*, Vol.11, 2010, p.19; Edward McWhinney, "Shifting Paradigms of International Law and World Order in an Era of Historical Transition," in Sienho Yee and Wang Tieya eds., *International Law in the Post−Cold*

notion of revolutionary change, or paradigm shift provides a useful framework to judge the evolution, current state, and potential future of international law including international human rights law and international criminal law.[105]

Indeed, there have been some co-shared views or approaches as kinds of paradigm for international legal scholars to explain and theorize the structure and order of international law. But, by looking back at classical types of international law, we can discover that the statist or state-centred paradigm has been used by the profession to discipline deviant practitioners, mainly by labelling them as utopian or idealist, and unworthy of serious attention either because they worked outside the paradigm or because they challenged prevailing patterns of statecraft.[106]

Since the late $20^{th}$ century, there have been many paradigm shift-talks in the international legal scholarship. We can categorizes paradigm shift-talks into some modes such as society / community paradigms, coexistence / cooperation paradigms, state-centrism / anthropo-centrism paradigms[107] and particularism / universalism paradigms.[108 · 109] Among these, society /

---

*War World: Essays in Memory of Li Haopei*(London and New York: Routledge, 2001), p.4.

105  *Ibid.*

106  Richard Falk, *op. cit.*, p.9.

107  'Anthropo-centrism' is interchangeably used with 'human-centrism' or 'people-centrism.' Anthropo-centrism means anthropo-centred approach or paradigm. The term 'approach' or 'view' is often interchangeably used with the term 'paradigm.'

particularism / coexistence / state–centrism paradigms have been based on statist approach and sound old–fashioned in the era of globalisation.[110] As the exceptions to these older paradigms have been multiplying for the past centuries, these paradigms have become less useful and newer, more appropriate paradigm for changing structure of international law is needed.

In this regard, Mosler argues that the basic principle which transformed international society into an international (legal) community was the agreement of the members to develop the rules and principles by which they are to be bound, which constitute the public order of the international community.[111] According to Armin von Bogdandy, the theory of international law can be described as a competition between the two paradigms of universalism and particularism.[112] Further, some scholars argue

---

108  Tilmann Altwicker and Oliver Diggelmann, "How is Progress Constructed in International Legal Scholarship?," *The European Journal of International Law*, Vol.25, No.2, pp.436–437.

109  Another example is provided by Cesare Romano's description of the developments in international adjudication. Romano identifies a shift from the consensual to the compulsory paradigm. According to Romano, 'compulsory jurisdiction' is used as a sort of synonym for the rule of law(Romano, "The shift from the Consensual to the Compulsory Paradigm in International Adjudication," *New York University Journal of International Law & Politics*, Vol.39, 2007, p.791.

110  Tilmann Altwicker and Oliver Diggelmann, *op. cit.*, p.436.

111  Hermann Mosler, *op. cit.*, pp.15–20.

112  Arnmin von Vogdandy and Serigo Dellavalle, "The Paradigms of Universalism and Particularism in the Age of Globalisation: Western Perspectives on the Premises and Finality of International Law," *Collected Courses of the Xiamen Academy of International Law*, Vol.2,

that international law establishes a dynamic legal order that has progressively developed from an order of peaceful coexistence to an order of cooperation of states and from an order concerned with narrowly construed state interests to an order that promotes the interests of the international community as a whole.[113]

Indeed, there have been persistent competitions between the older paradigms and the newer paradigms. In this regard, the shift form the older to newer paradigm in international law is really underway. It is noted that the need and justification for paradigm shift lies in that we are no longer justified or satisfied in explaining the structures and theories of international law in the light of older traditional paradigms based on Westphalian system. Therefore, it is urgent for the international legal scholars to

---

2009, p.45; Kate Parlett argues that it is commonly claimed that, historically, international law, being exclusively concerned with the rules applicable in inter-state relations, rarely engaged with individuals, but that over time, the international legal system has moved away from a state-centred approach to a more multifaceted or cosmopolitan system to engage with a wider range of actors, including individuals(Kate Parlett, *The Individual in the International Legal System: Continuity and Change in International Law*(Cambridge: Cambridge University Press, 2011), p.39.

113 Elena Katselli Proukaki, *The Problem of Enforcement of International Law: Countermeasures, the non-injured state and the idea of international community*(London and New York: Routledge, 2010), p.11; Further, Sienho Yee argues that one can reasonably say that the leimotif of international law was co-existence at the height of Cold War, co-operation during the period of d tente, and is now **co-progressiveness** in the post-Cold War era. ⋯ In his view, the ultimate goal of society or law including the international law of co-progressiveness is human flourishing(Sienho Yee, "Towards an International Law of Co-progressiveness," in Sienho Yee and Wang Tieya eds., *op. cit.*, pp.19-37).

revise the structure and scope of international law and develop new paradigms that may work for the problems we seek to solve.[114] But, it is not easy work. The design of a new paradigm is one step in the direction of revolutionary change, so the establishment or completion of new paradigm may be the work of the next several generations.

As Wolfgang Friedmann already explained in his classic 1964 work, *The Changing Structure of International Law*, "the principal preoccupation of the classical international law, as formulated by Grotius and the other founders, was the formalization, and the establishment of generally acceptable rules of conduct in international diplomacy."[115] Friedmann also explained that the changing demands of international society produced a demand for additional types of international law to cope with several dimensional changes such as democratization, industrialization, globalisation, and technological change or development.[116] The recognition that the structure of international society has undergone some basic changes, and that, correspondingly, international law is now developing on several levels must lead to a far-reaching reorientation in our conceptions of the science and study of contemporary international law.

---

114 Richard Falk, *op. cit.*, p.10.

115 Wolfgang Friedmann, *The Changing Structure of International Law*(New York: Columbia University Press, 1964), p.5.

116 *Ibid.*, pp.3-4.

# Ⅲ. Problematic Issues Concerning the Paradigm Shift in International Law

## 1. Reconceptualization of Sovereignty

Sovereignty is transformed nowadays.[117] It is well admitted that the shift in state sovereignty is already in process in terms of moving from a notion of absolute sovereignty to the notion of relative sovereignty.[118] Indeed, states' governmental authority is horizontally and vertically dispersed. Therefore, today's international law is constituted by polycentric decision-making structures and fragmented spheres of law. This has come to constitute what may properly be termed 'a new international law.'[119]

---

117 Some scholars argue that state sovereignty has been eroded or rather transformed, however, others insist that sovereignty is being sustained and the scope of state authority has increased over time. This debate in part reflects the fact that the term 'sovereignty' has been used in different ways by writers or arguers. According to Stephen D. Krasner, the term sovereignty has been commonly used in at least four different ways: domestic sovereignty, referring to the organization of public authority within a state and to the level of effective control exercised by those holding authority; interdependence sovereignty, referring to the ability of public authorities to control transborder movements; international legal sovereignty, referring to the mutual recognition of states or other entities; and Westphalian sovereignty, referring to the exclusion of external actors from domestic authority configurations (Stephen D. Krasner, *Sovereignty — Organized Hypocrisy —* (Princeton and New York: Princeton University Press, 1999), pp.3–42).

118 Gene M. Lyons and Michael Mastanduno eds., *Beyond Westphalia? — State Sovereignty and International Intervention*(Baltimore and London: The Johns Hopkins University Press, 1995); Michelle Sanson, *International Law and Global Governance*(Cameron May), p.301.

Current international legal discourse is grappling with the enormity of challenges posed by rapid restructuring of international law. A traditional image of international law is most linked to the concept of sovereignty, this being in a sense both constitutive and the central legal attribute of statehood. This conception of sovereignty has constituted the dominant structural premise of international law up until the present, constituting a paradigm of international law. Therefore, traditional international law has been mainly perceived as being concerned with the conditions of statehood and the rights and obligations of states in relation to other states.[120]

But, new international law encapsulates new structures of authority and new actors and interests.[121] Contemporary international legal discourse is an expansive and manifold field. The fragmentation of international law into specialized regimes gives rise to significant problem on unitary and coherent international legal order. Among a number of approaches to solve this problem, the way to establish a clear hierarchy of values through denoting certain norms *jus cogens* or *erga omnes* in international law has been suggested.[122] These concepts are based on the struggle for

---

119  Christoffer C. Eriksen and Marius Emberland eds., *The New International Law: An Anthology*(Leiden · Boston: Martinus Nijhoff Publishers, 2010), p.3.

120  *Ibid.*, pp.4-5.

121  *Ibid.*, p.8.

122  *Ibid.*, pp.9-10; Wilhelm G. Grewe, transl. and rev. by Michael Byers, *The Epochs of International Law*(Berin·New York: Walter de Gruyter,

overcoming a traditional paradigm in the sense that sovereignty is the central basis of legitimacy in international law and state consent or consensus constitutes the main basis of legal obligation.

In this regard, it is admitted that the concepts of *jus cogens* and the obligations *erga omnes* have signified the fundamental changes of the international community and international law. These concepts have been mainly shaped by the International Court of Justice(ICJ) and the International Law Commission(ILC) respectively. The concept of obligation *erga omnes* was introduced by the ICJ as an *obiter dictum* in the *Barcelona Traction* case where the ICJ suggested that the obligation not to commit or tolerate racial discrimination has an *erga omnes* character and therefore may be invoked by any state.[123] As mentioned above, traditional international law is based on consent and there is no hierarchy of obligations, so all obligations are of equal rank. In such a system there is no special place for community values that trump other norms such as in a domestic constitutional system. In order to fill this gap, the ILC introduced the concept of peremptory norms(*jus cogens*).[124]

Nowadays, these concepts have found their places in 1969

---

2000), p.716.

123  *Barcelona Traction, Light and Power Company, Limited*(New application: 1962) (*Belgium v. Spain*), Judgement of 5 February 1970 ICJ Reports 3, para. 33.

124  Menno T. Kamminga, *op. cit.*, p.6.

Vienna Convention on the Law of Treaties(VCLT)[125] and 2001 Draft Articles on Responsibility of States for Internationally Wrongful Acts,[126] which were drafted by the ILC. These concepts are based on the recognition of common interests and public order of international community. The incorporation of these new concepts in the international legal doctrine are now well rooted, and has contributed much to the groundbreaking developments of inter-national law.[127]

In his 1994 Hague Academy lecture, "From Bilateralism to Community Interest in International Law," then, Professor Bruno Simma examined ongoing tentative efforts in international law to

---

125 Article 53 【Treaties conflicting with a peremptory norm of general international law (*jus cogens*)】: A treaty is void if, at the time of its conclusion, it conflicts with a peremptory norm of general international law. For the purposes of the present Convention, a peremptory norm of general international law is a norm accepted and recognized by the international community as a whole as a norm from which no derogation is permitted and which can be modified only by a subsequent norm of general international law having the same character; Article 64 【Emergence of a new peremptory norm of general international law (*jus cogens*)】: If a new peremptory norm of general international law emerges, any existing treaty which is in conflict with that norm becomes void and terminates.

126 CHAPTER III (Articles 40 & 41) serious breaches of obligations under peremptory norms of general international law, and Article 48 【Invocation of responsibility by a State other than an injured State】 1. any state other than an injured state is entitled to invoke the responsibility of another state in accordance with paragraph 2 if; (a) The obligation breached is owed to a group of states including that state, and is established for the protection of a collective interest of the group; or (b) The obligation breached is owed to the international community as a whole.

127 Elena K. Proukaki, *op. cit.*, p.11.

overcome the traditional structures of bilateralism and give way to the formulation and pursuit of community interest.[128] It is now demonstrated that the changing nature of international law from a legal order confined to obligations of a reciprocal character to a legal order that safeguards fundamental community values and principles could hardly be disputed.

In December 2001, the International Commission on Intervention and State Sovereignty(ICISS) introduced the concept of responsibility to protect(RtoP). ICISS issued a report, *The Responsibility to Protect*, designed to meet the inherent tension between state sovereignty and the human protection against the atrocities committed by states.[129] In the words of one prominent member the ICISS, to cope with these severe human rights violations, the international community had to rethink sovereignty in terms of its essence being not so much control as responsibility.[130] Legalizing the RtoP needs a reconceptualization of the sovereignty and security of states.

RtoP is based on the concept of sovereignty not as a control but rather as a responsibility, and furthermore, based on a new

---

128 Hans-Peter Kaul and Eleni Chaitidou, "Balancing Individual amd Community Interests: Reflections on the International Criminal Court," in Ulrich Fasenrath *et al.*, *op. cit.*, p.975.

129 For understanding the RtoP in general, see Gareth Evans, *The Responsibility to Protect: Ending Mass Atrocity Crimes Once and For All*(Washington, D.C.: Brookings Institution Press, 2008)

130 Gareth Evans, "The Responsibility to Protect: Rethinking Humanitarian Intervention," *American Journal of International Law*, Vol.98, No.1, 2004, pp.78-80.

concept of human security rather than traditional concept of national security.[131] Human security is a newly articulated concept in which the individual, and not the state, is the referent object of security.[132] *The 1984 Human Development Report* of the UN Development Programme became the starting point for a new academic debate on the definition of security. Gradually a new approach to the function of security emerged, constituting a deepening and broadening of the traditional security function, that has led to a paradigm shift in security from one which is state-centred to one which is people-centred.[133]

This new conception of state sovereignty envisions a two-fold conception of state responsibility: a state is internally responsible to its citizens for the welfare and human security, and externally responsible to the international community for its internal actions. Furthermore, the Commission contemplated a kind of 'residual responsibility' on the part of the international community, to be activated: ( i ) when a particular state is clearly either unwilling or unable to fulfill its responsibility to protect; (ii) when a particular state ⋯ is itself the actual perpetrator of crimes or atrocities; or (iii) where people living outside a particular state are directly threatened by actions taking place there.[134]

---

131 Hisashi Owada, "Human Security and International Law," in Ulrich Fasenrath *et al., op. cit.,* p.512.

132 *Ibid.,* p.505.

133 *Ibid.*

It is admitted, as some critics say, that the concept of RtoP is a radical new approach, but is still ambiguous and controversial one. So, its potential status as a legal principle is uncertain. Nevertheless, it can be asserted that the evolution of legal obligations constituting RtoP towards their populations and other states point to an evolution towards international responsibility that might at some time crystallize into international law obligations to protect people.[135] If this trend in practice continues, the doctrine could indeed constitute an emerging norm of international law, *i. e.*, at least 'soft' law rather than mere moral norm. We may say that the principle of RtoP does represent a significant shift away from the prevailing state-centred approach and could, henceforth, provide a legal basis for the realization of human security and play a crucial role in the development of international law.

In tandem with the development of RtoP, the UN ILC concluded its work on drafting Articles on State Responsibility. The UN General Assembly endorsed these articles in 2001.[136] A chapter containing a new developing doctrine of international law for the aggravated state responsibility in case of serious breaches of obligations under peremptory norms of general international law

---

134 P. J. Glen, *op. cit.*, pp.23-24.

135 Susan Breau, *The Responsibility to Protect in International Law: An Emerging Paradigm Shift*(London & New York: Routledge, 2016), p.2.

136 ILC, Draft Articles on Responsibility of States for Internationally Wrongful Acts, November 2001, Supplement No. 10(A/56/10). Chapter IV.E.1 and UN Doc. GA Res. 56/83, 12 December 2001.

(*jus cogens*), which, it is argued embodies similar obligations to the RtoP.[137] In this regard, the developing part of both aggravated state responsibility and the RtoP is the idea of a state being responsible to a higher entity, *i. e.*, the international community. This may be estimated as the emerging paradigm shift, because instead of a voluntary assumption of international obligations, both the RtoP and aggravated state responsibility entail mandatory regimes of duties owed to a community of values, embodied in the international community.[138]

## 2. International Rule of Law

### 1) The Significance of the International Rule of Law

The ideal of the rule of law is well known from national constitutional law, however, it is admitted, nowadays, that it relates to the regulation of a community based on law and justice, not on power.[139] While the respect for the rule of law traditionally has been a requirement addressed to the domestic legal order, the relevance of the principle is increasingly acknowledged also as part of international law.[140]

---

137  Susan Breau, *op. cit.*, p.3.

138  *Ibid.*

139  Jan Klabbers, Anne Peters, and Geir Ulfstein, *The Constitutionalization of International Law*(Oxford: Oxford University Press, 2011), p.59.

140  *Ibid.*

Therefore, the great project for the 21$^{st}$ century among international legal scholars and politicians is to build the rule of law at the international or global level.[141] Because the international community still has no centralized governmental organizations for the realization of the rule of law, it is necessary to establish and promote the cooperative governance system for diverse actors and members in international arena.

But, in fact, there has been a question whether an international rule of law is possible. This question is inextricably linked to the traditional question of whether international law can be said to rule at all in the international arena. Simon Chesterman argues that when the rule of law is understood in the core, formal sense, one need only consider the international judicial systems and the processes of law-making to reasonably conclude that there is presently no such thing as the international rule of law, so, international law has yet to achieve a certain normative or institutional threshold to justify use of the term, rule of law.[142]

---

141 Historian Paul Johnson opined(in "Laying Down the Law," *Wall Street Journal*, 10 March 1999, A22) that the great undertaking of the last millennium was the establishment of the rule of law within nation states, and that the project for this new millennium is to build the rule of law on the international or global level(Brian Z. Tamanaha, *On the Rule of Law: History, Politics, Theory*(Cambridge: Cambridge University Press, 2004), p.127). As to the rule of law on the international level, see *ibid.*, pp.127-136.

142 Concerning the international rule of law, Simon Chesterman argues that it is helpful to distinguish between three possible meanings. First, 'the international rule of law' may be understood as the application of rule of law principles to relations between states and other subjects of

But, in contrast, Stephane Beaulac insists that the formal aspects of the rule of law are, to a large extent, already reflected in the international legal system. Beaulac pointed out, to support his view, the presence of norms having the characteristics of law and providing certainty, predictability, and stability to the system, and limiting the use of arbitrary power. In addition, Beaulac argues that international legal norms are adequately created and applied among states, and the international system has adjudicative enforcement of normativity, supporting this assertion by pointing out the existence of the ICJ.[143]

In fact, as Beaulac acknowledged, the limits of institutional elements of the international rule of law still remain. It is clear that the concept of the international rule of law is fraught with

---

international law. secondly, the 'rule of international law' could privilege international law over national law. Thirdly, a 'global rule of law' might denote the emergence of a normative regime that touches individuals directly without formal mediation through existing national institutions. Chesterman points that the second may be relevant to certain regional organizations such as the European Union which is very exceptional. The third approach accurately reflects the rise of quasi-administrative regimes that fall outside traditional domestic and international legal categories, but remains at an early stage of development. Therefore, he says that the first sense is the rule of law which may be applied in contemporary international arena. However, Chesterman argues that the cautious endorsements by the international society and organizations of the rule of law reflects the primitive nature of international law as a legal system(Simon Chesterman, "An International Rule of Law?," *American Journal of Comparative Law*, Vol.56, 2008, pp.356-358).

[143] Monica P. Moyo, "The International Rule of Law: An Analysis," *Minnesota International Law Journal*, Vol.23, 2014, pp.86-87.

both theoretical and practical application problems. In this regard, it is admitted that international community requires much more strengthened role of international law, *i.e.*, strengthened international rule of law. The strengthening or effectuation of international rule of law for realizing global governance is to be recognized as a crucial task for international law scholars and politicians to further the cooperative system for promoting community interests and values.

## 2) International Rule of Law and Paradigm Shift

The international rule of law demands: International society should be ruled by not only the active role of the States and IGOs but also the wide participation of NGOs on the basis of established international law; All the subjects and actors should rely on law as opposed to arbitrary power in international relations; International conflicts and disputes should be settled peacefully and justifiably by the international law and internationally agreed methods for settling international disputes rather than power or forcible means; It should be admitted that law can and should be used as an instrumentality for the cooperative international furtherance of social aims, in such fashion as to preserve the values of freedom and human dignity for individuals.[144]

---

144 Brian Z. Tamanaha, *op. cit.*, pp.127–136; Boo Chan Kim, *Global Governance and International Law: Some Global and Regional Issues*(BoGoSa, 2011), pp.49–50; William W. Bishop, "The International

It is admitted that the international rule of law is intimately linked with the humanization and constitutionalization of international law, and global governance which are to be examined later in relation to the paradigm shift in international law. The international rule of law should be applied and realized for the protection of human rights, as well as promotion of common values. Therefore, the aim or objective of the international law and organizations should be to protect and promote the human rights or fundamental rights and freedoms on international level.[145]

In this regard, in *The 2005 World Summit Outcome*, UN

---

Rule of Law," *Michigan Law Review*, Vol.59, 1961, p.553.

145 The post—World Ⅱ era has been the start of international protection of human rights. Especially, the UN Charter obligates member states to promote universal respect for human rights and not to discriminate on the basis of race, sex, language, or religion in implementing human rights obligations. Based on this broad obligation, the international community has extensively codified classical human rights for the protection of individual fundamental rights and freedoms. In addition, the international community has codified economic, social, and cultural rights directed at improving the economic, social, and cultural conditions of the individual to make the enjoyment of fundamental rights and freedoms more meaningful. More recently, the international community has attempted to define and codify group rights and rights of peoples, so—called 'third—generation rights.' These 'rights' or standards of achievement are intended to enhance the political, economic, social, and cultural self—determination and development of peoples to ensure the full and equitable participation of all nations, rich or poor, in the international community of states(Jost Delbruck, "A More Effective International Law or a New 'World Law'? — Some of the Development of International Law in a Changing International System," *Indiana Law Journal*, Vol.68, 1993, p.712).

member states unanimously recognized the need for universal adherence to and implementation of the rule of law at both national and international levels and reaffirmed their commitment to an international order based on the rule of law and international law.[146] UN General Assembly reiterated its reaffirming that human rights, rule of law and democracy are interlinked and mutually reinforcing, that they belong to the universal and indivisible core values and principles of the United Nations, and that the need for universal adherence to and implementation of the rule of law at both national and international levels and its solemn commitment to an inter‒ national order based on the rule of law and international law, which, together with the principles of justice, is essential for peaceful coexistence and cooperation among states.[147]

## 3. Humanization of International Law

### 1) The Meaning of the Humanization of International Law

Especially, since the establishment of the UN, international human rights law has been recognized as an important field of international law on the basis of the human values and human dignity. The concept of human rights and international human

---

146 Resolution adopted by the General Assembly(A/RES/60/1), para. 134.
147 Preamble of the Resolution adopted by the UN General Assembly (A/RES/62/70).

rights law have positively influenced various fields of traditional or general international law. Nowadays, international human rights law becomes part and parcel of the international law, and could help to renew the substance of international law and introduce a new paradigm in the international law. Although not all scholars agree as to the extent of the influence or impact of human rights law on the general international law, there seems to be consensus that human rights are a source of critical change in international law.[148]

In his work, *International Law*, Antonio Cassese points out that "the arrival of human rights on the international scene is, indeed, a remarkable event because it is a subversive theory destined to foster tension and conflict among states. Essentially it is meant to tear the veil that in the past protected sovereignty and gave each state the appearance of a fully armoured titanic structure, perceived by other states only 'as a whole,' the inner mechanisms of which could not be tampered with. Today, the human rights doctrine forces states to give account of how they treat their nationals, administer justice, run prisons, and so on. Potentially, therefore, it can subvert their domestic order and, consequently, the traditional configuration of the international community as well."[149]

---

[148] Vassilis P. Tzevelekos, "Revisiting the Humanization of International Law: Limits and Potential," *Erasmus Law Review*, June 2013 | No.1, p.63.

[149] Antinio Cassese, *International Law*, 2nd ed.(Oxford: Oxford University

Further, Cassese admits that the human rights doctrine has positively influenced various fields of traditional international law. It has helped to introduce a new paradigm in the international community, as the ICTY Appeals Chamber stated in 1995 in its seminal decision in *Tadić*(Introductory Appeal). In all these areas[150] the human rights doctrine has operated as a potent leaven, contributing to shift the world community from a reciprocity—based bundle of legal relations, geared to the private pursuit of self—interest, and ultimately blind to collective needs, to a community hinging on a core of fundamental values, strengthened by the emergence of community obligations and community rights and the gradual shaping of public interests.[151]

Some scholars including Theodor Meron use the term, 'humanization of international law' to explain the process of influencing of human rights and humanitarian law on general international law. In his work, *The Humanization of International Law*,[152] Meron points out that human rights are part and

---

Press, 2005), p.375.

150 Cassese illustrates the areas such as recognition of new states or governments, international subjects, customary law, the structure of international obligations, reservations to treaties, termination of treaties, *jus cogens*, international monitoring of compliance with law, enforcement, including countermeasures, the administration of international criminal justice, the laws of warfare or the humanitarian law of armed conflict(*ibid.*, p.396).

151 *Ibid.*

152 Meron wrote *The Humanization of International Law* on the basis of his Hague Academy lecture on international law in the age of human rights in 2003. This book contains eight chapters such as the first chapter(the

parcel of international law. The elaboration of human rights norms and institutions has produced no less than a revolution in the system of international law.[153]

## 2) Humanization of International Law and Paradigm Shift

Meron attempts in his work to demonstrate that the influence of human rights law has not remained or confined to one sector of international law, and that its influence has spread to many other parts, though to varying degrees. In the result, he concludes that the humanization of international law under the impact of human rights has shifted its focus above all from state-centred to individual-centred.[154] But, Meron adds that we must not exaggerate human rights' influence where there has been little or none.[155] Tzevelekos argues that despite human rights having impact on other areas of international law, this trend has in the past been somewhat inflated.[156]

---

humanization of the Law of War), the second chapter(Criminalization of Violations of International Humanitarian Law), the third chapter(the Law of Treaties), the fourth chapter(Humanization of State Responsibility: from Bilateralism to Community Concerns), the fifth chapter (Subjects of International Law), the sixth chapter(Sources of International Law), the seventh chapter(International Courts), the eighth chapter(UN Institutions and the Protection of Human Rights). See Thedor Meron, *The Humanization of International Law*(Leiden and Boston: Martinus Nijhoff Publishers, 2006).

153 *Ibid.*, p.1.
154 *Ibid.*
155 *Ibid.*

In this regard, it is necessary to explore and assess as to what areas of international law have been under humanization. In this regard, the Committee on International Human Rights Law and Practice of the International Law Association(ILA) carried out a review of the impact of international human rights law on general international law and published a volume, *The Impact of Human Rights Law on General International Law*[157] in 2009. In this volume, the Committee overall takes a kind of mitigated position, *i.e.*, 'reconciliation approach' rather than 'constitutionalist approach.'[158] Reconciliation approach means that the relation

---

156  Vassilis P. Tzevelekos, *op. cit.*, pp.62-65.

157  This volume is the culmination of four years of work by the Committee on International Human Rights Law and Practice of the ILA. The Committee was composed of human rights experts from some 30 countries nominated by their national ILA branches. The Committee was an appropriate forum to carry out a review of the impact of international human rights law on general international law. The impact of human rights law on general international law has been analysed in two earlier works: Bruno Simma, 'International Human Rights and General International Law: A Comparative Analysis' in Collected Courses of the Academy of European Law, Vol. IV-2(Kluwer, Dordrecht, 1993), pp.153-256 and T. Meron, The Humanization of International Law. The present volume includes the Final Report of the Committee as adopted by the 2008 Conference of the ILA in Rio de Janeiro, and a number of articles representing elaborated versions of selected papers that were prepared by individual members of the Committee and that formed the basis for the Final Report(Menno T. Kamminga & Martin Scheinen, *op. cit.*, p. v ). This volume contains several chapters which reviews the impact of international human rights law on the fields of international law such as the law of treaties, the structures of international obligations, formation of customary international law, state immunity, the right to consular notification, state responsibility, diplomatic protection.

158  See *infra* note 164

between the international human rights law and the general international law is two-way.[159]

However, the Committee considers that the impact of international human rights law on general international law is highly desirable in order to soften the international legal order's predominantly state-centred nature and to accommodate the special, non-reciprocal nature of international obligations in the field of human rights. According to Kamminga, the process of humanization of international law is a response to a deeply and widely felt need to make the international legal order more responsive to the needs of a wider range of actors than just states including the international community understood as referring to humankind as a whole and not just the community of states.[160] In this regard, the permeation of international human rights law through general international law constitutes a quiet and progressive revolution which focuses on shifting from the state-centred to human-centred paradigm.[161]

A paradigm shift is said to exist, consisting in the gradual abandonment of the classic conception of state sovereignty. But, humanization of international law is not fully completed and all the human rights norms can not become higher laws in the

---

159  Menno T. Kamminga, *op. cit.*, pp.1-4; Martin Scheinen, "Impact on the Law of Treaties," in Menno T. Kamminga & Martin Scheinen, *op. cit.*, pp.29-36.

160  Menno T. Kamminga, *ibid,*, p.21.

161  *Ibid.*, p.22.

hierarchical order of international law. The road is still under construction and the reality of humanization is an ongoing process.[162] We must, as of now, resist the triumphalist approach[163] or excessive human-rightism which is a kind of 'thick' constitutionalist approach that human rights have had and should have the strong impact on all the rest of international law like the peremptory norms of general international law (*jus cogens*),[164] however, the idea of humanization of international law may constitute a reality in the international legal order, and at the same time a potential for further development of international law.[165]


## 4. Constitutionalisation of International Law

### 1) The Meaning of Constitutionalism and Constitutionalisation

According to Jan Klabbers, fragmentation, verticalization, and constitutionalisation form the holy trinity of international legal

---

162  Vassilis P. Tzevelekos, *op. cit.*, p.66.

163  Theodor Meron, *op. cit.*, p.1.

164  Here, constitutional or constitutionalist approach means the argument that human rights law is something more than just one branch of international law, namely a constitutional dimension of international law, representing objectively binding rules, that is, norms that are legally binding upon states irrespective of their continuing will to be bound(Martin Scheinen, *op. cit.*, p.29). So, if we use the term 'thick' constitutionalist approach, it means something more than 'mere' constitutional approach.

165  Vassilis P. Tzevelekos, *op. cit.*, p.66.

debate in the early 21$^{st}$ century.[166] Traditionally, fragmentation of international law has been described as the existence of various fields or areas of international law, such as international environmental law, international economic law, international human rights law, international criminal law and so forth, among which there is no or hardly any relationship. In addition, proliferation of international courts and tribunals is regarded as one of its main factors.

In this regard, fragmentation basically refers to the profound systemic rupture in the structure of international law, reflected in the lack of well—developed and established hierarchy or other techniques to deal with normative conflicts and tensions between general international law norms and its specialized regimes, as well as between those regimes *inter se*.[167] This is why consti-tutionalism or constitutionalisation of international law as a theoretical approach has been applied and developed. In this perspective, it may said that the theories of constitutionalism and constitutionalisation of international law are based on a fragmentation of international law. Under this circumstance, the ILC also worked for avoiding the fragmentation of international legal system and guaranteeing consistency, and submitted a report *Conclusions of the Study Group of ILC on the Fragmentation*

---

166 Jan Klabbers, Anne Peters, and Geir Ulfstein, *op. cit.*, p.1.

167 Andrzej Jakubowski and Karolina Wierczyńska, eds., *Fragmentation vs the Constitutionalisation of International Law: A Practical Inquiry* (London and New York: Routledge, 2016), p.1.

*of International Law* to the UN General Assembly in 2006.

The strict concept of constitutionalism or constitutionalisation of international law still lacks clarity because of the diversity of definitions proposed by international legal scholars,[168] however, its significance grew in the legal discipline and became the subject of discussion. Regrettably, as of now, there is no consensus about the meaning of constitutionalisation of international law.[169] But, it must be noted that, in essence, the concept of constitutionalism and the concept of constitutionalisation are to be differentiated in the sense that the former is for advocating or making the normative case for a better and more just world, but the latter is for making a empirical case for a process or phenomenon in international law.[170] In other word, constitutionalism signifies an attitude or a frame of mind, but constitutionalisation means a process inspired by constitutionalism or constitutionalist thought.[171]

Today, constitutionalism is a value-laden concept and refers to the inclusion of basic substantive principles which goes beyond the simple articulation of formal rules and procedures of constitution.[172] Unlike the static language of the formal and

---

168 As to diverse definitions of constitutionalism and constitutionalisation, see Jan Klabbers, Anne Peters, and Geir Ulfstein, *op. cit.* pp.19-31.

169 Karolina Milewicz, "Emerging Patterns of Global Constitutionalization: Toward a Conceptual Framework," *Indiana Journal of International Law*, Vol.16, Issue 2, 2014, p.415.

170 Jan Klabbers, Anne Peters, and Geir Ulfstein, *op. cit.*, p.4.

171 *Ibid.*, p.10.

substantive characteristics that form the basis of constitutionalism, constitutionalisation indicates an underlying process or phenomenon which can be identified in the international arena. It embeds a time dimension which means that a constitution or constitutional elements can come into being as part of a process over time. In a word, it indicates a process encompassing the emergence, creation, and identification of constitutional elements.[173]

## 2) Constitutionalisation of International Law and Paradigm Shift

Nowadays, constitutionalism and constitutionalisation of international law become an academic and political agenda that identifies and advocates the unity or coherence of international law in order to overcome the fragmentation of international law through the application of (procedural and substantive) constitutionalist principles in the international legal sphere. In this regard, scholars of international law concur that the normative idea of constitutionalism and constitutionalisation of international law are recent phenomena, decisively changing the character of the international or world order.[174]

Among the diverse approaches, some scholars argue that there

---

172 Karolina Milewicz, *op. cit.*, p.419.

173 *Ibid.*, p.420.

174 *Ibid.*, p.414.

needs an international or global constitution,[175] or at least constitutional dimension of international law. Approaches for the normative idea of constitutionalism means that system of the rule of law and human rights protection system is to be established on the global scale.[176] In other word, the normative idea of global constitutionalism is considered to be a linkage of two specific sets of norms that evolve over time: the formal norms, which comprise primarily the principle of the rule of law, and the substantive norms, most importantly the guarantee of fundamental rights to human beings or individuals.[177]

Under this circumstances, the process of constitutionalisation of international law is underway regardless of the dimension of constitutionalism. Accordingly, this process changes the character of the international order and may bring about the normative idea of constitutionalism.[178] Such a value—laden constitutional approach is strongly linked to the recognition of individuals as the new subjects of international law *via* the promotion of

---

175 Several scholars have postulated a world constitution beyond the nation—state that is put into force by a world sovereign and legitimizes the exercise of global political power. In this regard, the UN Charter is referred to as the constitutional document of the international community. Accordingly, the UN is viewed as the primary institution that furnishes the international community with the necessary international organs(*ibid.*, p.424).

176 *Ibid.*, p.422.

177 *Ibid.*, p.423; Mattias Kumm, "The Legitimacy of International Law: A Constitutionalist Framework of Analysis," *European Journal of International Law*, Vol.15, 2004, pp.907–909.

178 Karolina Milewicz, *ibid.*, p.422.

fundamental or human rights[179] and touches upon the foundation of the hierarchical legal order and the development of core values in international law which are to be discussed in relation to the concepts of *jus cogens* norms and the obligations *erga omnes*.

In this regard, the feature of constitutionalisation is basically linked with the humanization of international law. In a sense, the theory of the humanization of international law might be seen as a contiguous or even complementary to the theory on the constitutionalisation of international law.[180] It seems that issues of the constitutionalisation of international law, the humanization of international law, and furthermore global governance are newly developed approaches which are deeply interconnected on the basis of the reconceptualization of sovereignty and the international rule of law, and they altogether become conspicuous evidences of paradigm shift in international law.[181]

---

179 *Ibid*.

180 Vassilis P. Tzevelekos, *op. cit.*, p.63,

181 According to Anne Peters, there are four important elements of constitutionalisation; First, the principle of sovereignty is being ousted from its position as a Letztbegründung(first principle) of international law. The normative status of sovereignty is derived from humanity, that is, the legal principle that human rights, interests, needs, and security must be respected and promoted. This normative status is also the telos of the international legal system. Humanity is foundational in a normative sense because states are not ends in themselves, but are composite entities whose justification lies in the fulfillment of public functions needed for human beings to live together in peace and security; Second, the principle of state consent is partly replaced by majoritarian decision—making. This is apt to improve the effectiveness of global governance, and thus contributes to output legitimacy of the system.

## 5. Strengthening of Global Governance

## 1) Significance of Global Governance

These days, social and economic processes operate pre—
dominantly at a global level, and the world is changing due to
processes of globalization. But, it is admitted that globalization
does not require world government, but require global
governance. As the $21^{st}$ century dawns, there is a desperate need
for more useful knowledge about global governance. States are
well aware that they themselves less able to deal with the array
of issues that face them. States admit that they can do so only
by working together with other entities and changing the modes
of modes of cooperation. Therefore, a multifaceted strategy for
global governance is required.

Recently, the concept of global governance has gone from the
ranks of the unknown to one of the central orienting themes in

---

Accepting the premise that the ultimate reference points of democracy
are natural persons, state majoritarianism is, in a democratic
perspective, ambiguous; Third, certain basic values, such as human
rights protection, climate protection, and maybe even free trade, seems
to have acquired universal acceptance, as manifested in the universal
ratification of relevant multilateral treaties. The formal acceptance of
universal treaties enshrining constitutional values is not the end, but
rather the beginning, of the constitutionalisation of international law;
Fourth, the settlement of international disputes is increasingly legalized
and juridified through the establishment of international courts and
tribunals with quasi—compulsory jurisdiction. The juridification is in
some regards merely a manifestation of the legalization of international
relations(Anne Peters, "The Merits of Global Constitutionalism," *Indiana
Journal of Global Legal Studies*, Vol.16, Issue 2, 2009, pp.398–399).

the practice and study of international affairs of the post—Cold War period. The intensifying connections between states and peoples are now frequently presumed to create the need for governance and rule—making at the global level.[182] Nowadays, only with global governance will states and peoples be able to cooperate on global issues, settle their problems or disputes, and advance their common interests and values.[183] The significance of global governance lies at this point.

Global governance means a governance at the global level. As the Commission on Global Governance[184] put it; "Governance is the sum of the many ways individuals and institutions, public and private, manage their common affairs. It is a continuing process through which conflicting or diverse interests may be accommodated and co—operative action may be taken. ⋯ At the global level, governance has been viewed primarily as intergovernmental relationships, but, it must now be understood as also involving non—governmental organizations(NGOs), citizens' movements, multinational corporations, and the global capital market."[185]

---

182 Michael Barnett and Raymond Duvall, "Power in Global Governance," in Michael Barnett and Raymond Duvall eds., *Power in Global Governance*(Cambridge: Cambridge University Press, 2008), p.1.

183 *Ibid.*

184 The Commission on Global Governance was an independent commission, meaning that it was not created by a resolution of the UN General Assembly. It operated officially as a non—governmental organization (NGO) but, as a practical matter, it was an instrument if the UN. It received the formal endorsement of UN Secretary—General, and funding from the UN Development Programme(UNDP).

But it must be noted that 'governance' is not synonymous with 'government.' As the report of the Commission on Global Governance makes clear, global governance is not world or global government. The Commission are not proposing movement towards world government.[186] But, both refer to purposive behaviour, to goal-oriented activities, to systems of rule; but government suggests activities that are backed by formal authority, by police powers to ensure the implementation of duly constituted policies, whereas governance refers to activities backed by shared goals that may or may not derive from legal and formally prescribed responsibilities and that do not necessarily rely on police powers to overcome defiance and to attain compliance. In its meaning, governance is a more encompassing phenomenon than government. It embraces not only governmental institutions, but also informal or non-governmental mechanism, whereby those persons and organizations within its purview move ahead, satisfy their needs, and fulfill their wants.[187]

---

185 The Commission on Global Governance, *supra* note 7, pp.2–3.

186 *Ibid.*, p. xvi.

187 James N. Rosenau and Ernst-Otto Czempiel eds., *Governance Without Government: Order and Change in World Politics*(Cambridge: Cambridge University Press, 1995), p.4; Charlotte Ku, *International law, International Relations and Global Governance*(London and New York: Routledge, 2012), pp.1–16.

## 2) Global Governance and Paradigm Shift in International Law

Nowadays, it is admitted that global governance is a kind of paradigm shift in international law and relations.[188] International law is to be changed in order to be part and parcel of global governance. Global governance is often exercised by authorities and through instruments which are not pertaining to classical categories of international law such as the soft law, NGOs, TNCs and so on.[189] Indeed, some or more of global governance is exercised through standards or code of conduct, many of which are made not through a formal intergovernmental process, but by means of informal gathering of members of international community or civil society.[190]

To establish and strengthen global governance on the basis of international rule of law, the humanization and consti-tutionalisation of international law is needed. It is necessary, both to ensure the promotion of human rights and common values in international community.[191] As with the humanization and the constitutionalization, global governance is not an event but a process to be underway for many years. Therefore, common vision

---

188 Charlotte Ku, *ibid.*, pp.17-36.

189 Jan Klabbers, *International Law*(Cambridge: Cambridge University Press, 2013), pp.304-305.

190 *Ibid.*, p.317,

191 Winston P. Nagan, "Global Governance: A New Paradigm for the Rule of Law," *Cadmus*, Vol.2, Issue 1, 2013, pp.161-168.

for the future and cooperative efforts of all the members of international community is needed.

In this regard, in its 1995 report, *Our Global Neighborhood*, the Commission on Global Governance, pointed out that the development of global governance is part of the evolution of human efforts to organize life on the planet, and that process will always be going on.[192] Further, the Commission stresses that these changes call for reforms in the modes of international cooperation, *i.e.*, the institutions and processes of global governance.[193] In addition, as the Commission pointed out in its report, the UN should be reformed or reorganized in order to play a more active role in building a global governance and strengthening the international rule of law as a *(de facto)* representative of international community.[194]

# Ⅳ. Conclusion

Since its inception, the modern international society has been changed into international community. Accordingly, the structure of international law has been transformed from state-centred

---

192 The Commission on Global Governance, *op. cit.*, p. xvi.

193 *Ibid.*, p. xiv .

194 *Ibid.*, pp.225-302; Thomas G. Weiss and Ramesh Thakur, *Global Governance and the UN: Unfinished Journey*(Bloomington and Indianapolis: Indiana University Press, 2010)

into human-centred on the basis of changing profile of state sovereignty and international society. This paper explains the concept of paradigm and the paradigm shift in international law, and continues to review the problematic issues concerning paradigm shift in international law, such as reconceptualization of sovereignty, the international rule of law, the humanization of international law, the constitutionalization of international law, and strengthening of global governance.

It seems that issues of the humanization of international law, constitutionalisation of international law, and furthermore global governance are newly developed approaches which are deeply interconnected based on the reconceptualization of sovereignty and the international rule of law, and they become conspicuous evidences of paradigm shift in international law. The new paradigm of international law such as community-based approach or human-centred paradigm is needed for international legal scholarship to explain the changing structure of international law and promote the community interests or values.

But, indeed, there have been persistent competitions between the older paradigm and the newer paradigm. In fact, the traditional, state-centred paradigm has still a lot of influence. In this regard, the shift form the older to newer paradigm in international law is still underway. However, it is emphasized that the need and justification for paradigm shift lies in that we are no longer justified or satisfied in explaining the structures and theories of international law in view of older traditional paradigm based on Westphalian system.

As of now, the shift from the older paradigm to the newer paradigm is not at all full-fledged, so the successful process of paradigm shift in international law remains to be seen. Therefore, it is urgent for the international legal scholars to reform the structure and develop new paradigm in international law in order to respond to the changing need of the international community.

# CHAPTER 4

# Global Governance and the United Nations

— focusing on the International Rule of Law —

## I. Introduction: the Role of the UN

The role of the United Nations(UN) in legal affairs — as spelled out in the Charter — is to promote the judicial settlement of disputes between States and encourage the development and codification of international law. A central task of the UN is the adjustment or settlement of international disputes by peaceful means in conformity with the principles of justice and international law, as called for in Article 1 of the UN Charter. And under Article 13 of the UN Charter, General Assembly's function is "encouraging the progressive development of international law and its codification."[195] Indeed, the United Nations and its members, from its foundation, regarded its role relating to the

---

195 The United Nations, *Basic Facts about the United Nations*(The United Nations, 1995), p.253.

international rule of law including the codification of international law as an important part of its tasks.

Its role relating to the international rule of law is very important
for the realization or effectuation of its aim or purpose, because
the purpose of the UN is to maintain international peace and
security, to develop friendly relations among nations based on
respect for the principles of equal rights and self-determination
of peoples, and to achieve international cooperation in solving
international problems of an economic, social, cultural, or
humanitarian character, and in promoting and encouraging
respect for human rights and for fundamental freedoms for all.[196]

The Charter of the UN is filled with a commitment to
strengthening the international rule of law, especially, in peace
and human rights affairs. In the Preamble, a pledge is made "to
establish conditions under which justice and respect for obligations
arising from treaties and other sources of international law can
be maintained." This broad world order goal is reaffirmed as a
'Purpose of the United Nations' in Article 1(1) where it is
undertaken to resolve international disputes in conformity with
the principles of justice and international law. I think, therefore,
it is very useful to consider what extent this mandate promoting
the international rule of law has been carried out, and to identify
areas of disappointment.

It is somewhat true that the UN has advanced the cause of

---

196 See the Preamble of the UN Charter.

peace and justice, and international law is playing a primary role in relation to these prospects. These days, the end of the Cold War or East–West rivalry between the United States and the former Soviet Union, and their respective blocs, should open wide the gates of opportunity for the effectuating the role of the UN. But, on the contrary, one might find a climate of skeptical assessment based on disappointing UN responses to a series of changes and challenges with which the international society now is confronted.[197]

Peace and security activity is still arguably the most controversial and challenging domain of UN activities.[198] In the first place, there is one view that we must review the legitimacy of the UN activity for the maintenance of the peace and security. The scope of inquiry undertaken here, therefore, must contain the role of law relating to UN operations — that is, law as a constitutional frame and as authoritative guidance with respect to contested action. The core issue of 'constitutionality' in peace and security actions has several additional dimensions that need to be addressed.

First, there is the question of double standards and selective action, not treating equals equally, that became especially salient over the years. Second, there is the crucial set of issues regarding the tension between respect for sovereign rights and a less statist

197 Thomas G. Weiss *et al.*, *The United Nations and Changing World Politics*(Westview Press, 1994), pp.83–88.
198 Richard A. Falk, *op. cit.*, pp.612–616.

definition of peace and security as illustrated by controversies about humanitarian assistance and the impact of such under- takings on Article 2(7)'s mandate not to intervene in matters essentially within 'the domestic jurisdiction' of member States. Third, there is a question, largely unexplored in the scholarly literature, of whether the United Nations, when it uses or authorizes force, should have its mandate more tightly constrained by law than comparable actions by States which are governed by the traditional law of war as set forth mainly in the Hague and Geneva Convention, as well as the two Geneva Protocols. Finally, there is the question of whether the latent potential already contained in the existing framework of UN law can be used to facilitate a process of global reform, or whether it is essential or more beneficial to alter or replace this framework by amending the Charter.

But, in this study, we should be concerned with 'the contributions' of the United Nations relating to the international rule of law. The United Nations is providing, through its sponsorship of law-making treaty negotiations and official conferences on major global challenges, the basis for the progressive development of international law responding to the rapidly evolving priorities and values associated with commitment to achieving a just and sustainable world order. Such contri- butions to the wider rule of law in the international society are indicative of a general UN disposition that also should be favorable to law in its own operations.

It is also relevant, in this wider sense, to note UN contributions to law—making and law application via the International Law Commission and the International Court of Justice. Both UN organs play major roles in enunciating and developing inter—national law cross a wide range of subject matters. Also, the law—declaring and law—making resolutions of the General Assembly, the status of which are a matter of persistent debate among internationalists, have exerted a definite, although uneven and controversial, influence on the growth of international law in the past half century. Over the past four decades, the United Nations has played a primary role in the codification of international law in various areas.[199]

In the background of this role, there are two broad world order concerns that condition the contemporary operative roles of international law. First is the emergence of a series of problems that overwhelm the problem—solving capacity of even the most powerful and activist sovereign States problems such as climate change, ozone depletion. reductions in bio—diversity, as well as transnational flows of disease, drugs, refugees, pollutants, crime, information and communication. Second, and more fundamental, the State has itself lost ground in relation to the projection of its authority—both directly and indirectly.[200]

Finally, we can find one more aspect of the UN relationship to

---

199 The United Nations, *Everyone's United Nations*(The United Nations, 1986), pp.365—397.

200 Richard A. Falk, *op. cit.*, pp.620—621.

the international rule of law. It is the role played by the United Nations in nurturing transnational democratic initiatives the manifold expressions of the voluntary and spontaneous actions of citizens and their organizations that are being generated by civil society.[201]


# II. The Function of the UN relating to the International Rule of Law

## 1. Overview[202]

In the strict sense of the term, neither the United Nations nor any of its Specialized Agencies was conceived as a legislative body. Their Charters and governing instruments contemplated that their objectives would be carried out mainly through recommendations aimed at coordinating or harmonizing the actions of their member States. Although it has often been emphasized that they are not legislatures, most UN organs have acted much like parliamentary bodies in their proceedings. As for applying and interpreting the international law, it takes place continually throughout the UN system. For a long time

---

201  *Ibid.*, p.616.

202  Christopher C. Joyner ed., *The United Nations and International Law*(Cambridge University Press, 1997), pp.3-19.

compliance and enforcement of international law were on the margins of UN concern. It is true that the task of UN law-making and law-applying carried on pretty much without serious consideration of means of ensuring compliance.

Nonetheless, we can get a clear view the whole array of the various compliance and enforcement processes used by UN organs by classifying them into several categories: First are the reporting and supervision procedures in a particular treaty or code of conduct. These procedures are most familiar in the human rights area. A second broad category of mechanisms for inducing compliances may be characterized as 'facilitative.' They include measures taken by the United Nations to assist States in carrying out obligations imposed by international law or by specific decisions of the organs. A good example is the use of armed peace-keeping forces to assist governments to comply with trans-border truce and cease-fire agreements.

A third category of compliance measures directly penalizes a law-breaking State by expelling it from the Organization or from taking part in some of the latter's activities. For example, the Charter provides for expulsion for persistent violations of the principles contained in the Charter. A fourth category of compliance measures is non-military enforcement action taken by the Security Council under Article 41 of Chapter VII of the Charter. This applies only when the Security Council has found a threat to the peace, or a breach of peace or act of aggression. Sanctions under Article 41 have come to be seen as the quintessential type of international enforcement.

The fifth category of compliance measures or enforcement is the use of armed force pursuant to Chapter VII of the Charter. It must be noted that the Security Council has applied its authority under Chapter VII by authorizing member States to use armed force as necessary to give effect to its decisions. The sixth category is the judicial settlement. It is of particular significance for legal order. And it is employed in both international and national tribunals. In this regard, the International Court of Justice is potentially the most important. In addition to these measures, 'self-help' or 'counter-measures' of States and public opinion of international society can be used in achieving compliance.

## 2. International Court of Justice(ICJ)

The ICJ, created in 1946 as the principal judicial organ of the United Nations, exists to settle disputes brought before it by States in accordance with international law. The International Court of Justice succeeded the Permanent Court of International Justice(PCIJ), which had functioned as the judicial arm of the League of Nations.

It gives judgements on contentious cases brought before it by States, and hands down advisory opinions at the request of UN organs and Specialized Agencies. Since its inception, States have submitted over 72 cases to it, and 22 advisory opinions have been requested by international organizations. Nearly all cases have been dealt with by the full Court, but since 1981 four have been referred to special Chambers at the request of the parties. Eleven contentious cases are pending.[203]

The disputes decided by the Court have dealt with a wide range of subjects, including: territorial rights; the delimitation of territorial waters and continental shelves; fishing jurisdiction; questions of nationality and the right of individuals to asylum; territorial sovereignty; the right of passage over foreign territory. The Court's advisory opinions have addressed such issues as: the competence of the General Assembly to admit a state to the UN; the capacity of the Organization to claim reparation for damages; the reservations that could be attached by a State to its signature on an international convention; appeals against judgements of the administrative tribunals that consider staff issues in the United Nations and the International Labor Organization(ILO); the presence of South African in Namibia; and the status of Western Sahara.[204]

Nevertheless, in a world of international legal disputes, the International Court of Justice, the principal judicial organ of the international community, has paradoxically few disputes on its docket. Viewed over the years, the Court has never been overworked. On the contrary, the general opinion is that its

---

203 The United Nations, *supra* note 195, p.253.
204 *Ibid.*, pp.253–257; Christopher C. Joyner, *op. cit.*, pp.366–374.

significant contributions to the settlement of international disputes and to the clarification and development of international law would be more significant if it had more business. But, anyway, it may be said that a decision by the International Court of Justice come fairly close to international legislation.[205]

In addition to the ICJ, the United Nations has patiently expanded its juridical functions by creating special international tribunals that deal with violations of humanitarian law. To replace domestic processes for trials, the Security Council created the war crimes tribunal for the former Yugoslavia in 1993,[206] and acted similarly to set up a special tribunal to deal with persons accused of committing crimes against humanity and genocide in Rwanda in 1994.[207] Both juridical bodies are *ad hoc*, criminal courts created by Security Council resolutions. Modeled after the 1945 Nuremberg Military Tribunal, the decisions of both tribunals are legally binding.[208]

---

205 Evan Luard, rev. by Derek Heater, *The United Nations: How It Works and What It Does?*(St. Martin's Press, 1979), p.87.

206 The formal name of this tribunal is the 'International Tribunal for the Prosecution of Persons Responsible for Serious Violations of International Humanitarian Law Committed in the Territory of the Former Yugoslavia Since 1991.' See, UN Security Council Resolution 827 of May 25, 1993.

207 The name of this Tribunal is the 'International Tribunal for Rwanda.' The sole purpose of the Tribunal is to prosecute persons responsible for genocide and other serious violations of international humanitarian law committed in Rwanda or committed in neighboring states by Rwandans during 1994. See, UN Security Council Resolution 955 of November 8, 1994.

These tribunals were explicitly created as part of an efforts to bring peace to war-torn territories, though they have been criticized for spending significant resources in order to prosecute few individuals with little lasting impact on the judicial institutions of the territory concerned. Hybrid tribunals, such as the Special Court for Sierra Leone and the Extraordinary Chambers in the Court of Cambodia, were intended to blend international supervision with development of national capacity but had limited success.[209]

## 3. International Law Commission(ILC)

The International Law Commission, established by the General Assembly in 1947 to develop and codify international law, develops new rules of international law and strives for the more precise formulation and systematization of existing customary international law. The mandate of the ILC is derived from a 1947 General Assembly resolution that established the Commission and approved its Statute. The General Assembly acted pursuant to Article 13(1)(a) of the UN Charter, which empowers it to "make recommendations for the purpose of: (a) promoting international co-operation in the political field and encouraging the progressive development of international law and its codification."

---

208 Christopher C. Joyner, *op. cit.*, pp.437-438.
209 Simon Chesterman, *op. cit.*, pp.349-350.

The Statute echoes that the Commission's task is "the promotion of the progressive development of international law and its codification."[210] And the progressive development of international law was defined as "the preparation of draft conventions on subjects which have not yet been regulated by international law or in regard to which the law has not yet been sufficiently developed in the practice of States."[211] Codification was to be "the more precise formulation and systemization of rules of international law in fields where there already has been extensive State practice, precedent or doctrine."[212]

The Commission meets annually in Geneva and is composed of 34 members, who serve in their individual capacities as legal experts, elected by the General Assembly so as to reflect "the principal forms of civilization and the principal legal systems of the world." Since 1949, when it held its first session, the Commission has prepared draft Articles on various aspects of international law, some chosen by the Commission itself and others referred to it by the General Assembly or the Economic and Social Council. Most of its drafts have been used as the basis for conventions adopted by the General Assembly or by international conferences. In other instances, the General Assembly has taken note of the Commission's work and brought it to the attention of member States for consideration.[213]

---

210 Statute of the International Law Commission, Art. I , para. 1.
211 *Ibid.*, Art. XV.
212 *Ibid.*, Art. XVII.

But, recently, a study by the UN Institute for Training and Research(UNITAR) asserts that the International Law Commission "is no longer playing the central role in the law—making process that it could and should play."[214] In this regard, the Chairman of the Commission stoutly defended its work before the General Assembly's Sixth Committee, pointing out that the International Law Commission "was constantly seeking to improve its working methods."[215]

## 4. The Human Rights Council

Originally, the Commission on Human Rights was created under the Economic and Social Council in 1947 with the goal of setting standards for international human rights, but as a subsidiary organ it had no authority to consider violations of human rights until 1967. Since then, it established and administered a number of extra—Conventional mechanisms for enforcing human rights. However, the Commission has long the subject of criticisms for

---

213 United Nations, *supra* note 199, pp.374—376.

214 Thomas M. Frank & Mohamed ElBaradei, "Current Development: The Codification and Progressive Development of International Law: A UNITAR Study of the Role and Use of the International Law Commission," *American Journal of International Law*, Vol.76, 1982, p.630.

215 The International Law Commission proposes legislation, but there is no body to pass it into binding law. Legislation, in the strict sense, does not yet exist at the international level. Evan Luard, rev. by Derek Heater, *op. cit.*, p.87.

its declining credibility and professionalism, and its ineffec-
tiveness.[216]

Therefore, by Resolution 60/251, the UN General Assembly
decided to establish, as a subsidiary organ, the Human Rights
Council[217] in Geneva, to replace the Commission on Human
Rights. The status of the Council will be reconsidered by late 2011
and it is possible at that time that it will become a full organ of
the United Nations like the Security Council and Economic and
Social Council, though at present, the Council remains a
subsidiary of the General Assembly.[218]

In terms of Resolution 60/251, the functions of the Council are
to:

"(a) Promote human rights education and learning as well as
advisory services, technical assistance and capacity— building,
to be provided in consultation with the consent of Member
States concerned; (b) Serve as a forum for dialogue on thematic
issues on all human rights; (c) Make recommendations to the
General Assembly for the further development of international
law in the field of human rights; (d) Promote the full
implementation of human rights obligations undertaken by
states and follow—up to the goals and commitments related to
the promotion and protection of human rights emanating from

---

216 Rhona K. M. Smith, *Textbook on International Human Rights*, 3rd
ed.(Oxford University Press, 2007), pp.57–58.

217 The Council consists of forty—seven members, The terms of Resolution
60/251 seek to ensure balance of member States.

218 Rhona K. M. Smith, *op. cit.*, p.58.

United nations conferences and summits; (e) Undertake a universal periodic review, based on objective and reliable information, of the fulfillment by each State of its human rights obligations and commitments in a manner which ensures universality of coverage and equal treatment with respect to all States; the review shall be a cooperative mechanism, based on an interactive dialogue, with the full involvement of the country concerned and with consideration given to its capacity—building needs; such a mechanism shall complement and not duplicate the work of treaty bodies; the Council shall develop the modalities and necessary time allocation of the universal periodic review mechanism within on year after the holding of its first session; (f) Contribute, through dialogue and cooperation, towards the prevention of human rights violations and respond promptly to human rights emergencies; (g) Assume the role and responsibilities of the Commission on Human Rights relating to the work of the Office of the United Nations High Commissioner for Human Rights, as decided by the General Assembly in its resolution 48/141 of 20 December 1993; (h) Work in close cooperation in the field of human rights with Governments, regional organizations, national human rights institutions and civil society; (i) Make recommendations with regards to the promotion and protection of human rights; (j) Submit an annual report to the General Assembly."

## 5. Security Council

Security Council is a principal organ which has played a primary role in maintaining international peace and security. Peace and security activities is arguably the most controversial and challenging domain of UN activity. It provides the public with a litmus test of the effectiveness of the Organization as a whole with respect to promoting the international rule of law and global concerns of the world community.

As mentioned above, Security Council may take measures relating to international rule of law, one of which is non–military enforcement action taken under Article 41 of Chapter VII of the UN Charter, the other is military enforcement action taken under Article 42 of Chapter VII of the UN Charter.

Indeed, especially during the Cold War era, the East–West rivalry and anachronistic, entrenched interests of the permanent members presently inhibited any dramatic enhancement of UN peace and security capabilities. There is still a reluctance to compromise this capability by allowing the autonomous capabilities of the UN to provide peace and security.[219] The fact that member States have not concluded agreements with the Security Council to make armed forces available at its call has limited the Council's power to mandate military action. It could do no more than authorize members to use troops as necessary to achieve prescribed goals.[220]

---

[219] Richard A. Falk, *op. cit.*, pp.638–639.
[220] Christopher C. Joyner, *op. cit.*, p.16.

## 6. The UN Commission on International Trade Law (UNCITRL)

In order to, at least reduce or remove, legal obstacles to the flow of international trade, the General Assembly, in 1966, established the UN Commission on International Trade Law (UNCITRAL). The Commission consists of 36 States representing the various geographic regions and principal legal systems of the world. Its mandate is to promote the progressive harmonization and unification of laws governing international commerce and trade.

The Commission prepares new international legal texts on trade law and encourages wider participation and uniform inter-pretation of existing international instruments. It also offers training and assistance in international trade law, particularly to developing countries. Since 1968, when it held its first annual session, UNCITRAL has concentrated on priority topics relating to international trade: international sale of goods; international payments; international commercial arbitration; and inter-national legislation on shipping. With regard to the international sale of goods, it has considered uniform legal rules governing sales contracts, time-limits and limitations, general conditions of sale and standard contracts.[221]

---

221 The United Nations, *supra* note 199, p.377.

## 7. General Assembly

The General Assembly studies international legal questions, and makes recommendations to encourage the development and codification of international law. Within the General Assembly, legal issues are considered by the Sixth (Legal) Committee. The General Assembly has also created subsidiary bodies, both permanent and *ad hoc*, to consider specialized legal matters. The reports of these bodies (principally, the ILC) are debated in the Sixth committee, which recommends action to be taken by the Assembly in plenary session.

In addition to considering and acting on reports of the ILC and UNCITRAL, the General Assembly also promotes the progressive development and codification of international law by conducting its own studies and assigning work to other subsidiary bodies. In 1967, it adopted a 「Declaration on Territorial Asylum」. In 1974, it adopted a definition of what constitutes aggression by one State against another. In 1970, after eight years of work, the Assembly adopted 「the Declaration on Principles of International Law concerning Friendly Relations and Co-operation among States in Accordance with the UN Charter」.[222]

At the fiftieth session of the General Assembly, the Sixth Committee reviewed the annual reports of the ILC, the UNCITRAL, the Special Committee on the Charter of the UN and on the Strengthening of the Role of the Organization (Special

---

222 *Ibid.*, pp.380-386.

Committee), and the Committee on Relations with the Host Country(Host Country Committee).

The Sixth Committee also considered a new item aimed at entrusting the Trusteeship Council with the common heritage of mankind, proposals for two new legal instruments relating to ( i ) the establishment of a permanent international criminal court, and ( ii ) the diplomatic courier and the diplomatic bag not accompanied by diplomatic courier, as well as other topics concerning international terrorism, review of the UN Administrative Tribunal's judgements, the UN Decade of International Law and the UN Programme of Assistance in the Teaching, Study, Dissemination and Wider Appreciation of International Law.[223]

## 8. Secretariat Legal Functions

The UN Office of Legal Afffairs is a UN agency, established in 1946, that performs several key functions in the area of intermational law. It is administered by Under–Secretary–General for Legal Affairs and Legal Counsel of the UN. Its responsibilities include advising the Secretariat and other organs on legal and constitutional questions; promoting and developing the rule of law in the affairs of the UN; maintaining and defending the legal interests of the Organization; and providing

---

223  Virgina Morris and M.–Christiane Bourloyannis–Vrailas, "The Work of the Sixth Committee at the Fiftieth Session of the UN General Assembly," *American Journal of International Law*, Vol.90, pp.491–500.

assistance to organs and conferences working in the legal field. It also provides legal services to the UN Development Programme (UNDP) and its subsidiary and affiliated programmes and funds, as well as other extra-budgetary administrative structures such as the United Nations Children's Fund.

The Secretariat of the UN also registers and publishes treaties, acts as a depository of international instruments, services the various legal bodies within the Organization and administers 'the UN Programme of Assistance in the Teaching, Study, Dissemination and Wider Appreciation of International Law.'[224]

# Ⅲ. UN Effort for Strengthening of the International Rule of Law

## 1. Overview

When the founders of the UN drew up the Charter, the international rule of law loomed as one of its central components. They established the International Court of Justice(ICJ) at The Hague as the 'cathedral of law' in the global system. But, States were free to take it or leave it, in whole or in part. The rule of law was asserted and, at the same time undermined. Each State could decide whether it was going to accept the compulsory

---

[224] The United Nations, *supra* note 199, pp.395-397.

jurisdiction of the Court.

Thus, from the outset, the ICJ was marginalized. International law includes the body of legal rules and principles that apply among States and also between them and other actors, including those of global civil society and other international organizations. The standing of international law is now unquestioned, though, the challenge today is to sustain the respect for law that has developed. It is true that, even though States are sovereign, they are not free individually to do whatever they want, it is also true that sovereign States are reluctant to obey the international law and further, submit their disputes to the judicial institutions like the ICJ as far as possible.

I think that the establishment of effective dispute settlement system with compulsory jurisdiction is an essential element in the rule of international law, but there has been a tendency for an increasing number of States accepting the optional clause to exclude from the jurisdiction of the Court matters of domestic jurisdiction as determined by themselves. However, international disputes between States should to be solved by, not the compulsory jurisdiction of the ICJ, but themselves, until a great feeling of confidence and solidarity between States can be established.

The establishment of the rule of law is recognized to be absolutely necessary, both to ensure protection of human rights and provide a firm basis for international peace and security, as well as economic and social cooperation. Indeed, the United

Nations has played a leading and dynamic role concerning the international rule of law. In this regards, it needs to strengthen and advance the compulsory settlement of international disputes by ICJ and other court or tribunal. But as a traditional international inter-governmental organization, the United Nations is dependent on the sovereign will of each of its members. Neither the Organization itself nor its Secretary-General possesses independent power of decision-making.[225]

So, many scholars think that the United Nations should be restructured or strengthened for the more role of the international rule of law than ever. I think also that the United Nations and its system should be fully reformed through the transformation of the Organization to bring greater unity of purpose, greater coherence of efforts, and greater agility in responding to an increasingly dynamic, changing, and complex world. To put it another way, the United Nations should promote world-wide democracy and international rule of law.[226]

---

[225] Gabriel M. Wilner, "The Role of the United Nations in the Maintenance of Peace before and after the Year Two Thousand: Introduction," *Georgia Journal of International and Comparative Law*, Vol.26, 1996, p.2.

[226] See *infra* note 238.

## 2. UN Decade of International Law[227]

The rule of law has been repeatedly heralded as the foundation for international order. On December 16, 1989 the General Assembly of the UN adopted Resolution 44/23 in which it proclaimed the 1990s 'Decade of International Law.' The idea for such a decade had officially been launched five months earlier, on June 29, 1989, at a Ministerial Meeting of the Non-Aligned Movement held in The Hague to commemorate the ninetieth birthday of the First Hague Peace Conference. In the Declaration issued at the end of this meeting, the UN General Assembly was requested to proclaim the Decade.

The proposal included the suggestion to hold Third (Hague) Peace Conference at the end of the Decade, in 1999. With the adoption of G.A. Resolution 44/23, the United Nations has taken over the initiative, and an open-ended working group of the Sixth (Legal) Committee of the Assembly will soon present its recommendations.

According to operative Paragraph 2 of G.A. Resolution 44/23, the main purpose of the Decade is as follows:

---

227 For more detailed information, see Marcel Brus, Sam Muller, Serv Wiemers ed., *The United Nations Decade of International Law* (Martinus Nijhoff Publishers, 1991).

a. To promote the acceptance of and respect for the principles of international law;

b. To promote means and methods for the peaceful settlement of disputes between states, including resort to and full respect for the International Court of Justice;

c. To encourage the progressive development of international law and its codification;

d. To encourage the teaching, study, dissemination and wider appreciation of international law.

Pursuant to operative Paragraph 3 of G.A. Resolution 44/23, the Secretary-General of the UN has requested member States, international bodies and non-governmental organizations to present him with their views on the programme of action to be taken during the Decade, including the possibility of holding a third international peace conference. On September 12, 1990, the Secretary-General present his report containing the first reactions.[228] On September 21, and October 8, two addenda were added. In general, the proclamation of the Decade was welcomed by all States, international organizations, and non-governmental organizations that have responded to the request of the Secretary-General to supply him with their views.

Thus far, the UN Decade has been organized into inclusive two-year terms: first term 1990–1992; second term 1993–1994;

---

228 United Nations Decade of International Law, Report of the Secretary-General, U.N. Doc. A/45/430(1990); U.N. Doc. A/45/430/ Add. 1(1990) and UN. Doc. A/45/430/Add. 2(1990). 13. U.N. Doc. A/45/430, at 6.

third term 1995-1996; and final term 1997-1999.[229] States have been invited to submitted suggestions for consideration by Sixth Committee of the General Assembly, in particular, with regard to the areas of international law which States considered ripe for codification or progressive development of international law. International organizations have been encouraged to report to the Secretary-General on ways and means for implementing multi-lateral treaties to which they are parties. And, both States and international organizations have been encouraged to publish summaries, repertoires, or yearbooks of their practice.[230]

---

[229] By its resolution 51/157 of 16 December 1996, the General Assembly adopted the programme of activities for the final term(1997-1999) of the Decade.

[230] Sompong Sucharitkul, "Legal Developments in the First Half of the United Nations Decade of International Law," *ASIL Interest Group on the UN Decade of International Law Newsletter*(Issue No.11), June 1996, pp.3-13.

## 3. The Reform of the UN[231]

The end of the Cold War has brought crucial changes in the world, resulting in a new emphasis on the international rule of law, establishing democratic institutions and concern for humanitarian needs, as well as human rights.[232] The post—Cold War world is beset by an epidemic of serious difficulties within States: persecutions, civil wars, rebellions, secessionist movements, genocide campaigns, and other such horrors. And the chaos, privation, and instability

---

231  There are some printed materials on U.N. Reform as follows: Erskine
Childers with Brian Urquhart, *Renewing the United Nations System*(Ford
Foundation & Dag Hammarskjold Foundation, 1994); Commission on
Global Governance, *Our Global Neighborhood*(Oxford University Press,
1995); Independent Working Group on the Future of the UN System, *The
United Nations in its Second Half—Century*(Yale University Press, 1995);
Tatsuro Kunugi, Makoto Iokibe, Takahiro Shinyo and Kohei Hashimoto,
*Towards a More Effective UN*(PHP Research Institute, 1996); Joachim
W. Miller, *The Reform of the United Nations*(Oceana, 1992); George
Soros(Chairman, Independent Task Force Sponsored by the Council on
Foreign Relations), *American National Interest and the United
Nations*(Council on Foreign Relations, 1996); South Centre, *For a Strong
and Democratic United Nations: a South Perspective on UN Reform*(South
Centre, 1996); The United Nations Commission on Improving the
Effectiveness of the United Nations, *Defining Purpose: the U.N. and
the Health of Nations*(US Commission, 1993); Harold Stassen, *United
Nations — A Working Paper for Restructuring* —(Lerner Publications
Company, 1994); Vicenc Fisas, *Blue Geopolitics — the United Nations
Reform and the Future of the Blue Helmets* —(Pluto Press with
Transnational Institute(TNI), 1995); Maurice Bertrand and Daniel Warner
eds., *A New Charter for a Worldwide Organization*(Kluwer Law Inter-
national, 1997).

232  Dick Thornburgh, "Today's United Nations in a Changing World,"
*American University Journal of International Law and Policy*, Vol.9,
1993, p.215.

generated by despotic regimes, failed and failing States, and dissolving societies are prominent features of our time.[233]

A new strategy for global governance involves reforming and strengthening the existing system of IGOs, and improving its means of collaboration with other subjects and actors in international society.[234] We have to notice that a vital and central role in global governance falls to people coming together in the United Nations, aspiring to fulfil some of their highest goals through its potential for common action.[235]

Although the role of non-governmental actors should not be underestimated, the United Nations among the international organizations must continue to play a central role in global governance. With its universality, it is the only forum where all the governments of the world come together on an equal footing and on a regular basis to try to resolve the world's most pressing problems. Over the years, the United Nations and its constituent bodies have made vital contributions to international communications and cooperation in a variety of areas, especially after the Cold War era. They continue to provide a framework for collaboration that is indispensable for global progress.[236]

---

233 Inis L. Claude, Jr., "Peace and Security: Prospective Roles for the Two United Nations," *Global Governance*, Vol.2, No.3, 1996, p.289.

234 Maurice Bertrand, "The Necessity of Conceiving a New Charter for the Global Institutions," Maurice Bertrand and Daniel Warner eds., *op. cit.*, p.10.

235 The Commission on Global Governance, *supra* note 7, p.225.

236 *Ibid.*, pp.2-6.

The United Nations has played a leading and dynamic role concerning the international rule of law and global governance, though, as an IGO, the United Nations is dependent on the sovereign will of each of its members. Neither the Organization itself nor its Secretary—General possesses independent power of decision or law—making and effectuation of law.[237] The International Court of Justice has jurisdiction only where the states that are parties to a dispute have agreed to submit their dispute to the Court. Many scholars, therefore, think that the United Nations should be restructured or strengthened for establishing the international rule of law and global governance.

The United Nations faces, therefore, not only unprecedented demands, but also great opportunities. That is why an effective and efficient United Nations — a United Nations which is focused, coherent, responsive and cost—effective — is more needed than ever. Now it is admitted that the United Nations should be reformed to be a more strong and effective Organization.

As mentioned above, the Commission on Global Governance issued its report, *Our Global Neighborhood,* early in 1995 — the year the United Nations turned 50. It was hoped that the jubilee would prompt a process of review and reform to improve the global governance, including institutional change at the United Nations. In the period since the publication of this report, reform

---

237 Gabriel M. Wilner, "The Role of the United Nations in the Maintenance of Peace before and after the Year Two Thousand: Introduction," *Georgia Journal of International and Comparative Law,* Vol.26, 1996, p.2.

has been on the agenda of the international community, and global governance has become part and parcel of the international discourse.

The Commission is convinced that the world is ready to accept "a set of core values that can unite people of all cultural, political, religious, or philosophical background ⋯. It is fundamentally important that governance should be underpinned by democracy at all levels and ultimately by the rule of enforceable law." The 'core values' upon which global governance is to be based include liberty and human rights. To implement, administer, and enforce global governance, the Commission has recommended a major restructuring of the UN system.

The United Nations and its system should be reformed through the transformation of the Organization to bring greater unity of purpose, greater coherence of efforts, and greater agility in responding to an increasingly dynamic, changing, and complex world. Especially, the UN should promote world-wide democracy and the international rule of law much more than it have promoted.[238]

Nowadays, it is admitted that the United Nations should be reformed to be a more strong and effective Organization. UN reform must reflect the realities of change, including the new capacity of global civil society in order to contribute to global

---

238 UN Secretary-General, "The Secretary-General Statement to the Social Meetings of the General Assembly on Reform," New York, 16 July 1997 (through the Internet: http://www.un.org).

governance.

Thus, then, the Secretary–General Boutros Ghali submitted his report *Renewing the United Nations: A Programme for Reform*, which has the most extensive and far–reaching reforms in the fifty–two–year history of the Organization. But, this report does not include other fundamental reform proposals for strengthening the international rule of law than reforming the Security Council, establishing an International Criminal Court, and enhancing its human rights programme.[239]

---

239 The actions and recommendations focus primarily on the following priority areas:
  - Esatblishing of a new leadership and management structure;
  - Assuring financial solvency;
  - Intergration of twelve Secretariat entities and units into five;
  - A changed management culture accompanied by management and efficiency measures;
  - Instituting a through overhaul of human resources policy and practices;
  - Promoting sustanied and sustainable development as a central priority of the United Nations;
  - Strengthening and focussing the normative, policy and knowledge-related functions of the Secretariat and its capacity to serve the United Nations intergovernmental bodies;
  - Improving the Organizations capacity for post–conflict peace–building;
  - Bolstering the international efforts to efforts to combat crime, druhs and terrorism;
  - Extending human rights activities;
  - Advancing the disarmanent agenda;
  - Enhancing response to humanitarian needs;
  - Effecting a major shift in the public information and communications strategy and functions;
  - Addressing the need for more fundammental change.
  See "Renewing the United Nations: A Programme for Reform" and for more detailed contents, see also "Report of the Secretary–General"(through the Internet: http://www.un.org)

But, indeed, there has been insufficient regard by UN planners for the reestablishment of the international rule of law and global governance. Therefore, I think that the United Nations should be fully and entirely reformed in order to play an active role in, not only maintaining international peace and security, but also widening the scope and role, and improving the effectiveness of international law in order to strengthen the international rule of law.

In the first place, the Security Council will need to be restructured if it is to play an effective role in future global peace management,[240] because recent peace–keeping and peace–enforcing experiences have indicated that the most fundamental requirement, and a primary objective, of a lasting peace is the reestablishment of democracy and the rule of law.[241] And, accordingly, some appropriate body should be mandated to explore ways in which international law–making can be expedited. In this regard, the International Law Commission should be revamped and have a wider capacity for international law–making. If so, it could formally coordinate international law–making, setting timetables and establishing lines of authority.[242]

The United Nations should establish an international moni–

---

240  Peter Mutharika, "The Role of the United Nations Security Council in African Peace Management: Some Proposals," *Michigan Journal of International Law,* Vol.17, 1996, p.537.

241  Mark Plunkett, "Reestablishing Law and Order in Peace–Maintenance," *Global Governance,* Vol.4, No.1, 1998, p.63.

242  The Commission on Global Governance, *supra* note 7, pp.329–331.

toring agency to integrate diverse monitoring functions and to bring the weight of the entire world community behind the effort to ensure compliance with the norms of peace, decisions of Security Council and the ICJ rendered to settle disputes, future arms constraints, environmental standards, and other rules as these are established.[243]

Above all, necessary condition for strengthening the international rule of law is an efficient compliance regime.[244] Many States and scholars have given thoughts to ways of increasing recourse to the ICJ. In 1971 the American Society of International Law(ASIL) established the Panel to study the ways of strengthening the role of the Court.

Those who wish to belong to the community of nations should be willing to abide by its rules and demonstrate their willingness by accepting the competence of the Court as its highest legal body. It is required that each member of the UN should accept the compulsory jurisdiction of the Court.[245] The American Bar Association(ABA) is also interested in the method of strengthening the role of the Court, especially the widening its advisory

---

243 Robert C. Johansen, "Reforming the United Nations to Eliminate War," *Transnational Law & Contemporary Problems*, Vol.4, 1994, pp.471–472.

244 The Commission on Global Governance, *supra* note 7, pp.325–326.

245 *Ibid.*, pp.308–313; According to Art. 36, para. 2 of the Statute of the ICJ, the States parties may "at any time declare that they recognize as compulsory *ipso facto* and without special agreement, in relation to any other State accepting the same obligation, the jurisdiction of the Court." As yet, the declarations, deposited by a total of 65 States, are decisions to accept compulsory jurisdiction under the optional clause.

jurisdiction.[246] In this regard, the Security Council should make greater use of the Court as a source of advisory opinions.

Although the Security Council is, of course, the supreme or primary organ of the United Nations, we need to consider whether the Security Council should subject its own decisions to judicial review by the Court, at least on procedural matters. If it did so, the Security Council would be in the same positions as several member States in their own jurisdictions, where courts can adjudicate on the legality of State action. I think it is necessary to give explicit power to the ICJ to review the legality at international law of Security Council.[247]

Up to the beginning of the 21st century, the absence of an International Criminal Court(ICC) discredited the international rule of law, because its role is to prosecute and punish persons responsible for international crimes such as genocide, crimes against humanity, and war crimes. Recent horrific human tragedies which we could see in Former Yugoslavia, Somalia and Rwanda have made it more imperative than ever to do so. Indeed,

---

246 Stephen M. Schwebel, "Widening the Advisory Jurisdiction of the International Court of Justice without Amending its Statute," *Catholic University Law Review*, Vol.33, 1984, pp.355-356.

247 The Commission on Global Governance, *supra* note 7, p.319. Some scholars assert that yet in many states, including the United States, this power of judicial review by the highest national courts has arisen even in the absence of explicit constitutional or statutory language. In addition, the UN Charter refers to the International Court of Justice as the Organization's 'principal judicial organ.' It can be argued that this implies a power of judicial review on the basis of the principle of implied power. See, *ibid.*, pp.319-320.

the concept of an ICC is an old one.

Efforts to establish such a court date back to 1945. A major step forward establishing the court was taken in July 1994, when the International Law Commission adopted the Statute for a proposed Court.[248] In June 1998 a diplomatic conference was held to finalize and adopt a treaty that would establish an ICC.

I'd like to suggest that a standby military force should be established, which can be composed of units from national military forces of member States to be available on call by Security Council under conditions carefully defined agreements to be concluded pursuant to Article 43 of the UN Charter. But the difficulties in obtaining military forces required for enforcement through the special agreements under Article 43 of the Charter have led to demands for new arrangements to ensure the availability of forces when required. For example, an independent force of volunteers has been prominently advocated, along with the idea of governmental standby forces on call by the Security Council.[249]

According to *Our Global Neighborhood*, it is recommended that a new Economic Security Council(ESC) would replace the existing Economic and Social Council(ECOSOC).[250] The International

---

248  *Ibid.*, p.323.

249  Christopher C. Joyner, *op. cit.*, pp.16–17.

250  According to *Our Global Neighborhood*, the new ESC would consist of no more than 23 members who would have responsibility for all international financial and development activities. Of great significance is the expansion of the concept of security: "All people, no less than

Monetary Fund(IMF), the World Bank, and the World Trade Organization(WTO) — virtually all finance and development activities — would be under the authority of this body. There would be no veto power by any nation, nor would there be permanent member status for any nation.[251] And to protect the environment, it is proposed that the Trusteeship Council ⋯ be given mandate of exercising trusteeship over the global commons.

The global commons include the atmosphere, outer space, the oceans beyond national jurisdiction, and the related environment and life-support systems that contribute to the support of human life. Its functions would include the administration of environmental treaties in such field as climate change, bio-diversity, outer space and the law of the sea. It would refer, as appropriate, any economic or security issues arising from these matters to the ESC or the Security Council.[252]

Lastly, to be an effective instrument of global governance in new century, the United Nations must be strengthened to take greater account of the emergence of global civil society. Global

---

all states have a right to secure existence, and all states have an obligation to protect those rights."(The Commission on Global Governance, *op. cit.*, p.84) "Where people are subjected to massive suffering and distress, however, there is a need to weigh a state's right to autonomy against its people's right to security."(*Ibid.*, p.71) "We believe a global consensus exists today for a UN response on humanitarian grounds in cases of gross abuse of the security of people."(*Ibid.*, p.89)

251  *Ibid.*, pp.266ff.
252  *Ibid.*, pp.251ff.

civil society is best expressed in the global non-governmental movement. As a group, NGOs are diverse and multifaceted. A major challenge for the global civil society is to create the public-private partnerships that enable and encourage non-State actors to offer their contributions to effective global governance.[253]

The Commission on Global Governance also recommends an 'Assembly of the People' which "should consist of representatives of organizations accredited to the General Assembly as civil society organizations ⋯. A forum of 300-600 organs of global civil society would be desirable and practicable."[254] A new 'Petitions Council' is also recommended, to consist of five to seven representatives of 'civil society,' for the purpose of reviewing petitions from NGOs in the field to direct to the appropriate UN agency for enforcement action.[255]

# Ⅳ. Conclusion

As mentioned above, it may be said that 'the rule of law' is to 'government' in domestic society what 'the international rule of law' is to 'global governance' in international society. The

---

253 *Ibid.*, pp.253-255.
254 *Ibid.*, pp.258-259.
255 *Ibid.*, p.260.

effectuation of the international rule of law for furthering global governance must be recognized to be really necessary in international society. States, international organizations including NGOs as well as IGOs, and individuals now face unprecedented demands and opportunities towards the new century or Millennium, and are required to promote the international rule of law and global governance.

I think that the United Nations, among lots of IGOs can most effectively promote the law-making process, encourage law observance and enforce the law in international society. Especially, the end of the Cold War gave new visibility to the United Nations and raised hopes for a more effective international legal order. Since the end of the Cold War, international society has been undergoing a thorough change, which results in a need for a new world order, establishing liberal and democratic systems and great concern for global governance.

As mentioned above, The United Nations and its system should be reformed through the transformation of the Organization to bring greater unity of purpose, greater coherence of efforts, and greater agility in responding to an increasingly dynamic, changing, and complex world.

It is one thing to propose reform, quite another to describe a mechanism for its realization. And UN reform is not an event; it is a process. It is a process that has been underway for years. Common vision for the future and positive political will on the part of international actors such as states, international organizations, as well as individuals is, therefore, indispensable requirement for the progress towards global governance.

# CHAPTER 5

# Global Governance and Non-Governmental Organizations

## I. Introduction: the Concept of the NGOs

International law historically governed only the conduct of States. But it is now generally applicable to international organizations. Further, in specified circumstances, it governs the conduct of individuals and corporations. International organizations can be sorted in a variety of ways. As mentioned above,[256] the traditional paradigm of organizational classification employs a 'functional' approach. International organizations are thereby: ( i ) public or private; (ii) administrative or political; (iii) global or regional; and (iv) either possess, or do not possess, supranational power.

In addition, it is usually said that there are two types of international organizations: intergovernmental organizations

---

256 See *supra* note 3.

(IGOs) and international non-governmental organizations(INGOs),[257] though the term 'international organizations' is usually used to describe an organization set up by agreement between two or more States.[258] Along with domestic NGOs, INGOs is pertaining to NGOs, which are established by private initiative as opposed to IGOs. In contrast to INGOs, IGOs are usually accorded 'international legal personality' that approximates that of the prime actors of statecentric international law because of their governmental status. International organizations, in the sense of IGOs, have existed since 1815, but it is only since the First World War that they have acquired much political importance. and the idea that they have international legal personality is even more recent.[259]

The development of the 'NGOs' concept is closely tied to the increase in formal 'private' organizations in the political process at national and international level. While their existence is not

---

257 NGOs are private in that they are separate from governments and have no ability to direct societies or to require support from them. But not evert organization that claims to be an NGO exactly fit this definition. Roughly speaking, there are three kinds of NGOs: ( i ) GONGO (government-organized nongovernmental organization); ( ii ) QUA-NGOs(quasi-nongovernmental organizations); ( iii ) DONGOs(donor-organized nongovernmental organizations). As for this, see Thomas G. Weiss & Leon Gordenker, "Pluralizing Global Governance: Analytical Approaches and Dimensions," Thomas G. Weiss and Leon Gordenker eds., *NGOs, The UN, & Global Governance*(Lynne Rienner Publishers, 1996), pp.20-21.

258 Peter Malanczuk, *Akehurst's Modern International Law*, 7th ed. (Routledge, 2000), p.92.

259 *Ibid.*

new, NGOs are now found in a wide variety of forms and contexts in a civil society. According to Wahl's definition, 'NGOs' are understood as formal private arrangements which operate in the political arena at both the national and international levels, and which possess the following characteristics: ( i ) a non—profit orientation; (ii) a claim to represent or act as advocate on behalf of public or special interests; (iii) relative organizational and financial independence *vis—à—vis* State apparatuses and enter—prises; (iv) a measure of professionalism and organizational durability.[260]

# II. the Role of the NGOs in Global Governance

INGOs also have existed for quite a long time. A case in point is the Red Cross established on 1864.[261] Nowadays, INGOs such as Amnesty International or Green Peace are very much in the news because their active role in international affairs. INGOs have in increasing numbers injected unexpected voices into international discourse about numerous global issues.

INGOs have proliferated considerably in the past decades and

---

260 Joachim Hirsch, "The Democratic Potential of Non—Governmental Organizations," Cho, Hee—Yeon and Joachim Hirsch eds., *The State and NGOs in the Context of Globalization*(Hanul Publishing Co., 2001), 2002, pp.11—13.

261 *Ibid.*, p.15.

are engaged in a broad variety of different areas, ranging from politics, the legal and judicial field, the social and economic domain, human rights and humanitarian relief, education, women, to the environment and sports.[262]

Especially during the last two decades, human rights advocates, gender activists, developmentalists, groups of indigenous peoples and representatives of other defined interests have become active in political work once reserved for representatives of States. Their numbers have enlarged the venerable, but hardly numerous, ranks of transnational organizations built around churches, labour unions and humanitarian aims.[263]

At present, domestic NGOs can hold, according to the UN Charter, official consultative status with the UN and UN Agencies, and with this status, they participate in various UN or UN-hosted world conferences. Further, domestic NGOs have also rights to petition at international human rights committee or commissions and participate in the enactment processes of international law-making. In this sense, there is no substantial difference between domestic NGOs and INGOs.

According to the Union of International Associations, the NGO universe includes well over 15,000 recognizable NGOs that operate in three or more countries and draw their finances from sources in more than one country; this number is growing all the time.[264]

---

262  Peter Malanczuk, *op. cit.*, pp.96-97.
263  Thomas G. Weiss and Leon Gordenker, *op. cit.*, p.17.
264  *Ibid.*; *The Yearbook of International Organizations for 1999-2000* gives

In their own ways, NGOs and IGOs grope, sometimes co-operatively, sometimes competitively, sometimes in parallel towards a kind of 'global governance.'

Like the NGO universe, global governance implies an absence of central authority, and the need for collaboration or cooperation among governments and others who seek to encourage common practices and goals in addressing global issues. The means to achieve a global governance also include activities of the UN, other IGOs and standing cooperative arrangements among States.[265] A new strategy for global governance involve reforming and strengthening the existing system of IGOs, and improving its means of collaboration with other subjects and actors in international civil society.[266]

As mentioned above, the Commission on Global Governance issued its report, *Our Global Neighborhood*, early in 1995 — the year the UN turned 50. It was hoped that the jubilee would prompt a process of review and reform to improve the global governance, including institutional change at the UN.[267] In addition, the

---

data in 6,076 'conventional' international organizations, of which 5,825 are nongovernmental as compared with only 251 inter—governmental units. See A. LeRoy Bennett & James K. Oliver, *op. cit.*, p.282.

[265] Thomas G. Weiss and Leon Gordenker, *op. cit.*, p.17.

[266] Maurice Bertrand, "The Necessity of Conceiving a New Charter for the Global Institutions," Maurice Bertrand and Daniel Warner eds., *op. cit.*, p.10.

[267] As for the UN reform for establishing global governance, see Kim, B. C., "Global Governance and the International Rule of Law," *Korean Journal of International Law*, Vol.45, No.2, 2000, pp.11–16.

Commission on Global Governance pointed that to be an effective instrument of global governance in new century, the UN must be strengthened to take greater account of the emergence of global civil society. NGOs priorities for UN Reform include democrati-zation vis-à-vis the major powers and international institutions and the participation of global civil society.

Global civil society is best expressed in the global non-governmental movement. A major challenge for the global civil society is to create the public-private partnerships that enable and encourage non-State actors to offer their contributions to effective global governance.[268] NGOs recognize that to play an enhanced, and more effective part in global governance, they will have to pay greater attention to the quality of their contributions and to the organization of their participation.

Some generalizing about NGOs(including domestic NGOs) that operate in global governance is necessary for a better under-standing of NGO roles. Some theoretical approaches to inter-national cooperation for global governance could aid in analysing NGO activity and in reaching conclusions.

First, although the role of NGOs in the international legal system or global governance is primarily an informal one, they have some effect on international policy-making or law-making in certain areas by adding additional expertise and making procedures more transparent, and a stronger effect with regard

---

[268] The Commission on Global Governance, *op. cit.*, pp.253-255.

to supervision and fact—finding as to the implementation of international norms.[269] Many NGOs probably exist to influence, to set direction for, or to maintain functions of governance or to operate where government authority does not. Donini points out that NGOs have even developed some roles in regard to the former diplomatic preserve of maintaining international peace and security. Nowadays, it is admitted that in any case NGOs are a strong presence at every contact point for transnational governance.[270]

Second, at least part of the activities of most NGOs falls into the category of operations. Operational NGOs are the most numerous and have the easiest fund—raising task. They are more and more central to international responses in the post—Cold War world. And most NGOs provide some services, if only to their members, while others concentrate on providing them to other organizations and individuals. The delivery of services is the mainstay of most NGO budgets and the basic for enthusiastic support from a wide range of donors. Such services include intangible technical advice as well as more tangible resources for relief, development and other purposes. Many NGOs operate development programmes; they have become increasingly active in migration and disaster relief, which may now be their most

---

269 Peter Malanczuk, *op. cit.*, p.97.

270 Leon Gordenker and Thomas G. Weiss, "NGO Participation in the International Policy Process," Thomas G. Weiss and Leon Gordenker, *op. cit.*, p.212.

important operational or advisory activities in total financial terms.[271]

Third, some NGOs make an educational and advocacy roles. The targets of operational NGOs are beneficiaries(or victims in emergences), whereas those for educational and advocacy NGOs are their own contributors, the public and decision makers. Educational NGOs seek primarily to influence citizens, whose voices are then registered through public opinion and bear fruit in the form of additional resources for their activities as well as new policies, better decisions and enhanced international regimes. Educational NGOs direct activities towards a broad public or towards specifically differentiated publics in order to persuade them to voice opinions on governmental policies in international organizations.[272] Educational NGOs can help to reinforce various norms promoted by IGOs through public education campaigns. This heightened awareness among public audiences can then help hold States accountable for their international commitments.[273] Advocacy NGOs pursue discussions with national delegates and staff members of international secretariats in order to influence international public policy. NGO advocacy may be generally described as unofficial participation by internal and external modes.[274]

---

271  Thomas G. Weiss and Leon Gordenker, *op. cit.*, pp.36-37.

272  *Ibid.*, p.38.

273  *Ibid.*

274  *Ibid.*, p.39.

Lastly, NGOs usually provide information to make the machinery work.[275] One of the greatest advantages of NGOs compared to government and multinational organizations is their first−hand knowledge and experience of people and conditions on the ground. For example, human rights organizations commonly identify their primary goals as monitoring and reporting of government behavior on human rights, particularly violations, building pressure and creating international machinery to end the violations and to hold governments accountable.[276]

# Ⅲ. The International Status of INGOs

## 1. Introduction

There are various categories of international actors who either govern or are governed by international law. These actors possess international legal personality — the legal capacity that carries with it certain entitlements and obligations arising under international law. The 'persons' with this legal personality include States, international organizations, and to some extent, private individuals within a State.[277]

---

275 *Ibid.*, pp.55−56.

276 *Ibid.*, p.56.

277 William R. Slomanson, *op. cit.*, p.57.

It is generally said that an international organization has legal capacity under international law if it satisfies three essential elements: ( i ) it must be a permanent association of State members with established objectives and administrative organs; (ii) an international organization must possess some power that is distinct from the sovereign power of its State members; and (iii) the association's powers must be exercisable on an international level, rather than solely under the national legal systems of its member States. Public international organizations, that is, IGOs possess a legal personality or capacity to exercise certain 'governmental' powers.[278]

From this perspective, although INGOs or domestic NGOs have been afforded a limited formal status in some international decision-making contexts, in general, they have not been accorded the status of international legal persons. Indeed, from a formal point of view, on a global level, there are no international legal standards governing the establishment and status of INGOs. Their legal status and capacity are governed by applicable domestic law. So, the relevant law is that of the State where a NGO is based and this may cause problems in the case of international activities because national laws are diverse and different.[279]

---

[278] *Ibld.*, p.109.

[279] Peter Malanczuk, *op. cit.*, p.97.

## 2. Legal Status of INGOs

Official acknowledgement of the importance of NGOs in the work of the UN remains a subject of controversy.[280] IGOs may agree to grant NGOs a certain consultative or observer status[281] and thereby a limited international status,[282] but it is said that this does not make them a subject of international law.[283]

Pursuant to Article 71 of the UN Charter, ECOSOC has extended 'consultative status' to NGOs satisfying certain basic criteria.[284]

---

280  Felice D. Gaer, "Reality Check: Human Rights NGOs Confront Govern-ments," Thomas G. Weiss and Leon Gordenker eds., *op. cit.*, p.51.

281  In 1991, the UN General Assembly granted the observer status to the ICRC. See Peter Malanczuk, *op. cit.*, p.97.

282  It can be said that the ICRC is not properly regarded as a NGO. Rather it is an international organization operating under unique legal and historical mandates independent of NGOs or for that matter the UN. Under international law the ICRC exercises its own mandates under the Geneva Conventions. These mandates and its absolute principle of neutrality sometimes places the ICRC at odds with NGOs and the UN in that it is intensely protective of its autonomy and special status. See A. LeRoy Bennett & James K. Oliver, *op. cit.*, p.285.

283  Peter Malanczuk, *op. cit.*, p.97.

284  The enhanced recognition of NGOs' role in international affairs can be detected from the fact that in 1994 about 1,000 NGOs had consultative status with the ECOSOC, as compared with only 41 in 1948. See *ibid.*; Consultations remain largely under ECOSOC control, in contrast to the fuller rights of participation available to IGOs in the UN system. NGOs can be granted status in one of three categories, designated as ' I ,"II,' and 'the roster.' Those in category I are supposed to have broad economic and social interests and geographical scope; those in category II have more specialized interests. The remainder of accepted applicants are listed in a roster for organizations that may make occasional contributions. For details, see Thomas G. Weiss and Leon Gordenker, *op. cit.*, p.22.

Recognition entitles an NGO access to ECOSOC proceedings and, for more prominent organizations, rights to lodge oral and written interventions as well as to propose agenda items. NGOs have also been afforded limited rights of participation at UN-sponsored world conferences in recent years, including at Rio(on the environment), Cairo(population), and Beijing(women). Conferences on multilateral pacts on climate change and endangered species have afforded NGOs a place as observers to treaty monitoring proceedings.

But in no institution save the International Labour Organi-zation(ILO) have NGOs been formally extended a status even approaching parity with that of States. Nor have NGOs been afforded standing in international judicial forums, with pro-minent exceptions at the level of regional organizations.[285] At the regional level within the framework of the Council of Europe, a common status for NGOs has been recently laid down in ⌜the European Convention on the Recognition of the Legal Personality of International Non-Governmental Organizations⌟.

The Convention, signed in 1986 and in force since 1991, recognizes, among the States which have ratified it, the legal personality and attached rights and duties as acquired by an NGO by its establishment in any one of the States parties.[286] But it is difficult to say that this Convention recognizes NGOs' 'inter-

---

285 William R. Slomanson, *op. cit.*, pp.5-6.
286 Peter Malanczuk, *op. cit.*, pp.97-98.

national' legal personality, though, it is still meaningful for member States to mutually respect the 'domestic' legal personality of each member's NGOs.[287]

Since the beginning of the last century, efforts have been made by bodies such as the Institute of International Law to improve the international legal standing of NGOs in general, though, such efforts have remained fruitless in formal view of the doctrine of sovereignty, NGOs are gradually being recognized to a limited degree, as a distinct legal entity in international society.

## 3. NGOs' Participation in International Law-making and Policy-making Process

As mentioned above, INGOs or domestic NGOs have been afforded a limited formal status in some international decision—making contexts. It could be admitted that NGOs have at least the capacity to participate in the norm—creating process of international law.[288] NGOs have, for the most part, actively participated in the norm—creating processes of Conventions on human rights, rights of women, humanitarian relief projects, and the environment.

---

287 Young Sam Ma, "International Legal Personality of NGOs," *Korean Yearbook of International Law*, Vol.4, 2004, p.153.

288 Christopher Tracy, "The Growing Role of Non—Governmental Organization," *American Society of International Law Proceedings*(April 1955), p.430.

In particular, NGOs have played an important role in the adoption of Conventions, such as drafting key articles, directly participating in negotiations, soothing frictions between different groups, and drawing out compromises in the norm-creating process of the UN Conventions relating human rights, humanitarian law, and environment.[289]

Especially, during the 1990s the movement for the international recognition of women's human rights has achieved some notable success in penetrating the international legal order and has become a model for non-governmental organization intervention. Such success is indicated by a number of key events: the affirmation at the Vienna World Conference on Huan Rights that human rights of women and of the girl-child are inalienable, integral and part of universal human rights; the adoption by consensus in the UN General Assembly of the Declaration on the Elimination of Violence against Women; the assertion at the Cairo Conference on Population and Development of the Reproductive Rights of Women; and the explicit inclusion of sexual crimes against women within the jurisdictions and indictment of the International War Crimes Tribunals for the former Yugoslavia and Rwanda and the Rome Statute for the International Criminal Court are perhaps the highlights.[290]

---

289 Young Sam Ma, *op. cit.*, pp.149-152.

290 Christine Chinkin, "Human Rights and the Politics of Presentation: Is there a Role for International Law," Michael Byers ed., *The Role of Law in International Politics*(Oxford University Press, 2001), pp.133-134.

# IV. The UN-NGOs Cooperation for Global Governance

It is necessary to note that there are evolving closer relationship between the UN system and NGOs in responding to complex world affairs such as humanitarian emergencies.[291] The UN and the NGO community share many basic principles, values and commitments to a more just, peaceful and humane world. In fact, over the years, NGOs have provided vital assistance to the UN in the conduct of its work, particularly in social, economic, and humanitarian areas.[292] They often provide independent monitoring, early—warning, and information—gathering services that can be especially useful in preventive diplomacy.

They can serve as unofficial or alternative channels of communication, and can help establish relationships that create the trust necessary to bridge political gaps. More and more, NGOs are helping to set public policy agendas — identifying and defining critical issues, and providing policy makers with advice and assistance. It is this movement beyond advocacy and the provision of services towards broader participation in the public policy realm that has such significance for governance.[293]

---

291 Andrew Natsios, "NGOs and the UN System in Complex Humanitarian Emergencies: Conflict or Cooperation?" Thomas G. Weiss and Leon Gordenker eds., *op. cit.*, p.67.

292 The Commission on Global Governance, *supra* note 7, p.254.

293 *Ibid.*, pp.254—255.

During this period of reform and restructuring, the UN recognizes NGOs as important allies and constituencies for its work, and for its capacity to achieve its goals in development, human rights, disarmament, and democracy and to respond to humanitarian crises. There is a need for NGO mechanism to link the national, regional and international levels of work. This requires increased NGO cooperation and coordination at the national level, and effective mechanism at the international level for more participation and cooperation of NGOs.

Therefore, the UN should remove some of the obstacles faced by NGOs in gaining access to institutions, discussions and informations. The UN system should maintain a flexible approach in its relations and cooperation with NGOs, and to NGO participation in the fora and bodies of the UN.[294]

# V. Conclusion

The effectuation of the international rule of law for furthering global governance must be recognized to be really necessary in international society. It is required both to ensure the protection of the human rights and to promote the common values and

---

294 UN Non-Governmental Liaison Service(NGLS), *The United Nations, NGOs and Global Governance: Challenges for the 21st Century*(NGLS, 1996), pp.9-11, 55-61.

welfare in world community. States, international organizations including NGOs as well as IGOs, and individuals now face unprecedented demands and opportunities in the new century or Millennium, and are required to promote the international rule of law and global governance.

Since the end of the Cold War, international society has been undergoing a thorough change, which results in a need for a new world order, establishing liberal and democratic systems and great concern for global governance. States, international organizations and individuals must cooperatively strive to ensure that the world community of the future is characterized by law and governance, not by lawlessness or anarchy.

Common vision for the future and positive political will on the part of international actors such as States, international organizations, as well as individuals is, therefore, indispensable requirement for the progress towards global governance. Though it is our firm conclusion that IGOs, *inter alia* especially the UN, must continue to play a central role in global governance, the UN or other IGOs can not do all the work of global governance.

Therefore, the obstacles faced by NGOs in gaining access to institutions, discussions and informations should be removed for their wide participation and active roles. It is admittedly advisable that INGOs should seek to obtain a formal (at least in a limited scope) international legal status (personality) at the universal level for their active role for strengthening global governance.

# CHAPTER 6

# Global Governance and Universal Jurisdiction

## I. Introduction

Only after the world witnessed the atrocities committed by Nazis during World War II, did the world begin to realize the necessity of protecting the human rights at international level. Until then, States had absolute sovereignty over their territory and population free from any interference. At trials in the International Military Tribunal at Nuremberg, Nazi leaders were punished for crimes against humanity as well as war crimes. Nuremberg trials paved a new road by holding individuals personally liable under international law, regardless of the office of the perpetrators.[295]

The United Nations(UN) Charter manifests that "promoting and encouraging respect for human rights"[296] is a primary purpose of

---

[295] Bruce Broomhall, *op. cit.*, p.19.

the UN. In 1948, the UN General Assembly adopted the 「Universal Declaration of Human Rights」 and the 「Convention on the Prevention and Punishment of the Crime of Genocide」. 「The International Covenant on Civil and Political Rights」 and 「the International Covenant on Economic, Social and Cultural Rights」 were adopted in 1966 and entered into force in 1976.[297]

The international efforts to promote human rights, however, have not been always satisfactory and the weak mechanism of enforcing human rights has been always problematic. As we know from the history since World War II, there have been many cases that cause gross human rights violation. These include atrocities in the Former Yugoslavia and Rwanda. In many cases, inter-national mechanism to prevent gross human rights violations could not function properly.

Atrocities in the former Yugoslavia and Rwanda gave inter-national community a momentum to devise a more systematic and effective way to cope with gross violations of human rights. In 1993, the UN Security Council established the International Criminal Tribunal for the Former Yugoslavia(ICTY) to prosecute persons responsible for serious violations of international humanitarian law committed in the former Yugoslavia since 1991. In 1994, it set the International Criminal Tribunal for Rwanda (ICTR) to charge persons with crime of genocide and other serious

---

296 UN Charter, Art. 1 (3).
297 Louis Henkin *et al.*, *Human Rights*(Foundation Press, 1999), p.279.

violations of international humanitarian law committed in Rwanda. The experiences of ICTY and ICTR helped a lot for international community to establish the International Criminal Court(ICC). In 1998, the world community witnessed the signing of the Rome Statute, establishing the ICC.[298]

Should national courts in liberal constitutional democracies enforce international law even when there is no specific authorization from the legislative or executive branches to do so? Does effective and fair global governance require the uniform application of international law—the proper institutionalization of an international rule of law? How should national courts approach the question whether to enforce international law when international law claims are made in cases before them?[299]

It is no longer sufficient to dismiss international legal claims on the grounds that international law is not really law. Claims denying the legal character of international law, invoking either State sovereignty — the lack of a sovereign on the international level — or the lack of centralized enforcement mechanisms, have generally failed. The core argument generally invoked in this context is the idea of the 'international rule of law.' The 'international rule of law' is a term with no fixed meaning today

---

298  William A. Schabas, *An Introduction to the International Criminal Court*, 2nd ed.(Cambridge University Press, 2004), pp.10–13.

299  Mattias Kumm, "International Law in National Courts: The International Rule of Law and the Limits of the Internationalist Model," *Vanderbilt Journal of Int'l Law*, Vol.44, 2003, pp.19–20.

and which is widely used to encompass all kinds of desirable features of the international legal order. The features of an international legal order such as protection of human rights, procedural legitimacy, fair and just social and economic redistribution, effective protection of the environment are likely to have been claimed to be part of the international rule of law.[300]

In the meantime, international society has developed various mechanisms that transcend the traditional or existing notion of international law. One of these schemes, for example, include universal jurisdiction. Universal jurisdiction allows a State to invoke jurisdiction against crimes committed in another jurisdiction where prosecution against the crimes is not provided. Although universal jurisdiction has been designed and developed to promote human rights and is a very useful tool, it also can be problematic. It allegedly denies traditional notion of States' territorial sovereignty and creates frictions among States.

The issue of universal jurisdiction was touched in the International Court of Justice(ICJ)'s *Congo v. Belgium case* as *obiter dictum* of some members of ICJ in 2000.[301] At that time

---

[300] *Ibid.*, pp.21–22. But the author pointed in this paper that the argument from the international rule of law is insufficient to justify as strong a role for national courts as an uncompromisingly internationalist position suggests(*ibid.*, p.31). I insist, however, that an effective institutionalization of the rule of law on the international level not only provides an asset to the international community as a whole, but also tens to limit the executive's opportunity to claim foreign affairs prerogatives and obtain power in a way that endangers and destabilizes national democracy.

Belgium had a law granting its courts universal jurisdiction over international crimes such as war crimes, crimes against humanity and genocide.[302] In 2000, a Belgian magistrate issued an international arrest warrant for Ndombasi Yerodia, the foreign minister of the Republic of Congo.[303] He allegedly committed grave breaches of the Geneva Convention of 1949 and its Additional Protocols, and crimes against humanity. This was the first universal jurisdiction case because the crime was not committed in Belgium and neither the perpetrator nor the victims were Belgian.[304]

But Congo complained, in the ICJ proceeding, that the warrant violated absolute immunity of Congo, but afterwards, abandoned

---

301  See *infra* note 306.

302  The Belgian magistrate derived his jurisdiction from the Belgian Law of June 16, 1993," 'Concerning the Punishment of Grave Breaches of the International Geneva Conventions of 12 August 1949 and of Protocols I and II of 8 June 1977 Additional thereto,' as amended by the Law of February 1999 'concerning the Punishment of serious Violations of International Humanitarian Law.' "But in August 2003, the Belgian legislature repealed the 1993 Act Concerning Grave Breaches of International Humanitarian Law, officially because 'the Act is systematically abused by persons and organizations with their own political agenda.' *See* Luc Reydams, "Belgium Reneges on Universality: The 5 August 2003 Act on Grave Breaches of International Humanitarian Law," *Journal of Int'l Criminal Justice*, Vol.1, 2003, p.679.

303  Mark A. Summers, "The International Court of Justice's Decision in Congo v. Belgium: How Has It Affected The Development of a Principle of Universal Jurisdiction That Would Obligate All States to Prosecute War Criminals," *Boston University Int'l Law Journal*, Vol.21, 2003, pp.63-65.

304  *Ibid.*, pp.65-68.

its position that the universal jurisdiction constituted a violation of the principle that a State may not exercise its authority on the territory of another State and of the principle of sovereign equality.[305] The ICJ eschewed any further comment, even in dicta, regarding the basis for Belgium's jurisdiction. In *Congo v. Belgium case*, several judges, however, expressed their opinion, in dicta, on universal jurisdiction separately and contradictorily.[306]

This study raises the question whether the rule of law on the international level is an attractive and realizable ideal, as in domestic legal system and whether and how universal jurisdiction enhances the international rule of law for global governance.

---

[305] In October 2000, Congo instituted proceedings in the ICJ, seeking to annul the international arrest warrant issued for Yerodia. Originally Congo alleged that (1) the universal jurisdiction excised by Belgium violated the principle of State sovereignty and sovereign equality, (2) the Belgian warrant violated immunity from criminal process of foreign ministers. Afterwards, Congo abandoned the claim based on State sovereignty. Therefore, the ICJ had no opportunity to directly review the issue of universal jurisdiction. *Ibid.,* p.68.

[306] *Congo v. Belgium,* 2002 *I.C.J. Rep.,* paras. 41-43; Three judges, Guillaume, Ranjeva, and Rezek concluded, in the words of Judge Guillaume, that "if the Court had addressed these questions regarding universal jurisdiction ⋯ it ought therefore to have found that the Belgian judge was wrong in holding himself competent to prosecute Yerodia Ndombasi by relying on a universal jurisdiction incompatible with international law."(*Ibid.,* para. 17) But three other judges, Higgins, Kooijmans and Buergenthal, wrote that "it would seem ⋯ that the acts alleged in Belgium's arrest warrant do fall within the concept of 'crimes against humanity' and would be within that small category in respect of which an exercise of universal jurisdiction is not precluded under international law."(*Ibid.,* para. 65) See Mark A. Summers, *op. cit.,* p.68 note 32.

# II. State Sovereignty and the International Rule of Law

The traditional notion of international law is based on State sovereignty. The Treaty of Westphalia is regarded as the foundation of the international system of States. It stipulated interstate norms and the relations of rulers and subjects. The Treaty was the result of Thirty Years War and became the cornerstone of modern European inter–State system, where a State had the absolute power to rule in its own territory and should be free from any intervention in the internal affairs.

In the Westphalian system, however, sovereignty is considered belonging to the ruling monarch, not the people. Since Westphalia, States began to respect State sovereignty as an international rule. It created the norm of territorial integrity, autonomy, and non–interference.[307] Since the 18th century, it was understood that sovereignty belonged to the people.

Until World War II, the inviolability of sovereignty was reinforced. Any interference in the States' internal affairs was not allowed. By emphasizing the inviolability of sovereignty, the treatment of one's own nationals became a purely domestic matter.[308] In the State–centric system, the basis for human rights

---

307 Anthony Sammons, "The "Under–Theorization" of Universal Juris- diction: Implication for Legitimacy on Trials of War Criminals By National Courts," *Berkeley Journal of Int'l Law*, Vol.21, 2003, pp.111, 115.

308 Rosalyin Higgins, *op. cit.*, p.97.

protection was closely related to State borders and limited by the principle of nationality. Neither other States nor other international organizations could intervene in it.[309] An individual could not bring a claim before international tribunal even if he or she was a victim of international wrongful acts.

The international legal order after World War II is also based on the notion of state sovereignty. Article 2 of the UN Charter provides that the UN is "based on the principle of the sovereign equality" and "[all] members shall refrain in their relations from the threat or use of force against the territorial integrity or political independence of any State." Further, it provides that the UN shall not intervene in domestic matters.[310]

On the other hand, one of the main purposes of the UN is to maintain international peace and security.[311] The development of international human rights after World War II, required a new notion of the State sovereignty. Treating their nationals is no longer States' internal affairs and perpetrators committing international crimes cannot hide any longer behind sovereign immunity.[312] State sovereignty is recognized by international community to promote international peace and security, in that sense, it is no longer absolute or unlimited. Gross violations of

---

309  *Ibid.*

310  UN Charter, Art. 2 (1), (4), (7).

311  UN Charter, Art. 1 (1).

312  Chris Brown, *Sovereignty, Rights and Justice: international political theory today*(Polity Press, 2002), p.218.

human rights are understood to threat international peace and security. Some scholars understand State sovereignty as an "allocation of decision making authority between and international regimes."[313]

The new notion of State sovereignty contributes to promote international rule of law by protecting human dignity and maintaining international peace and security through preventing gross violations of human rights. International community has realized that one of the effective ways to prevent gross violations of human rights is to hold individuals responsible for the crimes criminally liable. The international law mechanism to promote international human rights by holding individuals criminally liable includes the scheme of universal jurisdiction and various international tribunals including the ICC.

---

[313] Gregory H. Fox, "New Approaches to International Human Rights," Sohail H. Hashmi & Schail H. Hashmi eds., *State Sovereignty: Change and Persistence in International Relations*(Pennsylvania State University Press, 1997), p.107.

# Ⅲ. The International Rule of Law and Universal Jurisdiction

## 1. The Significance of Universal Jurisdiction

There are several bases that States can invoke criminal jurisdiction under international law. The territoriality principle allows a State to invoke jurisdiction when the act over which the State wishes to assert jurisdiction takes place on the territory of the State. The nationality or active nationality principle allows a State to invoke jurisdiction when the perpetrator of the crime is a national of the State. The passive personality principle allows a State to invoke jurisdiction when the victim of the offense is a national of the State.[314] Protective jurisdiction allows a State to invoke jurisdiction where important State's rights and interests were harmed.[315]

Universal jurisdiction allows a State to exercise jurisdiction over a criminal act even in the absence of territorial, nationality or other accepted contacts with the offender or the victim. The crime is so egregious that its nature entitles a State to exercise its jurisdiction to apply its laws.[316] The universal jurisdiction can

---

314 Anthony J. Colangelo, "The New Universal Jurisdiction: In Absentia Signaling Over Clearly Defined Crime," *George Journal of Int'l Law,* Vol.36, 2005, p.537.

315 Lee A. Steven, "Genocide and the Duty to Extradite or Prosecute: Why the United States is in Breach of Its International Obligations," *Vanderbilt Journal of Int'l Law,* Vol.39, 1999, pp.425, 427.

be used for a State to prosecute human rights violators, therefore, the development and expansion of universal jurisdiction are closely related to the development of human rights in international law.

Some scholars argue that universal jurisdiction is an exception to the basic principle that a State does not have any rights of criminal jurisdiction in respect of acts done abroad by aliens.[317] Higgins, however, states that it is "a well established norm, which stands alongside other norms of jurisdiction and is not an exception of international law."[318] Now, universal jurisdiction is accepted as one of bases, like other bases, on that a State can exercise jurisdiction.

On the other hand, an indiscriminate assertion of universal jurisdiction by States can cause a lot of conflicts among countries because it can be understood as an encroachment on the sovereignty of other countries.[319] If the rule of law means law and order,[320] this negative aspect of universal jurisdiction might endanger the international rule of law. It is not surprising that, for a long time, universal jurisdiction was only applied to piracy

---

[316] R. Higgins, *op. cit.*, p.57.

[317] F. A. Mann, "The Doctrine of Jurisdiction in International Law," *Recueil des Cours*(1964, I), 1. See R. Higgins, *op. cit.*, p.58, note 4.

[318] R. Higgins, *op. cit.*, p.58.

[319] Eugene Kontorovich, "The Piracy Analogy: Modern Universal Jurisdiction's Hollow Foundation," *Harvard Int'l Law Journal*, Vol.45, 2004, p.183.

[320] M. Neumann, *op. cit.*, pp.18-19.

and slavery.[321]

Therefore, it is worth reviewing the lists of crimes subject to universal jurisdiction, the bases of universal jurisdiction and its relation to the international rule of law, the role of national courts and the dynamics between national courts and ICC.

## 2. Crimes Subject to Universal Jurisdiction

There are two principal sources of international law that govern the exercise of universal jurisdiction: customary law and international agreement. And above and beyond customary and treaty law, are also the fundamental peremptory norms incorporated in the doctrine of *jus cogens*.[322] Before World War II, only piracy and slavery[323] were recognized as crimes subject to universal jurisdiction. Especially piracy is a crime that paradigmatically is subject to prosecution by any State based on principle of universality, and it is crucial to the origins of universal jurisdiction.[324]

---

321 M. Cherif Bassiouni, "Universal Jurisdiction for International Crimes: Historical Perspectives and Contemporary Practice," *Vanderbilt Journal of Int'l Law*, Vol.42, 2001, pp.81, 107-114.

322 Jon B. Jordan, "Universal Jurisdiction in a Dangerous World: A Weapon for All Nations Against International Crime," *MSU-DCL Journal of Int'l Law*, Vol.9, 2000, p.6.

323 R. Higgins, *op. cit.*, p.58.

324 Gabriel Bottini, "Universal Jurisdiction After the Creation of the International Criminal Court," *N.Y.U. Journal of Int'l Law & Policy*, Vol.36, 2004, p.527.

The development of various treaties and customary international law since World War II has expanded the category of
crimes subject to universal jurisdiction. Universal jurisdiction in
the form of the obligation to 'extradite or prosecute' was
recognized first in the four 1949 geneva Conventions, which
oblige all State Parties to prohibit 'grave breaches' of them. This
mechanism also became a characteristic feature of the terrorism-
related conventions of the 1960s and 1970s, as well as others that
followed. Finally, the Convention against Torture provides an
explicit duty to make the crime of torture as defined in the
Convention an offence under national law.

Thus, at least in the Geneva Conventions and the Convention
Against Torture, international law does provide a clear, mandatory form of 'universal' jurisdiction as between States Parties.
Where genocide, crimes against humanity and other war crimes
are concerned, one must turn to custom.[325] Indeed, these crimes
are widely considered to have attained the status of *jus cogens*,
or peremptory international legal norms.[326] Customary law is less
clear than conventional law, but it has the advantage of applying
to all States including non States Parties. A few crimes except
pricy and slavery that are deemed to be subject to universal
jurisdiction are as follows;

---

[325] B. Broomhall, *op. cit.*, pp.109–110.

[326] M. A. Summers, *op. cit.*, p.74; Theodor Meron, "International Criminalization of Internal Atrocities," *American Journal of Int'l Law*, Vol.89,
1995, p.558.

## 1) Crime of Genocide

The 1948 Genocide Convention states that States Parties should prevent and punish the crime of genocide.[327] Genocide is act of crime committed with intent to destroy, in whole or in part, a national, ethnical, racial or religious group.[328] The Convention itself does not provide for universal jurisdiction or the duty to extradite or prosecute and theoretically applies only to Contracting Parties. Therefore the Genocide convention has been widely criticized because of its jurisdiction clause.

Indeed, crime of genocide is, regardless of the Convention system, generally understood to be crimes subject to universal jurisdiction in customary international law.[329] Genocide is most likely crudest of crimes subject to universal jurisdiction and is a crime giving rise to universal jurisdiction as a matter of customary law. The fact that the Convention was unanimously adopted and widely ratified among States supports this argument.[330] Universal Jurisdiction over genocide has been recognized under customary law in the Nuremberg trials, the Eichmann and Demjanjuk judgements, and the Restatement of Foreign Relations Law.[331]

---

327 「Convention on the Prevention and Punishment of the Crime of Genocide」, Art. 1.

328 *Ibid.*, Art. 2.

329 B. Broomhall, *op. cit.,* p.110; M. A. Summers, *op. cit.,* p.74; Jon B. Jordan, *op. cit.,* p.6; G. Bottini, *op. cit.,* pp.537–538.

330 Lyal S. Sunga, *Individual Responsibility in International Law for Serious Human Rights Violations*(Springer, 1992), pp.72–73.

331 J. B. Jordan, *op. cit.,* p.17.

Furthermore the *Barcelona Traction Case*[332] states that the duty not to commit genocide is an obligation *erga omnes*, meaning all States having a legal interest.

## 2) War Crimes

Atrocities committed during World War II lead to the recognition of war crimes and genocide as crimes offensive enough to warrant universal jurisdiction. The Nuremberg trials was the central event recognizing universal jurisdiction over war criminals. The four 1949 Geneva Conventions[333] obliged all States Parties to prohibit grave breach of the Conventions. States Parties must search for person having committed grave breaches, regardless of nationality, and bring them to justice, or hand them over to another State Party for trials.[334] 1977 Additional Protocol also has the 'extradite or prosecute'(*aut dedere aut judicare*) provision with regard to grave breaches under the Conventions.[335]

The violations of 1949 Geneva Conventions are understood to

---

[332] *Barcelona Traction* Case(*Belgium v. Spain*), 1970 *I.C.J. Rep.* 3, para. 32.

[333] These include 「Geneva Convention for the Amelioration of the Condition of the Wounded and Sick in Armed Forces in the Field」, 「Geneva Convention for the Amelioration of the Condition of Wounded, Sick and Shipwrecked Members of Armed Forces at Sea」, 「Geneva Convention Relative to the Treatment of Prisoners of War」, and 「Geneva Convention Relative to the Protection of Civilian Persons in Time of War」

[334] Geneva Convention I, Art. 49; Convention II, Art. 50; Convention III, Art. 129 and Convention IV, Art. 146.

[335] 「Protocol I Additional to the Geneva Conventions of 1949」, Art. 2.

be crimes subject to universal jurisdiction among Contracting Parties because it provides the obligation of 'extradite or prosecute.' Further, war crimes committed in international and internal armed conflicts, as defined in the Geneva Convention, are generally deemed to be subject to universal jurisdiction under customary international law.[336] ICTY and ICTR, therefore, could have jurisdiction over crimes committed in internal armed conflicts.[337]

### 3) Torture

Torture is generally considered crime subject to universal jurisdiction only as a matter of international convention like hijacking, terrorism, and apartheid.[338] The Convention Against Torture stipulates the duty of each State Party to make all acts of torture punishable under its criminal law and the obligation of 'extradite or prosecute' among State Parties. Therefore, each State Party shall take such measures as necessary to establish its jurisdiction over the act of torture or extradite an offender to the State which have criminal jurisdiction over that offence if it does not submit the case to its competent authorities for the purpose of prosecution.[339]

---

336 B. Broomhall, *op. cit.*, p.110.

337 *Ibid.*

338 J. B. Jordan, *op. cit.*, p.17.

339 「Convention Against Torture and Other Cruel, Inhuman or Degrading

Accordingly, the crime of torture under the Convention is widely considered to be a crime subject to universal jurisdiction. But the crime of torture like hijacking, terrorism and apartheid have not yet received customary universal jurisdiction, because many of these crimes are subject to varying definitions from country to country.[340]

## 4) Crimes against Humanity

While there are certainly clearly defined 'crimes against humanity' that are subject to universal jurisdiction — *i.e.*, genocide and slavery —, the definitional problem of potentially expanding this class of international crime to encompass subjectively-determined conduct is great.[341]

Article 6(c) of the Nuremberg Charter defines 'crimes against humanity' as

> "murder, extermination, enslavement, deportation, and other inhumane acts committed against any civilian population, before or during the war, or persecutions on political, racial or religious grounds in execution of or in connection with any crime within the jurisdiction of the Tribunal whether or not in violation of the domestic law of the country where

---

Treatment or Punishment」, Arts. 4, 5, 6, 7.

340 So, one nation's definition of torture could be another nation's correctional system. See J. B. Jordan, *op. cit.*, p.23.

341 A. J. Colangelo, *op. cit.*, pp.586-587.

perpetrated."

Article 7 of the ICC Statute broadly defines 'crimes against humanity' as acts "committed as part of a widespread or systematic attack directed against any civilian population, with knowledge of the attack."

Unlike other crimes of universal jurisdiction, there is no specialized convention for 'crimes against humanity.' That is, there is no conventional system with regard to 'crimes against humanity.'[342] This has not prevented, however, the formation of a wide consensus among commentators that every State has the right to exercise their jurisdiction over crimes against humanity.[343] Although the bases of jurisdiction over crimes against humanity in Article 5 of the ICTY, Article 3 of the ICTR are territorial,[344] the category of crimes against humanity is well accepted as international crime and those crimes are understood to be subject to universal jurisdiction under customary international law.[345]

---

342 M. C. Bassiouni, *op. cit.*, pp.116–117.
343 G. Bottini, *op. cit.*, p.538.
344 *Ibid.*, p.119.
345 L. S. Sunga, *op. cit.*, pp.41–50; B. Broomhall, *op. cit.*, p.110.

## 3. Bases of Universal Jurisdiction and International Rule of Law

There are several arguments as to why universal jurisdiction is necessary. These arguments can be divided into two: pragmatic and humanitarian ones.

The pragmatic argument is based on the assumption that universal jurisdiction is justified because the perpetrator of the crimes would otherwise go unpunished. "Pirates being *hostis humani generis* (enemy of all mankind), are punishable in the tribunals of all nations. All nations are engaged in a league against them for the mutual defense and safety of all."[346]

As I stated above, universal jurisdiction was originally extended to piracy and slavery. The crimes of piracy and slavery were carried out on the high seas or in other areas that are not within the jurisdiction of any States. Such crimes would likely to go unpunished without universal jurisdiction because neither the territorial nor the nationality principle can be applied on the high seas.[347]

Humanitarian bases for universal jurisdiction are important in modern human rights development. Customary international law also allows a State to invoke universal jurisdiction based on the seriousness of the crimes committed.[348] Certain crimes are so

---

[346] *United States v. Smit*, 18 U.S. (5 Wheat) 153(1820), See Lee A. Steven, *op. cit.*, pp.425, 431.

[347] L. A. Steven, *op. cit.*, pp.431–435.

[348] *Ibid.*, p.435.

egregious that they threaten the peace and security of the international community as a whole. This kind of crimes includes war crimes, crimes against humanity. The serious nature of the crimes "threaten to undermine the very foundations of the enlightened international community as a whole; it is this quality that gives each one of the members of that community the right to extend the incidence of its criminal law to them ···."[349]

The arguments against universal jurisdiction are based on the various principles of international law. Among them, the most powerful argument is based on State sovereignty.[350] Universal jurisdiction, especially *in absentia*,[351] allegedly denies a rational distribution of competences among equal sovereign States and the principle of sovereign equality of States. However, States do not create "a chaotic and arbitrary method of enforcing international law" by invoking universal jurisdiction randomly.[352] States contemplate various criteria and take into account wide range of interests held by other States including one that the competent State might have.

I argue that the basis for universal jurisdiction must be sought

---

349 S. Z. Feller, "Jurisdiction over Offenses with a Foreign Element," M. Cherif Bassiouni & Ved P. Nanda eds., *A Treatise on International Criminal Law: Jurisdiction and Cooperations*(Thomas, 1973), pp.5, 32–33.

350 A. J. Colangelo, *op. cit.,* p.549.

351 Universal Jurisdiction *in absentia* is defined as invoking jurisdiction even when the defendant is not present in the territory of the acting State. See *ibid.,* p.542.

352 *Ibid.,* p.549.

from: ( i ) the nature of the crimes beyond any single State's capacity to prosecute the perpetrators[353]; (ii) *raison d' être* of State sovereignty in the international community. As I said above, international society is a legal community governed by the rule of law. State sovereignty is to be justified to the extent that international community allows in consideration of various factors including international peace and security.[354] Even though States have the authority to exercise sovereignty over its territory and its nationals, a State owes obligations toward international community to exercise it properly.[355]

The seriousness of certain crimes shows that the State lacks the capacity to prosecute the perpetrators and has failed in its obligations toward international community to protect its people. The invocation of jurisdiction by international community or a State representing international community is justified.[356] The exercise of universal jurisdiction by international community will promote international rule of law by holding individuals responsible for serious crimes liable.

---

353  A. Sammons, *op. cit.*, p.128.
354  *Ibid.*, pp.120–122.
355  *Ibid.*
356  *Ibid.*, p.33.

## 4. Is it Permissive or Mandatory?

Obviously States may invoke domestic jurisdiction when universal jurisdiction is allowed by international law. Then, the question of whether international law requires a State to exercise universal jurisdiction arises. The 1949 Geneva Conventions, which requires all States Parties to prohibit grave breaches of them, recognized universal jurisdiction by stipulating the obligation to 'extradite or prosecute.'[357] States Parties should search for persons alleged to have committed grave breaches, regardless of their nationality, and bring them before their own courts, or hand them over to another State Party for prosecution.[358] The Convention Against Torture stipulates a duty to make torture an offence under national law.[359] Each party must invoke jurisdiction over the crime when committed on its territory, by one of its nationals, against one of its nationals, or when the criminal is present on its territory and it does not extradite him or her.[360] These Conventions provide 'mandatory' universal jurisdiction among States Parties.

The issue becomes more complicated when it comes to crimes, by customary international law, subject to universal jurisdiction. Some scholars argue that, in customary international law, war

---

357 See Geneva Conventions, *supra* note 333.
358 B. Broomhall, *op. cit.*, p.109.
359 Convention Against Torture, Art. 4.
360 *Ibid.*, Arts. 6, 7, 12.

crimes, crimes against humanity and genocide only give rise to 'permissive' universal jurisdiction.[361] According to this view, the international community, which is often represented by the State requesting extradition of perpetrators of crimes subject to universal jurisdiction, has no right to demand that State arrest and prosecute the perpetrators of crimes subject to universal jurisdiction. They argue that the universality principle is 'exclusively' permissive, and never obligatory.

For example, Lyal S. Sunga states that "universal jurisdiction merely authorizes, rather than obliges States to prosecute and punish offenders. International law does not import a mandatory obligation upon State authorities to undertake prosecution."[362]

On the other hand, some scholars go beyond the above view on 'permissive' universal jurisdiction and argue with respect to some or all core crimes that such jurisdiction is 'mandatory' at customary law. Among them, Bassiouni argues that the prevention by States of war crimes, crimes against humanity and genocide is *jus cogens* that gives rise to obligations *erga omnes*.[363] He also argues that States have an obligation to adjudicate international crimes subject to universal jurisdiction.[364]

---

361 B. Broomhall, *op. cit.,* p.110.

362 L. S. Sunga, *op. cit.,* p.114.

363 M. Cherif Bassiouni, *Crimes Against Humanity under International Law*(Martinus Nijhoff, 1992), pp.510-527; Amnesty International, *The International Criminal Court: Fundamental principles concerning the elements of genocide*(Amnesty International, 1999).

364 M. C. Bassiouni, *ibid.*; Jodi Horowitz, "Regina v. Bartle and the

*Jus cogens* is defined as a "norm from which no derogation is permitted."[365] It is a norm accepted and recognized by the international community of States as a whole from which no derogation is permitted. The idea of obligations *erga omnes*[366] means that "all States have a legal interest regarding breaches of the obligations."[367]

According to this view, the duty not to commit war crimes, crimes against humanity and genocide is *jus cogens* from which no derogation is permitted and all States have a legal interest in prevention of those crimes. All States owe international community, which composed of States and is governed by rule of law, the obligation to adjudicate the perpetrators of inter-national core crimes.[368]

In *Congo v. Belgium case*, President Guillaume states that

---

Commissioner of Police for the Metropolis and Others *Ex Parte* Pinochet: Universal Jurisdiction and Sovereign Immunity for *Jus Cogens* Violations," *Fordham Int'l Law Journal*, Vol.23, 1999, pp.489, 525; R. Higgins, "The General International Law of Terrorism and International Law," R. Higgins & Maurice Flory, eds., *Terrorism and International Law*(Routledge, 1997), pp.13, 24.

365 「Vienna Convention on the Law of Treaties」, Art. 53.

366 It means obligations towards the international community. See Andre de Hoogh, *Obligations Erga Omnes and International Crimes: A Theoretical Inquiry into the Implementation and Enforcement of the International Responsibility of States*(Springer, 1996), pp.68-69.

367 *Ibid.*

368 Samantha v. Ettari, "A Foundation of Granite or Sand? The Inter-national Criminal Court and United States Bilateral Immunity Agreement," *Brooklyn Journal of Int'l Law*, Vol.30, 2004, pp.205, 222-238.

"universal jurisdiction *in absentia* as in the present case in unknown to international law."[369] Whereas, another separate opinion by Judges Higgins, Kooijmans and Buergenthal concluded that extraterritorial jurisdiction is 'mandatory' and States can exercise 'pure' universal jurisdiction.[370]

States can invoke universal jurisdiction only when it is the most egregious crimes under international law. Those crimes are the concern of all States and may threaten international peace and security.[371] All States must cooperate in bringing those who commit such offenses to justice. To achieve international co-operation in promoting and encouraging respect for human rights is one of the UN's purposes.[372] In order for the cooperation to be effective, States must either prosecute perpetrators of inter-national crimes who are within their custody or extradite them to States willing and able to prosecute.

In brief, universal jurisdiction flows directly from the fact that the core crimes of international criminal law rest on norms of *jus cogens* that give rise to obligations *erga omnes*.[373] In this

---

369  *Congo v. Belgium,* 2002 *I.C.J. Rep.* para. 12.

370  *Ibid.* paras. 59–60.

371  UN Charter, Art. 1 (1).

372  UN Charter, Art. 1 (3).

373  On the contrary G. Bottini insists that "while some argue that an international crime established by *jus cogens* norms is subject to universal jurisdiction, these two theories are, in fact, completely separate. ··· It is argued that States are entitled to exercise universal jurisdiction over offenses covered by obligation *erga omnes*. However, even if all States have a legal interest in a State's fulfillment of its

regard, I think that the exercise of universal jurisdiction especially over core crimes should be mandatory. It seems that the existing universal jurisdiction under customary international law is in transition from 'permissive' to 'mandatory' or 'obligatory' exercise.[374]

## 5. Dynamics between National Courts and ICC

### 1) The Role of National Courts

Even after the establishment of the ICC, the important role of national courts should not be disregarded. The ICC jurisdiction is complementary to national jurisdiction. One of the important roles that the ICC provides is to encourage domestic courts actively prosecute perpetrators of heinous crimes.[375] The complementary factor is the product of the compromise between State sovereignty and the interest of international community. Under the ICC system, the active role of national courts to protect

---

obligation to exercise criminal jurisdiction over a certain crime, that does not necessarily mean that other States also have jurisdiction over that crime." See G. Bottini, *op. cit.*, pp.518–519. I still think that although it is important to maintain distinctions between universal jurisdiction, *jus cogens*, and obligations *erga omnes*, the three concepts are based on the idea that members of the international community share common goals and fundamental values that shape an international public order. Therefore, the connections among those concepts are very clear.

374 B. Broomhall, *op. cit.*, p.112.
375 G. Bottini, *op. cit.*, pp.503, 546.

international human rights remains critical.

As I stated above, all States owe international community an obligation to prosecute or extradite perpetrators subject to universal jurisdiction. It means that, theoretically, international community, not individual States, has the right to exercise universal jurisdiction. Then, what is the relationship between national courts exercising universal jurisdiction and the holder of the right, international community? One of the ideas is that an individual State exercising universal jurisdiction undertakes the prosecution as the *de facto* agent for the international community.[376] The national court, however, is not under the direct control or guidance from any international body. Therefore, it is reasonably expected that the national court could be criticized for exercising its jurisdiction based on political motivation.[377] This accusation might harm the legitimacy of the process.

It is not true, however, that the prosecution by universal jurisdiction by a State is not controlled or guided by international community. The invocation of universal jurisdiction by an individual State can be reviewed by international community including International Court of Justice(ICJ).

In *Ndombasi Yerodia case*, the ICJ, in fact, held that "certain holders of high-ranking office in a State, such as the Head of

---

376 A. Sammons, *op. cit.,* p.137.
377 *Ibid.*

State, Head of Government, and Minister for Foreign Affairs, enjoy immunities from jurisdiction in other States, both civil and criminal."[378] The ICJ refused to recognize the arrest warrant issued by Brussel's magistrate based on universal jurisdiction.

National courts exercising universal jurisdiction may encounter many difficulties and these might make the application of universal jurisdiction less likely. First, national courts should find a legislative basis in order to invoke universal jurisdiction.[379] Without a proper statute allowing universal jurisdiction, prosecutors or judges of national courts might not invoke the principle. Second, acquiring evidence including witness testimony would be difficult because a lot of evidence that can be used to prove crimes, very often, are only available in another jurisdiction.[380] In order to overcome the evidentiary difficulties, mutual legal assistance might be helpful. Typically, treaties on mutual legal assistance allow the requested State to have a wide range of discretion in whether it gives legal assistance or not. National courts exercising universal jurisdiction might fail to collect enough evidence to prove the criminals guilty.

Prosecutors and judges exercising universal jurisdiction should take into account various factors. First, it is important whether the jurisdiction can secure the custody of the perpetrator or not.[381]

---

378 *Congo v. Belgium*, 2002 *I.C.J. Rep.*, paras. 58–61.
379 B. Broomhall, *op. cit.*, p.118.
380 *Ibid.*, pp.119–120.
381 *Ibid.*, p.123.

If it does not have the custody, the jurisdiction must obtain the custody from the relevant State, for example, by extradition. Second, if there is a State which has territorial or national jurisdiction and that State is willing to try the accused in a reasonable way, the invocation of universal jurisdiction must not be encouraged.[382] In decision making process as to whether to prosecute or not, attitude of victims, NGOs and international community should be considered.[383]

## 2) Universal Jurisdiction and the Jurisdiction of ICC

Universal jurisdiction is exercised unilaterally by a State, whereas the jurisdiction of ICC is based on States' delegation of the power to enforce particular international criminal law.[384] Universality principle gives States the authority to apply their own laws in the prosecutions of international crimes subject to universal jurisdiction. A problem that result from the exercise of universal jurisdiction is the possible prejudices inherent within the prosecuting State. Sometimes the opportunity to exercise universal jurisdiction is enticing that States will actually violate international law in order to take advantage of it.[385] The arguments of possible bias, such as complaint of intervention in

---

382  *Ibid.*, p.124.
383  *Ibid.*
384  A. Sammons, *op. cit.*, p.137.
385  J. B. Jordan, *op. cit.*, p.4.

the internal affairs can be raised against universal jurisdiction to the extent that the jurisdiction is unilateral.

In addition to developments in international criminal law, the 1990s also brought an expansion of the universality principle despite the objection to its function. This appears to be, at least in part, to the lack of international judicial and enforcement mechanisms.[386] But, now the Rome Statute promises to impact universal jurisdiction in particular and enforcement of inter-national criminal law in general. It is clear at the outset that the ICC and universal jurisdiction pursue similar goals.[387]

Both systems grant jurisdiction over offenses such as war crimes, crimes against humanity, and genocide. ICC has the jurisdiction over genocide, crimes against humanity, war crimes, the crime of aggression.[388] The Rome Statute, however, limits the ICC's jurisdiction to crimes committed on the territory of a signatory State or by a national of a signatory State,[389] in which case no universal jurisdiction issue arises.

The UN Security Council, however, can refer a case to the ICC even though the territorial and nationality connections do not exist.[390] It is understood that, where the UN Security Council initiates the case, the ICC has jurisdiction over crimes committed

---

386  G. Bottini, *op. cit.,* p.504.

387  *Ibid.,* p.505.

388  「Rome Statue of the International Criminal Court」, Art. 5.

389  *Ibid.,* Art. 12 (2) (a)−(b).

390  *Ibid.,* Art. 13 (b).

in non-party States by nationals of non-party States.[391] Some scholars argue that "given the problems and risks associated with the application of universal jurisdiction, the international community should eliminate universal jurisdiction in favor of the ICC."[392] They argue that the disappearance of universal jurisdiction will help make the ICC more effective.[393]

But, I do not agree with those arguments. The reasons are as follows: First, the crimes subject to universal jurisdiction and ICC jurisdiction are not the same.[394] For example, piracy is excluded from the ICC jurisdiction. Crimes excluded from the ICC jurisdiction must be governed by universal jurisdiction; Second, it is possible that customary international law or Conventions create new crimes subject to universal jurisdiction. The expansion of universal jurisdiction will strengthen international rule of law by enforcing international human rights norm in national courts; Third, the ICC jurisdiction is complementary in that national courts have primary jurisdiction. The ICC "shall be complementary to national criminal jurisdictions."[395] The ICC "shall determine that a case is inadmissible" if the case is investigated or prosecuted by a State which has jurisdiction over it, or when the case has already been investigated and the State has decided not

---

391  E. Kontorovich, *op. cit.*, pp.183, 187.

392  G. Bottini, *op. cit.*, p.541.

393  *Ibid.*

394  *Ibid.*, pp.523-541.

395  Rome Statute, Art. 17 (1).

to prosecute.[396] Trials by national courts should be encouraged; Fourth, the ICC can determine whether or not a State is unwilling to genuinely prosecute crimes, using a test of the good faith of national authorities.[397] It is not likely that national courts paralyze an ICC prosecution, invoking universal jurisdiction and prosecuting the perpetrators in bad faith.[398]

# Ⅳ. Conclusion

The on-going evolution of universal jurisdiction and estab-lishment of the ICC have shown the determination of inter-national community to protect the human dignity and value, and maintain international peace and security by preventing gross violations of human rights. They, however, cast great challenges to the traditional system of international law. Is universal jurisdiction compatible with the notion of State sovereignty? Does universal jurisdiction enhance the international rule of law? How does exercise of universal jurisdiction by national courts interact with international tribunals such as the ICC? These questions can not be answered easily.

---

396 *Ibid.*, Art. 17 (1).

397 *Ibid.*, Art. 17 (2).

398 On the contrary, G. Bottini argues that continued recognition of universal jurisdiction would paralyze an ICC prosecution. See G. Bottini, *op. cit.*, p.541.

One of the reasons for that is that most crimes subject to universal jurisdiction has emerged after World War Ⅱ and taken a position for relatively short period of time in international human rights law. The history of the ICC is in its nascent stage and more time and experience would be needed to formulate a more stable and well accepted system in international criminal law.

Expanding universal jurisdiction would contribute to streng-thening the international rule of law, rather than undermining it. Some of purposes of the UN includes maintaining international peace and security, and achieving international cooperation in promoting and encouraging respect for human rights.[399] Obviously the international crimes recognized by international community as subject to universal jurisdiction may threaten international peace and security, and human dignity.

Allowing the perpetrators of such crimes to go unpunished also undermines and, further, threatens international peace and security, and human dignity. If they go unpunished, it can be shown to possible perpetrators that international community will tolerate such crimes. It means that gross violations of human rights are likely to happen again, at any time.

At present stage, in conclusion, I want to note several points. First, the system of universal jurisdiction is a useful and effective mechanism to promote international human rights. Even though,

---

[399] UN Charter, Art. 1 (1), (3).

the ICC is a great achievement of international community, its effectiveness in trials and enforcement mechanism as well as its scope of jurisdiction falls short of that of national courts system. Universal jurisdiction strengthen the international rule of law.

Second, mandatory exercise of universal jurisdiction should be encouraged.[400] With full discretion in exercising the jurisdiction, a State's decision to prosecute is likely to be attacked as being politically motivated or biased. The common recognition of international community that the exercise of universal juris- diction is mandatory will contribute to deter possible gross human rights violation from recurring.

Third, the international system to enhance the effectiveness of universal jurisdiction should be framed. This includes legislating universal jurisdiction in national legal systems, concluding international conventions for extraditing perpetrators of inter- national crimes and facilitating legal assistance among States.[401]

Fourth, the function of national courts system exercising universal jurisdiction and that of the ICC is not exclusive. The function of national courts is primary and that of ICC is secondary. The role of both courts is functionally distributed and must be understood as a whole system to promote international human rights in international community.

---

400  B. Broomhall, *op. cit.*, p.112.

401  Especially, without proper procedure to obtain evidence in foreign jurisdictions, prosecuting the crimes subject to universal jurisdiction would be very hard. See *ibid.*, pp.120–121.

Finally, the positive attitude of States and international community in exercising universal jurisdiction is necessary. Although States' policy cannot be based only on humanitarian causes, human rights and humanitarian causes are international concerns and must be taken into account seriously in States' decision making process. Without bringing perpetrators of gross human rights violations to justice, international peace and security cannot be obtained.

# CHAPTER 7

# Global Governance and
# the Common Heritage of Mankind

## I. Introduction

In the process of global integration and globalization, international law lays down basic principles and rules governing the relationship among States and thus builds an important foundation for the functioning of international organizations, which, as one of its principal objectives, is to work for the observance of international law and its further development and codification.[402]

The international society or community has undergone vital changes and made developments in the twentieth century. As a matter of international expediency and common interest, States with divergent ideologies and political systems, economic and social levels of achievement, and religious backgrounds are

---

402 William L. Tung, *op. cit.*, pp. xi –xii, 26–29.

expected to move from passive coexistence to active collaboration and cooperation on the global basis.

In spite of different backgrounds and traditions, most States have been generally in common agreement on principles of internationalism rather than nationalism or colonialism, and furthermore on principles of globalism or universalism. The international community of the late 20th century faces an expanding need to develop universal norms to address global concerns and interests. Indeed, one of the most significant developments in international law during the 20th century has been the expanded role played by multilateral treaties addressed to the common concerns of States.[403] It is evident that, due to the development of international law and organizations, States are gradually becoming united into a world community.

There are new trends in the contemporary international law and world community. These new trends have emerged to meet the demands of cooperation and common welfare, and constitute a legal system or regime for promotion of cooperation and common welfare. The concept of the 'common heritage of mankind'

---

[403] Jonathan I. Charney, "Universal International Law," *American Journal of International Law*, Vol.87, 1993, p.529; The preamble and principles of the Charter of the UN represent public policy. The 'common heritage' regarding 'public' or 'collective' goods; the commitment to international cooperation; the condemnation of colonialism and genocide; the disapprobation of racism, and many other policies repeatedly expressed in resolutions of international organs are examples of international public policy. See Werner Levi, *Contemporary International Law: A Concise Introduction*(Westview Press, 1979), p.35.

(hereinafter often cited as 'CHM') is one of the strongly indicative of the new trends in international law.

What is the substance of the concept of 'common heritage of mankind'? Now, I am concerned with the new trends in international law and examination of the concept of common heritage of mankind, and further intend to investigate the content and principle of the common heritage of mankind.

# II. New Trends of International Law in the Globalization Era

There are a few areas of exclusive sovereign rights under international law, accepted in the early 20th century, that will continue to be modified and transformed quickly and wholly: ( i ) economic activities; (ii) human rights and responsibilities; (iii) protection of the natural environment;[404] and (iv) use of the natural resources; and so forth.

First, it will become increasingly difficult to disregard the effects of imports and exports of a State on other markets, or to close its markets or dominate other markets without some legal liability, witnessed now by the World Trade Organization(WTO)

---

404 Gerard J. Mangone, "The Dynamics of International Law for the Next Century"(unpublished paper) presented at Jeju National University on November 21, 1994.

system. Today, one can claim that there is universal consensus on global growth or common welfare as a goal of the world community. If this is so, then by necessary implication it can be said that such a consensus extends to such goals as: expansion of world trade; increased financial flows and ultimately a net transfer of resources or technology to developing countries; equitable distribution of world resources and wealth.

Second, Conventions on protection of human rights and the prevention or prohibition of genocide, war crimes or crimes against peace and humanity already approved, will be further strengthened through institutions like the European Court of Human Rights, the Inter-American Court of Human Rights, the UN Human Rights Council, and the ICC in addition to Declarations, such as the recent appeal against violence toward women, that lead eventually to international conventions. And the accountability of individuals to an international community has been strengthened. The role of individual as a carrier of responsibilities or obligations under international law is increasingly important. The attempted imposition of more obligations on individuals through international law has increased the number of crimes an individual could commit directly against international law, and for whose punishment any State or international tribunal has jurisdiction.[405]

Third, there happens an entirely new view of the relationship

---

405 Werner Levi, *op. cit.*, pp.157-58.

of human beings to their environment and the responsibility of States to preserve and protect plants, animals, air, and water. From the first international Convention of 1954 to prevent the pollution of the sea by oil, to the Conference on the Human Environment in Stockholm in 1972, to the UN Convention on the Law of the Sea of 1982, being in force 16 November 1994,[406] to the UN Conference on Environment and Development(UNCED) in Rio de Janeiro in 1992, States have been called upon to adopt laws and regulations to prevent and control pollution.

Fourth, in traditional international law, any State that possessed a territory and exercised actual control over it acquired a legal title to use the natural resources in the territory and moreover freely utilized the natural resources pertaining to the high seas or deep sea-bed, *i. e.* non-sovereign areas. The concept of territorial sovereignty allows a State to exercise its ultimate authority in the area. The absence of territorial sovereignty prevents a State from establishing for itself of granting to others

---

406  ⌜The Agreement on Implementation of the Sea-bed Provision of the Convention on the Law of the Sea⌟ was adopted by the UN General Assembly at a resumed forty-eighth session on July 28, 1994, by a vote of 121 in favor, none against, and 7 abstentions. Over fifty States have already signed the Agreement, including the United States and virtually all other industrialized States. The purpose of the 1994 Agreement is to enhance the prospects for widespread ratification of the Convention by responding to problems with the deep sea-bed mining regime in Part XI, particularly those that troubled industrial States, including the United States. See Bernard H. Oxman, "The 1994 Agreement and the Convention," *American Journal of International Law,* Vol.88, 1994, pp.687-696.

property rights in non–sovereign areas. In the past, the principle of *res nullius* and *res communis* have been available in con–nection with non–sovereign areas, with the *res communis* principle prohibiting the establishment of sovereignty in common areas, and *res nullius* allowing such sovereignty to be established pursuant to suitable criteria.

Modern development of technology has opened up areas beyond the traditional territorial jurisdiction of States. These areas are often described as 'international commons' or 'common spaces' and they are becoming a growing field for the development of international law. The concept of the high seas was the first to be developed as a common space or *res communis* beyond the territorial sovereignty of any State.

There are other extra–territorial spaces, such as deep sea–bed area, outer space, and Antarctic area. Nowadays, these areas or spaces are regarded as 'common heritage of mankind,' while the high seas is only regarded as *res communis* that means that every State can use a certain goods for its own purposes and its own interest. In the postwar era the 'common heritage of mankind' evolved as a new main principle of international law and had a highly innovating impact on modern international law.[407]

---

407 In addition to the 'common heritage of mankind,' 'permanent sover–eignty over natural resources' also evolved as a main principle of international(economic) law. At first glance these principles might look somewhat contradictory. But the principle of permanent sovereignty basically purports to establish exclusive jurisdiction of States over natural resources in areas where they can exercise sovereign rights,

Arvid Pardo, one of the founders of the common heritage of mankind concept under international law has claimed that it challenges the "structural relationship between rich and poor countries" and amounts to a "revolution not merely in the law of the sea, but also in international relations."[408] So, the concept of CHM could be extended and applied to the area of international space law and international law relating to Antarctica.

# III. Institutionalization of the Common Heritage of Mankind(CHM)

## 1. The Concept of the CHM

For a long time, the notion of sovereignty occupied only a modest place in the traditional law of the sea. Sovereignty was accepted for the internal waters and for a territorial sea of a limited width. Beyond the territorial sea the notion of the freedom of the high seas prevailed. The concept of the CHM is rather a new one, but not completely new for the world community. There

---

while the principle of the common heritage of mankind basically aims at sharing the world's natural resources through the international regime for the common areas or spaces. See Paul de Waart · Paul Peters · Erik Denters, *International Law and Development*(Martinus Nijhoff Publishers, 1988), pp.87–101.

408 Arvid Pardo, "Ocean, Space and Mankind," *Third World Quarterly*, Vol.6, 1984, pp.559–569.

are some important precedents for the concept of the CHM and some practices upon which the common heritage principle can draw: in religious doctrine the concept of 'stewardship'; in economic theory as well as in law, too, common goods, common lands, common property, *res communis*, social ownership.[409]

As explained above, *res communis* is a thing which is naturally common property and is incapable of being appropriated by any person. In traditional international law, *res communis* implied that every State had equal rights of use in the thing concerned, unregulated by other States. The *res communis* concept is not community-oriented, but geared to the self-interest of each and every member of the community. In addition, whereas the high seas were in theory open to all States, in practice, most poor countries did not greatly benefit from the economic, commercial, and military advantages occuring from their use, or at any rate they benefited from them to far less an extent than powerful or industrialized countries.[410]

The concept of CHM takes the idea one step further:[411] What may be used by all should be regulated by all. Whatever is the CHM must be subject to the wishes of the international community as a whole through the UN or some other regulatory body

---

409  *Ibid.*, p.95.

410  Antonio Cassese, *International Law in a Divided World*(Clarendon Press, 1986), pp.377-378.

411  David H. Ott, *Public International Law in the Modern World*(Pitman Publishing, 1987), p.126.

established specially for the purpose. This concept has been developed in connection with codification activities concerning the progressive development of international law within the framework of the UN system. The principle with this concept represents and forms an ideological basis or essential element of the 「UN Convention on the Law of the Sea」— from where it has found its way into national legislation relating to sea−bed activities.[412]

The concept of CHM was first propounded in an international forum as a standard by which to establish a new regulation for the exploration and exploitation of the resources of the high seas. The 「UN Convention on the Law of the Sea」 is universally recognized and accepted as one of the most significant

---

412  In 1967 Ambassador Arvid Pardo of Malta proposed to the UN General Assembly to declare the sea−bed and the ocean floor beyond the limits of national jurisdiction to be the CHM, which he presented as "a new legal principle, which we wish to introduce into international law." He proposed the creation of an organization to assure jurisdiction over this area as 'a trustee for all countries.' But among Western observers Arvid Pardo has sometimes been portrayed as an unworldly idealist. He has also been criticized for exaggerating the wealth in manganese nodules lying on the ocean floor and minimizing the cost of mining it. The maritime Powers remained skeptical about the meaning and content of the concept of CHM which, they thought, was 'not legal concept or principle' but merely embodied a 'moral commitment,' while the under−developed Countries insisted that it was the new consensus which had replaced the outmoded freedom of the seas in that area. See Clyde Sanger, *Ordering the Oceans — the Making of the Law of the Sea —* (University of Toronto Press, 1987), pp.18−20; R. P. Anand, *Origin and Development of the Law of the Sea*(Martinus Nijhoff Publishers, 1983), pp.203−204.

achievements of the international community in the field of codification and progressive development of international law. It has declared the Area(Deep Seabed) and its resources as the CHM. It also provides for the establishment of the International Seabed Authority, the body empowered to administer the CHM and to regulate its exploration and exploitation.[413]

Frakes has briefly identified five core components of the common heritage of mankind(CHM):[414] ( i ) There can be no private or public appropriation; no one legally owns common heritage spaces. (ii) Representatives from all nations must manage resources contained in such a territorial or conceptual area on behalf of all since a common area is considered to belong to everyone; this practically necessitating a special agency to coordinate shared management. (iii) All nations must actively share with each other the benefits acquired from exploitation of the resources from the commons heritage region, this requiring

---

413 Some commentators have observed the remarkable development of contemporary human rights in terms of third generation rights, *i. e.* 'solidarity' or group rights. The solidarity rights, with their emphasis of the aggregate, are said to include the right to self-determination, the right to enjoy other group processes or institutions, the right to development, the right to participate in and benefit from the CHM, the right to a healthy environment, and the right to humanitarian disaster relief. See Lung-chu Chen, *An Introduction to Contemporary International Law*(Yale University Press, 1989), p.211.

414 Jennifer Frakes, "The common Heritage of Mankind Principle and the Deep Seabed, Outer Space, and the Antarctica: Will Developed and Developing Nations Reach a Compromise?," *Wisconsin International Law Journal*, Vol.21, 2003. p.409.

restraint on the profit—making activities of private corporate entities; this linking the concept to that of global public good. (iv) There can be no weaponry or military installations established in territorial commons areas. (ⅴ) The commons should be preserved for the benefit of the furture generations, and to avoid a 'tragedy of the commons' scenario.

The concept of CHM has been further introduced into the outer space regime and, to a lesser degree, into the legal framework for Antarctica. Although attempts have been made to invoke this principle with respect to technology transfer and cultural property, the principle of the common heritage of mankind (hereinafter 'the CHM principle') has its main impact with respect to the establishment of an international administration for areas open to the use of all States.


## 2. Legal Instruments for the CHM

### 1) in Case of Deep Seabed Area

In the ˹UN Convention on the Law of the Sea˩, the CHM principle is set forth under different provisions: (ⅰ) The preamble provides that "…desiring by this Convention to develop the principles embodied in resolution 2749 (XXV) of 17 December 1970 in which the General Assembly of the United Nations solemnly declared *inter alia* that the area of the sea—bed and ocean floor and the subsoil thereof, beyond the limits of national juris—

diction, as well as its resources,[415] are the common heritage of mankind, the exploration and exploitation of which shall be carried out for the benefit of mankind as a whole, irrespective of the geographical location of States. ··· " ; (ii) Art. 136 provides that "the Area and its resources are the common heritage of mankind"; (iii) Art. 140 para. 1 provides that "activities in the Area shall, as specifically provided for in this Part, be carried out for the benefit of mankind as a whole, irrespective of the geographical location of States, whether coastal or land-locked, an taking into particular consideration the interests and needs of developing States and peoples who have not attained full independence or other self-governing status recognized by the United Nations in accordance with General Assembly resolution 1514 (XV) and other relevant General Assembly resolutions"; (iv) Art. 311, para. 6 provides that "States parties agree that there shall be no amendments to the basic principle relating to the common heritage of mankind set forth in Art. 136 and that they shall not be party to any agreement in derogation thereof."

## 2) in Case of Outer Space

In December, 1961, the UN General Assembly declared that "the

---

415 This area and its resources are the scope of the CHM — *ratione loci* —. About the general scope of the CHM, including *ratione loci, ratione materiae, ratione temporis, and ratione personae*, see E. D. Brown, The Area Beyond the Limits of National Jurisdiction(Graham & Trotman, 1986), pp.3-31.

exploration and use of the outer space should be only for the betterment of mankind and to the benefit of States irrespective of the stage of their economic or scientific development." States, it said, should be guided by the following principles: "(a) International law, including the Charter of the UN, applies to outer space and celestial bodies; (b) Outer space and celestial bodies are free for exploration and use by all states in conformity with international law and are not subject to national appro-priation."[416]

This CHM principle was extended to outer space in Art. 1[417] of the 「Declaration of the Legal Principles Governing the Activities of Sates in the Exploration and Use of Outer Space」(UN G. A. Res. 1962 (XXIII) of December 13, 1963). From there, it found its way into the 「Treaty on Principles Governing the Activities of States in the Exploration and Use of Outer Space, including the Moon and other Celestial Bodies」(hereafter the Outer Space Treaty), on January 27, 1967.

Art. 1 of this treaty provides that

"the exploration and use of outer space, including the moon and other celestial bodies, shall be carried out for the benifit and in the interests of all countries, irrespective of their degree of economic or scientific development, and shall be the

---

416 Edmand J. Osmañczyk, *Encyclopedia of the United Nations and International Agreements*(Taylor & Francis Inc., 1985), p.587.

417 Art. 1 provides that "The exploration and use of outer space shall be carried on for the benefit and in the interests of all mankinds."

province of all mankind."

In the discussion on the drafting of the Outer Space Treaty the two terms 'province of all mankind' and 'common heritage' were repeatedly compared with each other. The formulation 'province of all mankind' was looked upon as being more closely related to the principles of the freedom of outer space and the prohibition of appropriation.

The reference to the common heritage concept is more explicit in Art. 11, para. 1 of the 「Agreement Governing the Activities of States of the Moon and other Celestial Bodies」(hereafter 'the Moon Treaty'), on December 5, 1979, which provides that "the moon and its natural resources are the common heritage of mankind, which finds its expression in the provisions of this agreement, in particular in para. 5 of this article."

And the Art. 4, para. 1 of this treaty combines the two terms:

"the exploration and use of the moon shall be the province of all mankind and shall be carried out for the benefit and in the interests of all countries irrespective of their degree of economic or scientific development."

As used in the Moon Treaty, both terms have a different emphasis although they have the same objective. Art. 4, para. 1 emphasizes the cooperation of the States parties in all their undertakings concerning the moon and other celestial bodies, whereas Art. 11. together with Art. 5, provides the CHM principle with legal content.

The Moon Treaty in making provision for the exploitation of the natural resources of the moon and other celestial bodies, ordained that this should be accomplished through an international institution charged with fixed responsibilities. The implementation of such responsibilities was to produce advantage to mankind and to the common interest.

### 3) in Case of Antarctica

Antarctica is also subject to a so-called international law of 'common spaces' and is to be regarded as part of the 'common heritage of mankind.'[418] Thus, its legal status of the Antarctica is analogous to that of outer space under the 1962 UN Declaration and Outer Space Treaty and of the deep sea-bed under the Law of the Sea Convention. But, as far as the legal regime of Antarctica is concerned, the CHM principle has been invoked to a lesser degree.

In this regard, the Antarctic Treaty was signed in Washington, DC., December 1, 1959. The preamble of this treaty provides that

" ··· recognizing that it is in the interests of all mankind that Antarctica shall continue forever to be used exclusively for peaceful purposes and shall not become the scene or object of

---

418 Jonathan I. Charney, *The New Nationalism and the Use of Common Spaces*(Osmun Publishers, 1982), p.184.

international discord."

And at the 11th Consultative Meeting to the Antarctic Treaty, held on June–July 1981, the Antarctic Treaty Consultative Parties only emphasized in Recommendation XI–1, para. 5(d) that "the Consultative Parties, in dealing with the question of mineral resources of Antarctica, should not prejudice the interests of all mankind in Antarctica." Apart from that, the CHM principle has been used during the discussions in the UN on Antarctica to question the authority of the Antarctic Treaty Consultative Parties to negotiate and conclude a treaty concerning the exploration and development of antarctic mineral resources.

The UN General Assembly Res. 38/77 of December 15, 1983 adopted without vote, reaffirmed the conviction "that in the interest of all mankind, Antarctica should continue forever to be used exclusively for peaceful purposes, and that it should not become the scene or object of international disputes."[419]

## 3. Content of the CHM Principle

### 1) Introduction

The CHM principle constitutes a distinct basic principle providing general but not specific legal obligations with respect to the utilization of areas beyond national jurisdiction. It

---

419 Edmund J. Osmañczyk, *op. cit.*, p.41.

conflicts with the principle of sovereignty as it raises the ideas of common interests or international public utility and the obligation to cooperate. However, it still is up to each State to decide how to ensure that activities subject to the principle are carried out for the benefit of all mankind. State practice with respect to these methods is reflected in numerous statements made at the Third UN Conference on the Law of the Sea, in the UN General Assembly and in the UN Conference on Trade and Development(UNCTAD), as well as in the national legislation of States interested and involved in the use of areas beyond national jurisdiction.

An analysis of the agreements mentioned above and the various related resolutions of the UN General Assembly reveals that the CHM principle is not and is not intended to be fully defined in all its aspects. However, in some respects, the CHM principle provides clear rules.

## 2) Legal Meaning of the CHM Principle[420]

According to Art. 137 of the 「UN Convention on the Law of the Sea」,

"no State shall claim or exercise sovereignty or sovereign

---

420  Rüdiger Wolfrum, "Common Heritage of Mankind," in : R. Bernhardt (ed.), *Encyclopedia of Public International Law*, Installment 11(1989), p.67.

rights over any part of the sea-bed and the ocean floor and subsoil thereof, beyond the limits of national jurisdiction or its resources, nor shall any State or natural or juridical person appropriate any part thereof. No such claim or exercise of sovereignty or sovereign rights nor such appropriation shall be recognized."

The Moon Treaty as well as the Outer Space Treaty follows the same approach.

⌜Convention on the High Seas⌟ of April 29, 1958 already prohibits any occupation of the high seas including the respective sea-bed.[421] Art. 136 of the UN Convention, however, goes one step further. It states that no such claim or exercise of sovereignty or sovereign rights or such appropriation shall be recognized. Thus, the prohibition of occupation and appropriation has been given a legal status the effect of which is similar to that of *jus cogens*.

Moreover, Art. 137 is phrased as an obligation of all States and not only the States parties to the Convention. In addition, one of the objectives of the CHM principle is to preserve the present legal status of the international commons against all States and all private persons.

As explained above, the CHM principle introduces a revolutionary new positive element into the law of the sea by indicating that

---

421 Art. 2 of the Convention on the High Seas provides that "the high seas being open to all nations, no State may validly purport to subject any part of them to its sovereignty.…"

the control of the sea-bed is vested in mankind as a whole. Mankind, in turn, is represented by the International Sea-Bed Authority which is the institution through which States parties organize and control deep sea-bed activities. Thus, the States parties are meant to act as a kind of trustee on behalf of mankind as a whole.

## 3) Regime of Exploration and Exploitation[422]

It was accepted from the outset that the CHM principle was meant to embrace the peaceful use of the international commons as well as the protection of the environment. The regime of utilization, furthermore, establishes the duty of all States to cooperate internationally in the exploration and exploitation of the deep sea-bed and its mineral resources as well as outer space and its celestial bodies.

The regime of exploration of the Area established by the UN Convention can be summarized as follows: All activities of exploration and exploitation of the Area must be organized, carried out and controlled by the International Sea-Bed Authority;[423] The activities shall be carried out either by the

---

422 Rüdiger Wolfrum, *op. cit.*, pp.67-68.

423 This rule is adhered to primarily by the developing States, but the United States and many other developed nations defines the exploration and exploitation of resources of the deep sea-bed as a freedom of the high seas. Developed nations including the United States assert that, unless or until a state agrees to be bound otherwise, it may authorize or engage

Enterprise,[424] or by State parties, or by State enterprises, or by natural or juridical persons having the nationality of, or being controlled by, a State party.

A corresponding duty of States to cooperate in the peaceful exploration and utilization of outer space including celestial bodies has been formulated as a principle immanent in space law. And the status of Antarctica is analogous to that of outer space and sea-bed area. As a part of CHM, Antarctica is also subject to legal regulation only by some international institution or authority representative of the interests of all the world's States, and all States are entitled to share in the benefits of any resource exploitation in this area.[425]

Controversy over the utilization system concerning the deep sea-bed centered upon the question of how to make sure that deep sea-bed mining benefits all mankind. According to Art. 140 of the UN Convention, the activities in the sea-bed area should be carried out for the benefit of mankind as a whole, taking into particular consideration the interests and needs of developing States.

---

in the exploration and exploitation of deep sea-bed resources, provided that such activities are conducted with reasonable regard for the rights of other Sates or persons to engage in similar activities and to exercise the freedoms of the high seas. See Louis B. Sohn & Kristen Gustafson, *The Law of the Sea*(West Publishing Co., 1984), pp.173-174.

424 The Enterprise is an organ of the Authority charged not only with the exploration and exploitation but also with transporting, processing, and marketing the minerals recovered from the Area.

425 Jonathan I. Charney, *op. cit.*, pp.184-193.

The following more specific demands have been formulated in the UN Convention: equal participation of all States, sharing of revenues, transfer of technology, preferential treatment, protection against adverse effects and cooperation. The UN Convention attempts to reach the objective of equal participation by the following means: ( i ) restrictions imposed upon potential deep sea-bed miners; (ii) affirmative action benefiting non-mining States; and (iii) conferring of jurisdiction over deep sea-bed mining on the International Sea-Bed Authority so that all States parties can equally, though indirectly, participate therein. This utilization system represents an attempt to provide for distributive justice. The means to achieve an equal distribution of the resources of the sea-bed can be attributed to two different approaches, based either on the idea of preferences or the idea of compensation.

The legal regime of outer space, especially existing under the Moon Treaty, does not provide for such an elaborate system of utilization. Art. 11, para. 7(d) of the Moon Treaty only declares that one of the main purposes of the international regime shall be the equitable sharing by all States parties in the benefits derived from those resources, whereby the interests and needs of the developing countries, as well as the efforts of those countries which have contributed either directly or indirectly to the exploration of the moon, shall be given special consideration. It can hardly be argued that the three specific means invoked by the UN Convention are a mandatory consequence flowing from the

CHM principle in general.

The introduction of the term 'mankind' combined with the word 'heritage' indicates that the interests of future generations have to be respected in making use of the international commons. More specifically, it requires that deep sea-bed or outer space activities should avoid undue waste of resources and provides for the protection of the environment.


# IV. Summary and Conclusion


Throughout the world today, and especially during the second half of this century, most States, individuals, and international organizations have been much more concerned with and affected by common interests and welfare. Some, therefore, have concluded it is possible to speak of a world community(Gemein-schaft) rather than an international society or a 'world arena' (Gesellschaft).[426]

Indeed, many changes in our world contribute to the intro-duction of new legal principles into the consciousness and norms of the international or world community. A current illustration

---

[426] cf. Arvid Pardo & Carl Q. Christol, "The Common Interest: Tension Between the Whole and the Parts," R. St. J. Macdonald Douglas M. Johnston ed., *The Structure and Process of International Law: Essays in Legal Philosophy, Doctrine and Theory*(Martinus Nijhoff Publishers, 1986), pp.643-60.

of this trend has been the attention given to the general needs or common interests of all human beings, as reflected in the formation and promulgation of the CHM principle.

The introduction of the concept of CHM no doubt represents a great deal advance in the international or world community. It marks the passage from the traditional postulate of sovereignty to that of cooperation and integration. In other words, the expression 'common heritage of mankind' succinctly expresses the new model of world community which has gradually emerged since 1945. The concept of CHM involves the substitution of the traditional ideas of territorial sovereignty, national interest and free exploitation with the ideas of world community on the basis of globalism or common interests, international management and equitable sharing of benefits.[427]

Although we cannot always expect every State to behave in a logical, rational and consistent manner, and yet deny that every State is primarily motivated by self-interest and national expediency on the basis of nationalism, the CHM principle has gained legal status in international law remarkably quickly as a new general principle of customary international law.

While the specific rights and obligations to be derived from the CHM principle are not at all clear, we can conclude at least as

---

427 Felipe H. Paollilo, "The Future Legal Regime of Seabed Resources and the NIEO: Some Issues," Kamal Hossain ed., *Legal Aspects of the New International Economic Order*(Nichols Publishing Company, 1980), pp.165-166.

follows:[428]

( i ) The concept of the CHM as a basic principle has entered into the corpus of contemporary international law. States, therefore, should respect the CHM principle with regard to the Antarctica, outer space, deep sea-bed and the resources pertaining to these areas or spaces;

(ii) The CHM principle includes the right of equal or non-discriminatory access to and the principle of non-appropriation of the areas and resources in question in accordance with the applicable international regime and treaties;

(iii) The CHM principle includes orderly and safe development and rational management of the resources of the areas in question and equitable sharing by States in the benefits derived therefrom; an international regime should be established by a generally accepted treaty of universal character, with the appropriate machinery for the regulation and control of the exploitation of the resources of the area in question, taking into particular consideration the interests and needs of developing countries;

(iv) The protection, preservation and enhancement of the natural environment for the present and future generations is the responsibility of all States. All States have the responsibility to ensure that activities within their jurisdiction or control do not cause damage to the environment of other States or of areas

---

[428] Paul de Waart *et al.*, *op. cit.*, pp.415–416.

beyond the limits of national jurisdiction. All States should cooperate in evolving international norms and regulations in this field.

# CHAPTER 8

# Global Governance and the Dispute Settlement System

— focusing on the Law of the Sea and Korean Perspective —

## I. Introduction

As is generally known, international law provides the conceptual framework in which the international community and international relations are seen and understood. In this sense, international law is fundamental to the understanding of the world and the conduct of international relations. However, a conflict or dispute may be arisen between international actors including States and non-State entities. Compared with 'conflict' which means a general state of hostility between the parties, the term 'dispute' is used to signify a specific disagreement relating to a question of rights or interests in which the actors or parties proceed by way of claims, counter-claims, denials and so on.[429]

---

429 John Collier and Vaughan Lowe, *The Settlement of Disputes in*

「The UN Convention on the Law of the Sea」[430] actually extended States' control over the seas and increased States' responsibilities, has led to extremely overlapping national claims and conflicts over maritime utilization including international navigation.[431] With the enforcement of the UN Convention and the growing importance of the sea,[432] there are increasingly many potential disputes arising out of the law of the sea.

---

*International Law — Institutions and Procedures* —(Oxford University Press), 1999, p.1. In the *Mavrommatis Case*, the International Court defined dispute as "a disagreement on a point of law and fact, a conflict of legal views or interests between two persons." 1924 P.C.I.J. Ser. A. No.2, pp.11-12. J. G. Merrills also defined dispute in this perspective as "a specific disagreement concerning a matter of fact, law or policy in which a claim or assertion of one party is met with refusal, counter-claim or denial by another." See J. G. Merrills, *International Dispute Settlement*(Sweet & Maxwell, 1984), p.1.

430 「UN Convention on the Law of the Sea」, Dec. 10, 1982, U.N. Doc. A/CONF. 62/121. (South) Korea already ratified the Convention on January 29, 1996. China and Japan also ratified the Convention in June, 1996.

431 New international regimes of the oceans include: the twelve-nautical territorial sea; innocent passage through the territorial sea; transit passage through straits used for international navigation without the discretion of the coastal State to deny passage on bases not bearing on the tangible consequences of passage; archipelagic baselines; archipelagic sea lanes passage; the new 200nauticalmile exclusive economic zone, giving principal legislative authority to the coastal State over living and non-living resources and environmental protection in the zone; traditional navigation and overflight freedoms in the EEZ; the laying of cables and pipelines; and the definition of the seaward limit of the continental shelf regime. Jonathan I. Charney, "Entry into Force of the 1982 Convention on the Law of the Sea," *Virginia Journal of International Law*, Vol.35, Winter, 1995, pp.383-385.

432 Hanns J. Buchholz, *Law of the Sea Zones in the Pacific Ocean*(the Southeast Asian Studies, 1987), pp.1-7.

It is difficult to enumerate all the disputes, but some broad areas of dispute may be identified. Disputes in the law of the sea can be divided into two categories: ( i ) disputes relating to the area of national jurisdiction, such as disputes arising from the delimitation of boundaries, disputes arising from activities within national zones and (ii) disputes relating to the areas beyond national jurisdiction, such as disputes over the exploitation and management of the deep sea-bed resources.[433]

In a different way, R. R. Churchill and A. V. Lowe point out some examples: ( i ) adjacent or opposite States may disagree over the boundaries separating their respective maritime zones; (ii) one State may claim the right to conduct naval manoeuvres in the exclusive economic zone(EEZ) of another State which denies that such a right exists; (iii) a fisherman may challenge the right of a foreign State to arrest him for fishing fifty miles from its coasts.[434]

These three examples mentioned above illustrate different kinds of dispute which may arise. For the purposes of settlement, the important distinction is between the first two examples, which represent inter-State or international disputes, and the third, which represents disputes between a State and an individual.

---

[433] Yogesh K. Tyagi, "The System of Settlement of Disputes under the Law of the Sea Convention: An Overview," *The Indian Journal of International Law*, Vol.25, No.2, 1985, pp.193–196.

[434] R. R. Churchill and A. V. Lowe, *The Law of the Sea*(Manchester University Press, 1983), p.291.

Disputes of the latter kind, however, may become translated into international disputes proper.[435]

There is a widespread assumption that in a successful legal system, disputes should be avoided, or at least resolved quickly, peacefully and further, justifiably by the international law and internationally agreed methods. However, recourse to legal processes for the adjustment of conflicts and settlement of dispute is just optional in contemporary international law system because of decentralized characteristics of international society.[436]

The traditional and also contemporary methods for the settlement of these disputes such as negotiation, good offices, mediation, inquiry, conciliation, arbitration, judicial settlement, and other peaceful means may be utilized for the dispute settlement. But the selection of method may be left to the choice of the dispute parties. Even the jurisdiction of the ICJ remains still optional or non-compulsory because of sovereign States' reluctance to submit their disputes to legal institutions.

The UN Convention, however, contains the most sophisticated and detailed system for international dispute settlement never seen before. The regime for the settlement of disputes of the Convention strengthens all of the substantive portions of the Convention. The treatment of dispute settlement in the UN Convention is remarkable and innovative, for it demonstrates the

---

435 *Ibid.*
436 *Ibid.*, p.3.

issues which arise in attempting to create a regulatory framework for a major area of State activity as well as the means by which such issues can be handled by the contemporary international community. The provision of machinery for the settlement of disputes positively is included as an integral part of the Convention and arrangement of dispute settlement methods for securing binding decisions is actually extensive and active.[437]

The Republic of Korea(hereinafter, cited as 'Korea'), now, is concerned with diverse problems or disputes relating to the law of the sea. They are mainly arising among the coastal countries in the Northeast Asian Seas.[438] Under the system of dispute settlement of the Convention, Korea, as a party to the treaty, should accept any or more of the compulsory procedures through a written declaration at the time of signing, ratifying or acceding to the Convention or thereafter.

Therefore, I'd like to review the traditional methods of dispute settlement and the new system for dispute settlement relating to the law of the sea contained in the UN Convention, and suggest

---

437  J. G. Merrills, *op. cit.*, pp.136−137.

438  In the widest term, the East China Sea means the Northeast Asian Sea, and comprises the East Sea, the Yellow Sea, the East China Sea(in the narrowest term), and the Sea of Okhotsk. And the States involved here include Korea, North Korea, People's Republic of China(hereinafter 'China'), Taiwan, Japan, and Russia. David M. Ong, "The Dispute Settlement Mechanism of the 1982 UN Convention on the Law of the Sea: Implications for East Asia," Dalchoong Kim *et al.* eds., *Convention on the Law of the Sea and East Asia*(Institute of East and West Studies, 1996), p.205.

the desirable methods for settlement of disputes involving Korea relating to the international rule of law.

# II. Settlement of Disputes under the Traditional Law

The traditional and also contemporary methods for the settlement of these disputes are direct negotiation, good offices, mediation, inquiry, conciliation, arbitration, judicial settlement, and solution by resort to regional agencies or arrangements, or other peaceful means of the parties' own choice.[439]

## 1. Non-Adjudicatory System for Dispute Settlement

Occasionally a dispute relating to law of the sea between a State and an individual can be submitted to the municipal court. When the foreign laws applied to an individual are thought uncompatible with international law, he may attempt to take the issue with the arresting officer or, if that is unsecessful, with the municipal

---

439 Article 33 of the UN Charter; "The parties to any dispute, the continuance of which is likely to endanger the maintenance of international peace and security, shall, first of all, seek a solution by negotiation, enquiry, mediation, conciliation, arbitration, judicial settlement, resort to regional agencies or arrangement, or other peaceful means of their own choice."

court before which he is brought for trial.[440] In this case, the problem of the relationship between municipal and international law is of great importance.[441]

It may be that municipal courts insist upon enforcing the legislation which is alleged to conflict with international law. If so, if the dispute is to be pursued, it must be taken up on behalf of the aggrieved individual and continued as a dispute between States. A State could take up such a case by exercising 'the right of diplomatic protection,' which extends to the State's nationals. Under general international law, an injury to a State's nationals is deemed to be an injury to the State.[442] In the absence of 'genuine link' of nationality of this kind, diplomatic protection may not be exercised.[443]

Disputes which arise immediately between States, rather than between individuals and States, are on the international plane from the outset. Examples are boundary disputes, such as the Korea—Japan continental shelf dispute, and cases involving the armed forces, which are considered to embody the sovereignty of the State, such as the Corfu Channel dispute between the United

---

440 R. R. Churchill and A. V. Lowe, *op. cit.*, pp.291—292.

441 *Ibid.*, p.292.

442 Thomas Buergenthal and Harold G. Maier, *Public International Law* (West Publishing Co., 1990), pp.5—7.

443 This is known as 'the genuine link theory.' Furthermore, diplomatic protection is a right, and not a duty of a State: the individual has no right to insist upon his State exercising diplomatic protection on his behalf; nor, indeed, to prevent his State from doing so. R. R. Churchill and A. V. Lowe, *op. cit.*, pp.292—293.

Kingdom and Albania. International disputes of this kind never go before municipal courts, it being a rule of international law that no State should be required to submit to the courts of another.[444]

Once the disputes arises on the international plane, it is normal to seek a settlement by direct or diplomatic negotiation between the parties. The various methods peaceful settlement are not set out in any order of priority, but first mentioned, negotiation, is also the principal means of handling disputes threatening the maintenance of international peace and security and all other disputes as well.

If negotiations do not resolve the dispute, it may be necessary to involve a third party. This may involve no more than the provision of good offices or mediation, or the third party may play a more conclusive role, settling disputed questions of fact or law, or both. Although it is quite possible to distinguish mediation and good offices from negotiation, in practice, they are very much part of the same process.

Good offices are a preliminary to direct negotiations between the parties. The person offering his good offices will attempt to persuade the parties to negotiate each other. Mediation is simply a continuation of this, and often the mediator is a person, again approved by both parties, who takes part in the negotiations.

---

444 See Article 33 of the UN Charter, and the 1982 「Manila Declaration on Peaceful Settlement of Disputes between States」, UN GA Res 37/10, (1982)).

His/her task is to suggest 'the terms of a settlement' and to attempt to bring about a compromise between the two opposing views.[445]

The commissions of inquiry which is a fact—finding machinery, is most often intented to establish the factual basis for a settlement between States. Occasionally, a conciliation commission may be established to propose a settlement to the dispute. Conciliation commissions are different from commissions of inquiry because the latter do not produce concrete terms for dispute settlement. Conciliation could be regarded either as a 'non—judicial' or a 'semi—judicial' procedure for the settlement of disputes.[446]

## 2. Arbitration and Judicial Settlement

A State is not bound to go to an international tribunal unless it has accepted previously that tribunal's jurisdiction or agrees by a special agreement(so called *compromis*) to submit a particular dispute to the tribunal. Arbitration is the determination of a dispute between States through a legal decision of one or more arbitrators or of a tribunal chosen by the parties.[447] Arbitration

---

445 Martin Dixon, *Text on International Law*(Blackstone Press Ltd., 1990), p.161.

446 *Ibid.*, p.165.

447 The International Law Commission(ILC) has defined arbitration as "a procedure for the settlement of disputes between States by a binding award on the basis of law and as a result of an understanding voluntarily accepted." *Ibid.*, p.165.

is one of the oldest methods used to settle international disputes. An arbitral award is final and binding on the parties, unless the treaty states otherwise. The parties may agree to set up an *ad hoc* arbitral tribunal whose composition and terms of reference they jointly determine. Alternatively, there may be a standing tribunal with jurisdiction over disputes arising between the States in question. Also, treaties may provide for disputes to be settled by special arbitral procedures(e.g., the 1964 European Fisheries Convention, and the 1969 Intervention Convention).

Some States have preferred to take the matter to the International Court of Justice(ICJ). But, this has the disadvantage that the parties cannot determine the composition of the Court, this being set in advance in accordance with the Statute of the ICJ. On the other hand, because a number of States have opted under Article 36 (2) of the Statute to accept the jurisdiction of the ICJ in advance of any specific dispute arising, and because this acceptance cannot be withdrawn once proceedings have been instituted against that State, this system does have some advantages.[448]

States may also bind themselves in advance to submit all disputes arising from a particular treaty to the ICJ. There are many treaties containing such compromissory clause which relate to the law of the sea,[449] and an attempt was made to adopt this

---

448  R. R. Churchill and A. V. Lowe, *op. cit.*, pp.294-295.

449  Several conventions concluded under the auspices of the International Matime Organization(IMO) contain provisions authorizing the sub-

system in respect of the four Geneva Conventions on the Law of the Sea. An optional protocol provided that all disputes arising from the interpretation or application of the these Conventions should be referred to the ICJ, unless the parties agreed within a reasonable time upon some other means of peaceful settlement.

Just over thirty States have accepted this obligation: its unpopularity, like that of declarations under Article 36 (2) of the Statute of the ICJ, derives mainly from an unwillingness on the part of States to accept an open-ended obligation to submit disputes — whose nature it is almost impossible to predict — to a particular settlement procedure.[450]

## 3. Review of the Traditional System

The existing mechanism for the dispute settlement in the law of the sea has proved to be inadequate in both theory and practice. First of all, parties to disputes are not bound to accept a particular procedure for the settlement of disputes. The obligation of States is to settle the dispute peacefully, but not to settle the dispute obligatorily. A State cannot be compelled to submit its dispute to a third party for settlement unless it has

---

mission of such disputes to the ICJ or to an arbitral tribunal. Among them are 1954 Oil Pollution Prevention Convention, Article 13, 1969 Convention on Intervention on the High Seas, Article 8 and its Annex, Article 13-19. Louis B. Sohn and Kristen Gustafson, *The Law of the Sea*(West Publishing Co., 1984), pp.238-239.

450  R. R. Churchill and A. V. Lowe, *op. cit.*, p.295.

given its consent in some or other. Apparently, the absence of a general obligation to settle disputes is reflected by the fact that the jurisdiction of the ICJ and other international tribunals is not compulsory. Secondly, there are reasons to believe that the most widely–used procedure of diplomatic(or direct) negotiation usually produces a political compromise, not necessarily a solution based on law and equity.[451]

Arbitration has largely relied on the parties to disputes in the procedures of settlement. The parties control not only the composition of the court of arbitration but they also lay down the rules to be applied. These tactics often lead to split awards of a controversial nature.[452]

The ICJ has failed to become a World Court in the true sense of the term,[453] because it does not carry the confidence and full faith of the socialist countries and a large number of developing nations, nor does it provide *locus standi* of the non–State entities. As a result, it cannot be utilized directly by Trans–national Corporations(TNCs) and international organizations which are going to be active participants in the sea–bed mining activities. Above all, the implementation or enforcement of any settlement always depends on the good–will of the parties to disputes.

---

451  J. G. Merrils, *op. cit.*, p.58.
452  Louis B. Sohn, "Settlement of Disputes Arising out of the Law of the Sea Convention," *San Diego Law Review*, Vol.12, 1975, pp.503–504.
453  Y. K. Tyagi, *op. cit.*, p.193.

# III. New Dispute Settlement System in the UNCLOS

## 1. Introduction

Taking this limitations of traditional system for dispute settlement into account, from the beginning of the negotiations leading to the UN Convention, many States have insisted that effective and compulsory means be provided for settling law of the sea disputes, while one view during the Third UN Conference on the Law of the Sea(hereinafter 'the third UN Conference') was that the same approach as the optional Protocol to the Geneva Conventions should be adopted.[454]

After long-standing difficult negotiations, however, an intricate system for the settlement for law of the sea disputes was devised. Indeed, the provisions on settlement of disputes incorporated in the UN Convention took shape since the end of the 1974 session of the UN Conference in Caracas, where a working paper[455] was presented by a group of States representing all regions containing several features.[456] Binding dispute settlement was made an

---

[454] J. G. Merrills, *op. cit.*, p.119.

[455] UN Doc. A/CONF 62/L. 7(1974).

[456] These features are as follows:
1. Obligation to settle disputes under the Convention by peaceful means;
2. Settlement of disputes by means chosen by the parties;
3. Clause relating to other obligations with respect to dispute settlement;

integral part of the Convention, not trucked away in an optional protocol.[457]

The UN Convention is a comprehensive effort at codification of the legal system regarding the ocean and the legal norms governing oceanic activities of various actors. For the settlement of disputes, the Convention has adopted a broad and comprehensive system which reflects a general approach as well as a functional approach.[458] And under the UN Convention, a few old

---

4. Clause relating to settlement procedures not entailing a binding decision;
5. Obligation to resort to a means of settlement resulting in a binding decision;
6. The relationship between general and functional approaches;
7. Parties to a dispute;
8. Local remedies;
9. Advisory jurisdiction;
10. Law applicable;
11. Exceptions and reservations of the dispute settlement provisions. See A. O. Adede, "Settlement of Disputes Arising Under the Law of the Sea Convention," *American Journal of International Law,* Vol.69, 1975, p.800; J. R. Coquia, "Settlement of Disputes in the UN Convention on the Law of the Sea," *Indian Journal of International Law,* Vol.25, No.2, 1985, p.174.

457 John King Gamble, Jr., "The 1982 UN Convention on the Law of the Sea: Binding Dispute Settlement?," *Boston University International Law Journal,* Vol.9, Spring, 1991, p.56.

458 The rapid development and change of maritime law in the past decades has brought about several proposals for the creation of courts or arbitral tribunals specialized in the law of the sea and competent to decide all or certain disputes in this field. In the course of the Third UN Conference on the Law of the Sea, all aspects of the traditional law of the sea were reconsidered and, in this connection, a complex system of institutions for the settlement of disputes was elaborated. Rudolf Bernhardt, "Law of the Sea, Settlement of Disputes," Bernhardt(ed.), *Encyclopedia of*

institutions and procedures have been retained in their existing form, a few more have been adapted to the new circumstances and many new institutions have been established for the effective settlement of disputes arising out of the interpretation and application of the Convention.

The dispute system of the UN Convention has three aspects: ( i ) it encourages peaceful settlement of disputes; (ii) it provides a variety of non-binding methods for fact-finding and conciliation, and offers other special dispute settlement vehicles; and (iii) it establishes a system for compulsory dispute settlement that will lead to the binding resolution of disputes arising under virtually all of the provisions of the Convention.[459]

Part XV of the UN Convention contains the main provisions of settlement of disputes. The said Part enumerates the general obligation of States parties, the procedure of non-compulsory and compulsory methods of settling disputes and the limitation on the subject matter of the jurisdiction of the compulsory methods of dispute settlement.

The UN Convention contains detailed provisions for conciliation (Annex V), the Statute of the The International Tribunal for the Law of the Sea(ITLS), and on Arbitration(Annex VII). The provisions of the Convention will certainly be the beginning of the successful attainment of the objectives set forth in Article 2, Section 3, of

---

*Public International Law* Instalment 1, 1981, p.134.
459 Jonathan I. Charney, *op. cit.*, p.391.

the UN Charter and in the implementation of the methods provided for in Article 33 of the UN Charter.

The provisions will also implement ⌜the Declaration of Principles Governing the Sea−Bed and Ocean Floor and the Subsoil thereof beyond the Limits of National Jurisdiction⌟, under which "the parties to any dispute relating to activities in the area and its resources shall resolve such dispute by any of the means mentioned in Article 33 of the UN Charter and such procedure for settling disputes may be agreed upon in the international regime to be established." The duty to settle disputes is now emphasized in the Convention.

Indeed, more effective legal procedures for the settlement of disputes are necessary to avoid political and economic pressures that improve many international conflicts. The settlement of disputes through purely legal channels will really give meaning to the principle of equality before the law. Moreover, the settlement of disputes through courts or tribunals will develop a more precise jurisprudence and make the law uniform.

A precise and uniform jurisprudence on the law of the sea can be achieved by making the system of settlement of disputes an integral part of the UN Convention. The fear that the compulsory and binding third−party procedure runs counter to the sovereignty of States, is misplaced, for to agree to be so bound is just an exercise, not a denial of that sovereignty.

## 2. General Provisions

The new system for the settlement of disputes under the UN Convention can by analysed in three categories: ( i ) General procedure with general obligation; (ii) compulsory—general procedures; and (iii) compulsory—special procedures. Indeed, it has been anticipated in the Convention that parties may fail to settlement their disputes through exchange of views or other non—binding(Conventional or non—Conventional) peaceful means.

In order to meet that case, a set of four compulsory procedures entailing binding decisions has been incorporated in the Convention. They are as follows: ( i ) the ITLS; (ii) the ICJ; (iii) an arbitral tribunal constituted in accordance with Annex Ⅶ of the Convention(Arbitration); and (iv) a special arbitral tribunal constituted in accordance with annex Ⅷ of the Convention(Special Arbitration).

Article 279 of the UN Convention provides that States parties are obliged to settle any dispute between them governing the interpretation or application of the Convention by peaceful menas in accordance with Article 2 (3) of the UN Charter and shall seek a solution by the various means indicated in Article 33 (1) of the UN Charter. Initially, the parties are afforded the right to agree at any time to settle a dispute between them relating to the interpretation or application of the Convention by peaceful means of their own choice.[460] The parties have the obligation to proceed

---

460 Article 280 of the Convention.

expeditiously to exchange views regarding the settlement of a dispute by negotiation in good faith or other peaceful means.

In fact, a number of States have agreed through regional or bilateral agreements or some other instruments to settle their disputes through methods of their choice. Article 282 of the Convention provides that if the States parties to a dispute agree through a general or bilateral agreement or otherwise, such dispute, if requested by any party to such dispute, shall be submitted to a procedure that entails a binding decision, in lieu of the procedures of part XV of the Convention, unless the parties otherwise agree.

It can be readily seen that at least a concept of freedom of choice exists which allows parties to be free to agree if a dispute has arisen that it be referred to a new procedure that will best solve such dispute. When a dispute arises between States parties concerning the interpretation or application of the Convention, the parties to a dispute shall proceed expeditiously to an exchange of views regarding its settlement by negotiation or other peaceful means.[461]

### 3. Non-Compulsory and Compulsory Conciliation

One of the non-compulsory methods suggested in the UN Convention is conciliation. Conciliation is the process of settling

---

461 Article 285 of the Convention.

a dispute by referring it to a commission of persons whose task is to elucidate the facts after hearing the parties, endeavor to bring them to an agreement, and to make a report containing the proposals for a settlement. The proposals do not have binding character of an award or judgment.

But, it must be emphasized here that settlement of disputes through conciliation is given special place in the Convention as a deliberate attempt to encourage States to settle their disputes through such informal procedures instead of relying on costly judicial settlement.[462] If the State parties to the dispute fail to reach a settlement through otherwise agreed dispute settlement procedures, one of them may then invite the other to the non-binding conciliation procedure under Article 284. Such conciliation may take place in accordance with the procedure laid down under Annex V of the Convention. If this invitation is accepted, conciliation procedure can be started from the choice of the conciliators. Generally, this type of conciliation is the 'non-compulsory conciliation.'

On the contrary, there are some cases which allow one of the State parties to the dispute unilateral submission to conciliation procedure. Under Article 297 (2) (b),[463] Article 297 (3) (b),[464] and

---

462 Jorge R. Coquia, *op. cit.*, pp.174-175.

463 A dispute arising from an allegation by the researching State that with respect to a specific project the coastal State is not exercising its rights under Articles 246 and 253 in a manner compatible with this Convention shall be submitted, at the request of either party to conciliation under Annex V, Section 2, provided that the conciliation commission shall

Article 298 (1) (a) ( i )[465] of the Convention, this type of conciliation, which is called 'compulsory conciliation,' can be instituted. In this respect, compulsory conciliation is often the substitute, for example, for disputes regarding fisheries management in the EEZ, consent to foreign marine scientific research in the EEZ and

---

not call in question the exercise by the coastal State of its discretion to designate specific areas as referred to in Article 246, Paragraph 6, or of its discretion to withhold consent in accordance with Article 246, Paragraph 5.

464 Where no settlement has been reached by recourse to Section 1 of this Part, a dispute shall be submitted to conciliation under Annex V, Section 2, at the request of any party to the dispute, when it is alleged that: ( i ) a coastal State has manifestly failed to comply with its obligations to ensure through proper conservation and management measures that the maintenance of the living resources in the exclusive economic zone is not seriously endangered; (ii) a coastal State has arbitrarily refused to determine, at the request of another State, the allowable catch and its capacity to harvest living resources with respect to stocks which that other State is interested in fishing; or (iii) a coastal State has arbitrarily refused to allocate to any State, under Articles 62, 69 and 70 and under the terms and conditions established by the coastal State consistent with this Convention, the whole or part of the surplus it has declared to exist.

465 Disputes concerning the interpretation or application of Articles 15, 74 and 83 relating to sea boundary delimitations, or those involving historic bays or titles, provided that a State having made such a declaration shall, when such a dispute arises subsequent to the entry into force of this Convention and where no agreement within a reasonable period of time is reached in negotiations between the parties, at the request of any party to the dispute, accept submission of the matter to conciliation under Annex V, Section 2; and provided further that any dispute that necessarily involves the concurrent consideration of any unsettled dispute concerning sovereignty or other rights over continental or insular land territory shall be excluded from such submission;

certain international maritime boundary disputes. The compulsory conciliation procedures by themselves can promote settlement of dispute, which should be primary objective for the peaceful order of the sea.

## 4. Compulsory Procedures Entailing Binding Decisions

One of the most significant innovations in the new Convention is the obligation of State parties to a dispute to submit to compulsory procedures entailing binding decisions. This procedure will be followed where no settlement has been reached by recourse to the non-compulsory methods provided for in Section 1 of Part XV of the convention. Article 286 of the Convention opens the way for compulsory procedures.

Three alternatives are now provided in addition to a special arbitral tribunal to be especially constituted under Annex VIII of the Convention. When signing, ratifying, or acceding to the Convention, or at any time thereafter, a State may choose by declaration one of the means for settlement of disputes, namely: the ITLS, the ICJ, an arbitral tribunal constituted in accordance with Annex VII of the Convention, and the special arbitral tribunal constituted in accordance with Annex VIII for one or more of the categories of disputes specified therein.

When an international organization and one or more of its member States are joint parties to the dispute, the organization shall be deemed to have accepted the same procedures for the settlement of disputes as the member States. The law applicable to disputes submitted shall be the UN Convention and such other rules of international law not incompatible with the Convention. This declaration shall remain in force unless revoked within three months duly deposited with the Secretary-General of the UN.

However, a declaration shall not affect or be affected by the obligation of a State party to accept the jurisdiction of the Sea-Bed Disputes Chamber of the ITLS to the extent and in the manner provided for in Section 5 or Part XI. If a State party to a dispute is not covered by a declaration, it is deemed that it had accepted arbitration in accordance with Annex VII of the Convention. Likewise, the parties which have chosen the same procedure are limited to use such procedure unless the parties otherwise agree. In the event that the parties have not accepted the same procedure(or one party has not accepted any procedure), their dispute is to be submitted to an arbitration in accordance with Annex VII, unless the parties agree otherwise. Any new declaration or revocation shall not affect the proceedings of a case already submitted to a court or tribunal which had acquired jurisdiction over the said case.[466]

The UN Convention provides access to the dispute settlement processes not only for State parties, but also for non-State entities having a legal relationship with the International Seabed

---

[466] J. R. Coquia, *op. cit.*, pp.176-177.

Authority, the organization that is charged with regulating deep seabed mining. Anyway, the existence of the compulsory dispute settlement regime will accomplish several objectives: To encourage the peaceful settlement of disputes; encourage international respect for the Convention law; and provide a vehicle to clarify legal ambiguities in the Convention text.

Among the new institutions created by the Convention is a new Court, the International Tribunal for the Law of the Sea(ITLS). The ITLS has its own Statute which forms Annex Ⅵ of the Convention. The idea that disputes of a particular type are best handled by tribunals set up for the purpose is nothing new — the machinery of the European Convention on Human Rights is a well-established example — and the Convention's arrangement for special arbitration clearly reflect the same impulse.[467]

The ITLS is the central forum established by the UN Convention for the peaceful settlement of disputes relating to the law of the sea. The jurisdiction of the Tribunal comprises all disputes and all applications submitted to it in accordance with the Convention and all matters specifically provided for in any other agreement which confers jurisdiction on the Tribunal. The Tribunal has exclusive jurisdiction, through its Seabed Disputes Chamber, with respect to disputes relating to activities in the international seabed area. Unlike the ICJ, the Tribunal is open to international organizations in certain circumstances and under the same

---

[467] J. G. Merrills, *op. cit.*, p.130.

provision may be used by States which are not parties to the Convention.

The creation of the ITLS may be thought to indicate a certain lack of confidence in the International Court of Justice,[468] though, the ICJ, as a principal jurisdictional organ of the UN, is still one of the courts or tribunals that may be chosen under the dispute settlement mechanism of the Convention.

## 5. Limitations and Optional Exceptions

It is of great importance to note that the Convention does not provide compulsory and binding settlement procedure for all kinds of disputes, because the dispute settlement system of the Convention has many 'limitations' and enshrines an innovative provision for 'optional exceptions' to applicability of its compulsory procedures. Many types of disputes are left out of the dispute settlement provisions of the Convention and are left to the discretion of the coastal State.

Article 297 of the Convention provides the limitations on the compulsory dispute settlement provisions. The limitations on the compulsory procedure exempt certain types of disputes that arise out of the coastal States' exercise of sovereignty with respect to the uses of the EEZ. While, the disputes relating to the EEZ contained in Article 297 are automatically exempt from disputes

---

468 J. G. Merrills, *op. cit.*, p.130.

settlement procedures, another group of disputes may be excluded from dispute settlement procedures by filing a special optional declaration.[469]

Parties to the Convention are entitled to declare, on or after signature, that they will not accept any or all of the Article 287 procedures in respect of any or all of three specified categories of dispute.[470] Two of these disputes concerning military activities and disputes in respect of which the UN Security Council is exercising its functions are rooted in the need for deference to States' sovereign rights and to international settlement procedures. These categories are subject only to the general obligation to reach a settlement by peaceful means agreed by the parties. The third category is that of delimitation disputes or concerning historic bays or titles, which are excepted from the general regime because of lack of agreement on the delimitation criteria and procedures at the third UN Conference.[471]

If a State declares that it will not accept compulsory settlement of disputes over the boundaries of its territorial sea, EEZ or continental shelf, it must nonetheless accept 'compulsory conciliation' if no agreement is reached within a reasonable time. Futhermore, disputants are obliged to negotiate an agreement on the basis of the conciliation commission's report; if they do not do so, they must agree upon some other procedure for settling

---

469  J. G. Merrills, *op. cit.*, p.243.
470  Article 298 of the Convention.
471  J. G. Merrills, *op. cit.*, pp.243–245.

the dispute — a rather insubstantial obligation.[472]


# IV. Desirable Method for the Settlement of Dispute involving Korea

## 1. Existing Maritime Disputes involving Korea

Korea is one of the coastal States of the Northeast Asian Sea. Among them are Korea, North Korea, Japan, China(including Taiwan), and Russia. These coastal States have had many territorial and maritime conflicts or disputes in this semi-enclosed sea.[473] They are arising, or likely to arise, out of delimitation of sea boundaries or conflicting maritime claims of jurisdiction, troubles over fisheries, preservation of marine environment, and military activities in the national zones, passage through the straits, and conflicting claims as to the territorial sovereignty over island. Korea, now, is concerned with diverse problems or disputes relating to the law of the sea as mentioned above. Some of these disputes have been solved, while, many of these still remain to be solved.

Maritime boundaries are yet to be agreed on between Korea and

---

472 R. R. Churchill and A. V. Lowe, op. cit., p.299.
473 Hanns J. Buchholz, op. cit., pp.57-71; see also Choon-ho Park, East Asia and the Law of the Sea(Seoul National University Press, 1983)

China, as well as between Korea and Japan. One reason for the growing disputes relating to the boundary delimitation is that the distance between the coasts of any two countries in this area does not exceed 400 nautical miles. The problems of boundary delimitation of the overlapping EEZ or continental shelf shall be the focal point of them. But, above all, the most fundamental reason of the legal difficulties concerning maritime boundary delimitation disputes basically arise from the different justifications by the protagonists concerning the breadths of their overlapping maritime claims. China base its claim on the geomorphologic criterion of 'natural prolongation of land territory,' while Japan depends on the 'distance criterion.' But, Korea rather ingeniously relies on both these criteria.[474]

Historically, maritime relations among the coastal countries of the Northeast Asian Sea have been characterized by conflict rather than cooperation.[475] Maritime relations including fishery relation in the postwar years were tense, acrimonious, and occasionally even violent. Korea and Japan, however, have already had two Delimitation Agreements of 1974 and Fisheries Agreement of 1965 in the East Sea and the East China Sea, one

---

[474] David M. Ong, *op. cit.*, pp.206–209; Wei–chin Lee, "Troubles under the Water: Sino–Japanese Conflict of Sovereignty on the Continental Shelf in the East China Sea," *Ocean Development and International Law,* Vol.18, No.5, 1987, pp.592–595.

[475] Tsuneo Akaha, "From Conflict to Cooperation: Fishery Relations in the Sea of Japan," *Pacific Lim Law and Policy Journal,* Vol.1, Summer, 1992, pp.225–280.

of the two Delimitation Agreements is a partial continental shelf boundary agreement, and the other is a 'joint development zone' agreement. Korea, Japan, and China already proclaimed their EEZ respectively. Korea and Japan already concluded their negotiation for the revision of the 1965 Fisheries Agreement according to the new EEZ system of the UN Convention. The new Fisheries Agreement between Korea and Japan came into force in January, 1999.

Korea and China also had held negotiations to establish a Fisheries Agreement governing maritime affairs in the West (Yellow) Sea for five years. In the result, two countries signed the Fisheries Agreement in August, 2000, which came into force on June 30, 2001. In this Agreement Korea and China agreed to introduce three zones — exclusive, transitional and provisional — in the Yellow Sea, transitional zone, the second of which, being that it would exist between the exclusive and provisional zones, eventually was merged into the exclusive fishing zones of each of the two countries 5 years after the Agreement's entry into force. Then, two countries agreed to set up a transitional zone because negotiators maintain a difference of opinion on the width of the provisional zone.[476]

But, in the process of concluding the Fisheries Agreement between Korea and China, they agreed not to set the exclusive fishing zones on the basis of their territorial baselines because

---

[476] See *Korea Times*, Nov. 11, 1998.

neither of the two countries recognizes the unilaterally proclaimed baselines of the other. The two countries' exclusive and transitional zones on the Yellow Sea will be of equal size. Meanwhile, the provisional zone will remain in force until the two countries conclude negotiations to set the delimitation of EEZ.

Therefore, indeed, they are required to negotiate for setting the borderline between two countries' EEZ including the continental shelf as well as the fisheries zone according to the Convention.

Korea has taken position that since the seabed and its subsoil of the Yellow Sea are composed of a common continental shelf in which the natural prolongation of territories of Korea and China overlap each other, so the problem of boundary delimitation should be solved by the application of 'the equidistance principle.' On the contrary, China has the position that the large part of the continental shelf of the Yellow Sea is pertaining to China, because the seabed and subsoil of the Yellow Sea has been made of the sediments washed down into it from Yellow River and Yangtze River of China.[477]

Therefore, it does not seem easy for Korea to compromise with China to settle the existing or anticipated disputes of delimitation relating to the EEZ as well as setting their baselines.

There is also a problem relating to the international straits in the Northeast Asian Sea. Open navigation and overflight through

---

[477] Seong, Ho Jhe, "Some Delimitation Issues in the Maritime Areas Surrounding the Korean Peninsular," *Ocean Policy Research*, Vol.11, No.1, Summer, 1996, pp.99–128.

straits used for international navigation and for connecting one part of the high seas or an EEZ to another part is established by the Convention's regime of transit passage. This new regime has gained general acceptance and has become in part practice among States bordering the straits as well as shipping States. There are several major straits in the Northeast Asian Sea, among them Korea Strait and Jeju Strait are likely to raise some conflicts or problems involving the system of passage of the Convention through the international straits.

The Jeju Strait has some legal issues which need to be reviewed in light of the Convention. The legal status of the Jeju Strait has been a subject matter of considerable discussion. There are two basic legal issues involved in the Jeju Strait: ( i ) whether it is an international strait which allows the right of transit passage for foreign ships; (ii) what methods should be used in the adoption of sea lanes and traffic separation schemes and regulating the passage of foreign ships. As for the Korea Strait, especially the extension of the territorial sea limit from three miles to twelve in the Strait would raise an important legal and policy problems.[478]

---

[478] In the Korea Strait, both Korea and Japan have restricted their maritime claims in certain sections of the Strait to three miles, so that a channel between their territorial sea, which allows the right of free passage for all foreign ships, exists. In this respect, the Korea Strait can not be regarded as 'international strait' under the Convention. For details, see Chi-Young Pak, "UNCLOS and the Korean Straits," Dalchoong Kim *et al.* eds., *op. cit.*, pp.55-84.

However, the most complicating factor in the Northeast Asian Sea is the existence of disputed islands.[479] Among them is Dok-do, which is the target of the most intractable bilateral territorial dispute. Indeed, Korea-Japan dispute on the territorial sovereignty over Dok-do presents a political threat to the stability of the Korea-Japan's diplomatic relation including fisheries regime. The dispute over Dok-do has been an issue between Korea and Japan since 1952. But though two countries are persisting in their own arguments, it seems that they apparently have preferred to avoid raising the issue during the negotiation between them. In recent negotiation for the revision of 1965 Fisheries Agreement between two countries, it seems that they agreed on its discounting in the delimitation of maritime boundary.

## 2. Desirable Method for Dispute Settlement under the UN Convention

Disputes likely to arise under the Convention can be simplified as follows: ( i ) Category I —disputes which can readily be solved by the parties when left to their own devices; (ii) Category II —difficult and protracted disputes where resolution is possible if

---

479 These islands are Senkaku/Diaoyutai islands disputed between China, Taiwan, and Japan, the Kuril islands disputed between Japan and Russia, and Dok-do disputed between Korea and Japan. David M. Ong, *op. cit.*, pp.209-210.

the disputants are provided the proper opportunities; (iii) Category III-disputes involving vital national interests where the parties are unwilling to agree to binding procedures.[480]

Category I disputes are the most numerous, and many of those appear to be susceptible to the traditional legal or diplomatic means of settlement pursued by States. Though, of course, the traditional methods of settlement considered above can be used in this type of disputes, the new system for dispute settlement of the Convention also should and could be utilized, if there is no solution. Especially, the litmus test of the dispute settlement system of th Convention is how many Category II disputes will be resolved, while nothing can be done as to Category III disputes under the dispute settlement system.

Therefore, except the dispute over the territorial sovereignty of Dok-do pertaining to Category III, the new system of the Convention, outlined above, is necessarily a matter of thorough review and speculation to Korea. The Convention may do well because of the wide array of choices provided. The Convention system could resolve many disputes, but most would fall within Category I disputes which would have been solved anyway.[481]

In the first place, as mentioned above, Article 279 of the Convention provides that State parties are obliged to settle any dispute between them by peaceful means in accordance with

---

480 John King Gamble, Jr., *op. cit.*, p.57.
481 *Ibid.*

Article 2 (3) of the UN Charter and shall seek a solution by the various means indicated in Article 33 (1) of the UN Charter. Consequently, Korea would be free to utilize the non-Conventional procedures.

But, it must be noted that if Korea fails to settle disputes through the general peaceful means, it is obliged to settle disputes through the compulsory procedures under the Convention. Under the system for dispute settlement of the Convention, Korea is free to accept any or more of the compulsory procedures: the ITLS; the ICJ; an arbitral tribunal; a special arbitral tribunal through a written declaration at the time of signing, ratifying or acceding to the Convention or thereafter.

Further, Korea can declare in writing that it does not accept any one, or more, of the compulsory procedures entailing binding decisions, with respect to one or more of the following three categories of disputes: ( i ) disputes concerning sea boundary delimitations; (ii) disputes concerning military activities; and (iii) disputes in respect of which the Security Council of the UN is exercising its functions.

Bearing in mind that East Asian States are generally reluctant to submit to compulsory judicial procedures for international disputes,[482] though, certain advantages exist in formal inter-

---

[482] The 'zero-sum' nature of judicial decision, where one party wins and the other loses, causes much of the reluctance of States to entrust their vital interests to international judicial settlement. Furthermore, East Asian countries are 'face-loving' countries in the cultural and historical sense. Wei-chin Lee, *op. cit.*, p.596.

national judicial settlement,[483] and it is perhaps advisable that these States make declarations upon ratification to the effect that they are willing to submit to an arbitral tribunal established in accordance with Annex VII. The reason for this is that under this procedure, these States will be able to exert maximum influence over the choice of personnel in the composition of any arbitral tribunal that is constituted.

It is also desirable to East Asian States to state that in relation to the specific issues covered by Annex VIII, they will also accept the special arbitration procedure.[484] Special arbitral tribunals constituted under Annex VIII can deal only with disputes concerning fisheries, protection and preservation of the environment, marine scientific research or navigation, including pollution from vessels and by dumping.[485] It is of importance to note that the ITLS, which specializes in law of the sea issues and also has a 'Special Chamber for Seabed Disputes,' serves more as a specialized court on law of the sea, and as a supplement to the ICJ.

From this perspective, for the effective and final settlement of disputes, I think it is desirable that Korea should accept three

---

483 Because a decision would be coming from the ICJ, it would relieve political leaders of much of the blame for an unfavorable result. Moreover, submissions can be employed to 'depoliticize'the dispute, allowing the legal issue to be isolated from its political overtones, and facilitating dispassionate settlement of the dispute and acceptance of the ultimate solution. *Ibid.*, p.596.

484 David M. Ong *op. cit.*, pp.221-223.

485 Article 1, Annex VIII of the Convention.

compulsory procedures other than the ICJ: the ITLS, arbitration, and special arbitration among four compulsory procedures.[486] But the ICJ will be still one of the options under the dispute settlement system of the Convention, because, if the ICJ gives the best service, therefore, it will be able to be selected by Korea in its change of the declarations. As for the optional exceptions, it is desirable that Korea should take cautious attitude as to declaration of optional exception; accordingly it should utilize compulsory procedures in the settlement of the above three categories of disputes, since removing these disputes from the compulsory dispute settlement procedures would reduce an opportunity of settling such disputes in need of peaceful resolution.[487]

---

[486] But yet, Korea did not declare any choice of procedures at the time of signature or ratification. Therefore, it is assumed that Korea chose 'arbitration procedure' according to the Convention. As for the lists of choice of the procedures under Art. 287 and declarations of optional exceptions under Art. 298 of the Convention, and as to the list of the choice of procedure under Art. 30 of the Agreement for the Implementation of the Provisions of the Convention relating to the Conservation and Management of Straddling Fish Stocks and Highly Migratory Fish Stocks and optional exceptions, see http://www.un.org/Depts/los/settlement_of_disputes/choice_procedure.htm

[487] Mark W. Janis, "Dispute Settlement in the Law of the Sea Convention: The Military Activities Exception," *Ocean Development and International Law Journal*, Vol.4, No.1, 1977, pp.51−65.

# V. Conclusion

As reviewed above, the UN Convention innovatively and substantially advances international dispute settlement by including compulsory jurisdiction system for the strengthening the international rule of law in this globalization era. The dispute settlement system of the Convention stands as an important accomplishment for 'international law of dispute settlement.' The system has been praised but also been subjected to some criticism.

Indeed, it seems that the provisions relating to the dispute settlement are complex and ponderous. It is regrettable that certain disputes are either excluded from compulsory binding dispute settlement under the Convention or may be excluded at the option of States. If the most important objective of international law is to be the peaceful settlement of international disputes, therefore, the dispute settlement system of the Convention should be improved for the effective role.

Relating to dispute settlement in Northeast Asian Sea, for the effective and final settlement of disputes, it is desirable that Korea should accept any one or more of compulsory procedures entailing binding decisions and take a cautious attitude as to declaration of optional exception.

But, I think, above all, the best mechanism for the settlement of disputes is the prevention of disputes. The necessary task of all the coastal States of Northeast Asian countries including Korea is to build up a stable and cooperative maritime regime or regional international organization such as Association of Southeast Asian Nations(ASEAN) that may provide the institutional basis for a future regional system for prevention and settlement of disputes. This can be linked to the system for dispute settlement of the Convention in order to improve the existing mechanism of dispute settlement involving the Northeast Asian countries.

We should be concerned about taking the appropriate preventive measures and also try to find more effective and equitable methods for solution to disputes in the Northeast Asian Sea.

# CHAPTER 9

# Global Governance and
# Human Rights

— focusing on the Political Rights of Koreans in Japan —

## I. Introduction

As mentioned above, traditionally, the rule of law centered on governance within and by the nation State and only the municipal legal system was the paradigm for the effectuation of the rule of law, however, to a considerable extent, global governance has grown alongside the activities of individuals and organizations whose predominant concerns have been not only international security but also the promotion of respect for human rights.[488]

For a long time we have an aspiration for a just world order represented by ideal of global governance. Human rights are those rights possessed by an individual that cannot be withheld or

---

[488] Roger Brownsword, ed., *Global Governance and the Quest for Justice Volume 4: Human Rights*(Hart Publishing, 2004), pp. v−vii(preface).

withdrawn by the State. Many scholars have typically referred to this significant features of International Human Rights as the "protection of individuals and groups against violations by governments of their international guaranteed rights ⋯."[489]

In this perspective, this Chapter discusses the problem of the legal status of Koreans Residents in Japan focusing on the political rights at local level.

## 1. Background of the Problem

The issue of Koreans(or Korean Residents) in Japan[490] is an old problem deriving from Japan's illegal occupation of Korea during the first half of the 20th century. It is an unresolved legacy of the colonial relationship between these two countries as well as an issue of the rights of foreigners and minorities under international law.[491] The legal status of Koreans in Japan was

---

489  William R. Slomanson, *op. cit.*, p.494.

490  While there are many other expressions used to refer to ethnic Koreans (for more information on this subject, see Kim, Kyeong Deuk (hereinafter 'Kim, K. D.'), "The Overseas Koreans Act From the Perspective of Koreans in Japan and Future Directions," *Korea–Japan Ethnic Studies*, No.5, 2003, p.131, note (1)), in this paper, the term 'Koreans(Korean Residents) in Japan' will be mostly employed.

491  A dictionary definition of minority would be an aggregate or a group of people distinct from mainstream members of a society in their ethnicity, religion, language, nationality or other important social and cultural attributes, who further perceive themselves as separate and distinct from the latter. See *The New Encyclopedia Britannica*, Vol.27, p.356; Arnold Rose, 'Minorities,' David L. Sills(ed.), *International*

addressed at the time of the normalization of diplomatic ties between Korea and Japan in 1965, and ensconced in a bilateral treaty specifically devoted to it, 「The Treaty on the Legal Status and Treatment of People of the Republic Korea Residing in Japan」 (hereinafter the 'Legal Status Treaty').

This agreement, however, failed to bring improvements to the status of Koreans living in Japan, in any fundamental fashion. In 1991, the foreign ministers of the two countries signed a Memorandum of Agreement(hereinafter the 'Memorandum'), to introduce amendments to the Legal Status Treaty. This Memorandum left out some of the essential questions touching the legal status of Koreans in Japan, such as their right to participate in public life in the host State. The current legal status of Koreans in Japan does not offer them sufficient protection against potential human rights abuses, and much remains to be done in this direction. As permanent residents of Japan, these Koreans are *bona fide* members of the Japanese society.[492] Yet, they face severe discrimination at many levels and

---

*Encyclopedia of the Social Sciences*, Vol. 10, p.365. In the broad sense of the term 'minority' can refer to not just a community of people with a common racial or ethnic background, distinct from the rest of a society, formed over a long period of time, but also any community of people residing in countries other than their country of origin, for political or economical reasons, such as refugees, foreigners and stateless persons. See Kim, B. C., "The Rights of Minority under International Law," *Journal of East Asian Studies*, Vol.8, Jeju National University, 1997, p.2.

492 Koreans in Japan may be considered to have a dual identity, in that they are Korean citizens living abroad at the same time as residents

do not receive the same treatment as Japanese citizens.

This essay will begin by an examination of the current legal status of Korean permanent residents of Japan, followed by a discussion of issues surrounding the political participation of foreign residents in a general legal context. It will then explore the background and current status of the movement to win the right to participate in local politics for Koreans in Japan and discuss future directions for it.

## 2. Legal Status of Koreans in Japan

The term 'Koreans in Japan,' as used in this paper, refers to all Korean nationals who settled in territories under Japanese jurisdiction during the illegal occupation of Korea by Japan, and to their descendants. All ethnic Koreans residing in Japan, regardless of their current citizenship (Korea or Choseon), are considered 'Koreans in Japan.'[493] The Korean community in Japan

---

of Japan and members of Japanese society.

493 Whilst there are varying views on who should be considered 'Koreans in Japan,' for the purposes of this paper, we will limit the scope of Koreans in Japan to ethnic Koreans possessing Korean citizenship who are in Japan as permanent residents. In a more general context, 'Koreans in Japan' commonly embraces all ethnic Koreans, including those who emigrated to Japan prior to the establishment of the government of the Republic of Korea, and those who had Korean citizenship, but renounced it later, and their direct descendants. However, it may be more appropriate to exclude from a discussion of the legal status of Koreans in Japan those ethnic Koreans who are currently Japanese by virtue of their citizenship, as this topic deals with issues that do not directly

is unlike that of any other foreigners residing in Japan, insofar as their initial settlement in Japanese territories has a specific historical origin, namely the illegal occupation of Korea by Japan.[494] The first wave of Korean immigrants to Japan began during the 1910s, following the so-called land survey project by the Japanese colonial government, expropriating land from local landlords and thereby depriving the peasantry of land to cultivate. New waves of Koreans left their homeland for Japan after the 1931 Manchurian Incident and in the wake of the Sino-Japanese War, and at the onset of the Second World War in the Pacific. The total number of Koreans in Japan eventually grew to over 2 million. With the conclusion of the war in 1945, about three-fourths of Korean immigrants returned home. But

concern them. Indeed, one mustn't forget that Korean permanent residents in Japan are resident aliens from the viewpoint of the Japanese state. See "Ethnic Koreans' Rights of Participation in Local Politics," Translation by Suh, Yong Dal(hereinafter 'Suh, Y. D.') & Kim, Yong Ki(hereinafter 'Kim, Y. K.'), *Journal of Management And Economics*, Vol.33, No.1, 2000, pp.183–184; See Choi, Yeong Ho(hereinafter 'Choi, Y. H.'), "Ethnic Koreans' Rights of Participation in Local Politics: The Korean and Japanese Views," *Youngsan Collective Paper Series*, Vol.7, Youngsan University, 2001, p.2. Cho Sang Gyun's discussion of the legal status of Koreans in Japan, however, englobes all residents in Japan having Korean ethnic affiliations, including Koreans who are naturalized Japanese and Japanese nationals born to an ethnic Korean parent and a Japanese parent. See Cho, Sang Gyun(hereinafter 'Cho, S. G.'), "The Legal Status of Ethnic Koreans in Japan," *Korea Journal of Northeast Asian Studies*, Vol.33, 2004, p.372.

494 On this topic, see Moon, Kyeong Su(hereinafter 'Moon, K. S.'), "The Origin of the Ethnic Korean Community in Japan," *Journal of East Asian Studies*, Vol.9, Jeju National University, 1998, pp.179–198.

for various reasons, some 500,000 stayed on, even after the December 1946 deadline for repatriation. These Koreans and their descendents form the backbone of the current ethnic Korean community in Japan.[495]

'Permanent foreign residents' is a term used in Japan to mostly refer to ethnic Koreans, as Koreans make up the largest minority group with foreign backgrounds.[496] During the Japanese occupation of the peninsula, Korean people were given the status of Japanese citizens, if only in name. However, Koreans who remained in Japan

---

495 See Lee, Kwang Gyu(hereinafter 'Lee, K. G.'), *Koreans in Japan*(Iljogak, 1993), pp.16-46; Chung, In Seop(hereinafter 'Chung, I. S.'), *The Legal Status of Ethnic Koreans in Japan*(Seoul National University Press, 1996), pp.1-6. Citizenship was bestowed both in Korea and Japan, through patrilineal descent, which was one reason why the number of Koreans in Japan constantly remained around 600,000 since the mid 1950s. In 1985, the citizenship law in Japan was amended to open the door to citizenship also for individuals born to a foreign-born father and a Japanese mother. This has resulted in a gradual decline in the number of Korean nationals residing in Japan, a trend that is expected to continue into the future. Korea also adopted the rule of bilineal descent in 1997. However, this is not likely to affect the situation of Koreans in Japan in any direct or indirect manner. See Lee, Chang Hee(hereinafter 'Lee, C. H.') (editor), *International Law Issues Between Korea and Japan*(Asayeon, 1998), pp.111-118.

496 The term 'resident alien' is used in Japan to refer to all foreign nationals who have an established residence in Japan, whether or not their lifestyle and social interaction are de facto the same as Japanese citizens. Resident aliens in Japan fall into three large categories: ( i ) Koreans, Chinese and Taiwanese who were forced, directly or indirectly, to move to Japan; (ii) descendants of the latter who were born and grew up in Japan; and (iii) tax-paying foreign nationals who resided in Japan for three years(the minimum number of years of residence required for naturalization under international law) or longer and have an established residence in Japan. Suh, Y. D., *op. cit.*, p.185.

after the end of the war were discriminated against at multiple levels. With the entry into force of the San Francisco Peace Treaty on April 28, 1952, the Japanese government declared that it would thenceforth treat all Koreans in Japan as foreign nationals, paying no regard to the special circumstance in which they came to settle in the country in the first place. The right to political participation, previously recognized to Koreans in Japan, was also revoked,[497] and other legal hurdles were created with regard to their residency status, causing not only hassles but instability.

The legal status of Koreans in Japan improved somewhat with the signing of the 1965 Legal Status Treaty, guaranteeing them among others the right to permanent residency.[498] Yet, changes brought by the Legal Status Treaty were very far from

---

[497] The right of political participation ceased to be granted to Koreans in Japan already prior to 1952, with the 1945 and 1947 amendments to Japan's House of Representatives Election Law and the 1947 amendment of the Local Government Law. However, attempting to restore the right of political participation as recognized during the colonial era would be a move fraught with misgivings and risk. Doing so may be taken as a tacit acknowledgement of the legality of Japan's colonial rule of the Korean peninsula. See Choi, Y. H., "Ethnic Koreans In Japan and Their Response to the Changing Landscape of Right of Political Participation in Post-War Japan," *Journal of Korea Political Science Association*, Vol.34, No.1, 2000, p.196; Kim, K. D., "The Question of Citizenship for Ethnic Koreans in Japan and Their Right of Participation in Local Politics,"(Seoul National University School of Law Center for Public Interest and Human Rights Law; http://jus.snu.ac.kr/~bk21) p.1.

[498] The Legal Status Treaty contains provisions related to ( i ) eligibility for permanent residency; (ii) forcible deportation; and (iii) education and minimum living standard, which will not be given detailed treatment in this essay.

fundamental. Discrimination against ethnic Koreans continued in Japan and often flared into diplomatic rows between the governments of the two countries. The Convention Relating to the Status of Refugees(hereinafter the 'Refugee Convention'), ratified in 1981, resulted in a minor easing of Japanese immigration control regulations and the abolition of nationality requirement for accessing 'child rearing support,' opening the door to related social security benefits for Koreans in Japan.[499]

However, issues detrimental to the welfare of Koreans in Japan such as restrictions related to access to permanent residency, the Japanese Deportation Law and discrimination in education and employment still await resolution. To settle the '1991 issue'[500] and

---

[499] Following its signing of the Refugee Convention, Japan amended the Immigration Control Law, renaming it "Immigration Control and Refugee Recognition Law," and also introduced partial changes to the Alien Registration Law. Articles 23 and 24 of the Refugee Convention stipulate that refugees legally residing in a signatory country must be given the same treatment as its nationals concerning public relief and assistance. On the subject of the treatment of Koreans in Japan following the ratification of the Refugee Convention, see Kim, Eung Ryeol(hereinafter 'Kim, E. R.'), "The Refugee Convention and Treatment of Koreans in Japan," *Journal of Asian Studies*, No.88, 1992, pp.77-102.

[500] Whilst the right to permanent residency was recognized to Korean residents in Japan in 1965, in the context of the normalization of Korea-Japan relations, the Legal Status Treaty did not address the question of legal status of children and descendants of those who became permanent residents by virtue of the same treaty. The two countries agreed to meet and discuss this question, if and when there is a request to the effect from the Korean side within 25 years from the conclusion of the 1965 bilateral treaty. The last date for the Korean side to express a desire to reopen the discussion on the legal status of descendants being January 1991, this issue is frequently referred to as the '1991 issue.'

supplement the content of the Legal Status Treaty, the Korean government met with its Japanese counterpart, and their negotiations resulted in the adoption of the January 1991 Memorandum.[501] The 1991 Memorandum was not a legally binding, formal treaty, but a typical gentlemen's agreement. However, Tokyo(or Japan) immediately went ahead to carry out its commitments under this Memorandum. Japan honored its commitments by enacting the Special Law on Immigration Control and the Law on the Registration of Foreigners. For other commitments related to concrete formalities, administrative orders were issued to government agencies concerned.

To carry out Japan's Memorandum commitments, on April 26, 1991, the Diet passed the Special Law on Immigration Control.[502] The new law was proclaimed on May 10 of the same year and entered into force some six months later, on November 1. The legislation simplified the complex classification system put into place following the 1952 Peace Treaty, regarding nationals of Japan's wartime occupied territories and their descendants, that are mostly Koreans and Taiwanese.[503] 'Treaty permanent residency,' in other

---

See *ibid.*, pp.79–80.

[501] For more information on Japan's ethnic Korean policy and Korean residents' evolving legal status, see Hosaka, Y., "The Legal Status of Koreans Residing in Japan: Review of Recent Amendments to the Nationality Law and Immigration Law," *Journal of Peace Studies*, Vol.8, No.1, Korea University, 2000.

[502] The full title of this law is the 「Special Immigration Control Law Concerning Individuals Who Lost Japanese Citizenship with the Entry into Force of the Treaty of Peace with Japan」.

words, the right to permanent residency pursuant to the Legal Status Treaty, was replaced by 'special right to permanent residency,' recognized to all nationals of occupied territories who have resided in Japan since before the end of the war and lost their Japanese citizenship with the ratification of the Peace Treaty and their Japan-born descendants, as long as they continue to live in the country at the time of the entry into force of this law.[504]

Due to the special historical circumstance surrounding their initial settlement in Japan, ethnic Koreans are granted a somewhat more stable legal status than other foreigners living in Japan. Their legal status, however, is undeniably distinct from that enjoyed by Japanese citizens. Ethnic Koreans are discriminated against both under civil and public laws.[505] The Japanese public law system not only does not recognize ethnic Koreans' right to political participation, but also does not guarantee their rights to education and employment, thereby hindering them from playing an active role in Japanese society

---

[503] The scope of application of this law, created to fulfill Japan's 1991 Memorandum commitments, is not limited to Koreans who became permanent residents by virtue of the 1965 Legal Status Treaty, but extends to all foreign nationals who settled in Japan under similar historical circumstances, including ethnic Koreans linked to North Korea and Taiwanese residing in Japan.

[504] Article 3 of the Special Law on Immigration Control.

[505] Cf. Hosaka, Y., *op. cit.*, pp.6–7; Lee, C. H., *op. cit.*, pp.102–111; Chung, I. S., *op. cit.*, pp.68–504; Kim, B. C., "Participation of Korean Residents in Japanese Local Politics," *Local Government Law Journal*, Vol.2, No.2, 2002, pp.120–125; Cho, S. G., *op. cit.*, pp.371–391.

as fully—fledged citizens, with the same rights as their Japanese counterparts.

# II. Legal Issues Surrounding Political Rights of Foreign Residents

## 1. What Is the Political Rights and Who Enjoys It?

The legitimacy and legality of the power formed and exercised by a State reside in the consent given by the people. This consent is, in turn, made possible through guaranteeing political freedom and rights to political participation to the people governed by a State. Rights of political participation, guaranteed as one of the basic constitutional rights, are generally understood as subjective civil rights, pertaining to the direct participation by citizens in the formation of political will and process of policymaking of their government, and in elections or votes as members of an electoral or voting college, and their eligibility to be appointed to a public function.[506] These rights are based on the doctrine of the sovereignty of nationals,[507] which has been also used by many countries to deny the freedom of political activities and rights of

---

506 Kwon, Yeong Seong(hereinafter 'Kwon, Y. S.'), *Introduction to the Study of Constitutional Law*(Bobmunsa, 2006), p.570.

507 See Hur, Yeong(hereinafter 'Hur, Y.'), *Korean Constitution*(Pak-youngsa, 1999), pp.137—138.

political participation to aliens,[508] reserving them to their own nationals.[509]

However, strictly speaking, rights of political participation reserved for 'citizens' concern only national politics, not local politics. In today's era of local autonomy and self-government, nationality is becoming less and less relevant as a barrier to political participation. Independently of participation in the formation of political will and policy-making or establishment of national institutions, all individuals domiciled within the jurisdiction of a local government have the right to vote in elections of local councils and heads of local governing bodies as well as the right to be elected as a member of a local council or head of a local governing body.

Rights of participation in local politics may be therefore defined as the rights of local residents to weigh in on political issues touching their own regions.[510] Rights of participation in local politics, furthermore, must guarantee the right to participate in

---

508 The term 'foreigner' is generally used to designate individuals who do not possess the nationality of the country where they reside or travel and refers both to those with the nationality of another country and to those without any nationality. The scope of foreigners includes special foreigners and refugees, in addition to 'general foreigners.' For more information on this subject, see Kim, Hee Gon(hereinafter 'Kim, H. G.'), "Foreign Residents' Rights to Participate in Local Politics," *Journal of Public Land Law Studies,* Vol.7, 1999, pp.288-289.

509 Kwon, Y. S., *op. cit.*, p.580; Chung, I. S., *op. cit.*, p.397.

510 See Suh, Po Geon(hereinafter 'Suh, P. G.'), "Japanese Debate on Foreigners' Rights to Political Participation," *Journal of Public Law,* Vol.30, No.5, 2002, pp.173-175.

a regional referendum on important decisions touching the governance of a region or its residents.

Local voting rights, just like national voting rights, were in the past a privilege reserved only for citizens. However, the doctrine or conception of human rights prevailing today and related laws tend toward erasing the distinction between citizens and non-citizens, prescribing the equal treatment of resident foreign nationals to citizens and recognition of equal rights. In keeping with this trend, an increasing number of countries are granting political freedom and rights of political participation to aliens residing on their soil, albeit in a limited scope.

Many European countries have already extended local voting rights to foreign nationals having resided on their soil for a certain number of years, or are moving toward it, in the context of promoting local autonomy. This development reflects a major mentality shift with regard to the relevance of nationality as concerns local politics; in other words, the belief that decision-makers in local governance should be the residents or inhabitants of a region, and that their right to influence local politics as directly-interested parties must not be limited or restricted by their nationality status.

## 2. Legal Basis for Political Rights of Foreign Residents

### 1) The Treatment and Rights of Foreigners under International Law

Nation—States, while they enjoy full discretion as to the admission of foreigners onto their soil, also have obligations under international law, with regard to foreigners already admitted into their territories; namely, the treatment of foreigners must meet certain required standards, and the government is responsible for extending basic protection necessary for their safe stay within the country.[511] All countries have their own established rules concerning the treatment and rights and duties of foreigners residing within their borders, in accordance either with the international minimum standard or the standard of national treatment.[512] International human rights law requires States to treat all individuals under their jurisdiction (including foreigners and minority members) without discrimination, by guaranteeing certain levels of rights. However, few international law scholars expect a country to treat foreigners in exactly the same manner to its own nationals. Many of them believe that national treatment of foreigners is a requirement concerning only basic human rights. In other words, the prevailing view is that countries are free to deny political rights to foreigners, insofar

---

511 Peter Malanczuk, *op. cit.*, p.256.
512 Brownlie, I., *Principles of Public International Law*, 5th ed.(Oxford University Press), 1999, pp.524—530.

as these rights directly relate to national sovereignty, as well as rights to exercise certain professions.[513]

The denial of rights of political participation to foreigners, therefore, had long been perceived as not constituting a discriminatory treatment prohibited under international law. To put it otherwise, nationality as a basis for refusing voting rights to foreigners was long viewed as a 'rational basis for discrimination.' This had been the dominant view also in the legal interpretation of international human rights treaties.[514] For example, Article 2 of the Universal Declaration of Human Rights,[515] citing wrongful grounds for discrimination, omits nationality from a list including "race, color, sex, language, religion, political or other opinion, national or social origin, property, birth or other status."[516] The omission of the term 'nationality' has been widely treated as the evidence that discriminating against non-nationals

---

513 Kim, Dae Sun(hereinafter 'Kim, D. S.'), *International Law*, 11th ed. (Samyoungsa, 2006), p.430; Kim, Cheong Geon(hereinafter 'Kim, C. G.'), *International Law*(Pakyoungsa, 1998), pp.566-568; Tabata, M., *Lectures on International Law* I(Yushindo, 1984), p.233.

514 Examples include 「the Universal Declaration of Human Rights」, 「International Covenant on Civil and Political Rights」, 「American Convention on Human Rights」, 「African Charter on Human and People's Rights」, and 「the International Convention on the Elimination of All Forms of Racial Discrimination」.

515 Article 2: "Everyone is entitled to all the rights and freedoms set forth in this Declaration, without distinction of any kind, such as race, color, sex, language, religion, political or other opinion, national or social origin, property, birth or other status. …"

516 'National origin,' cited under Article 2, does not mean 'country of origin,' but 'ethnic origin.'

on the basis of nationality is permissible.[517] Even those inter-national treaties espousing the doctrine of equal treatment of nationals and non-nationals, which, for this reason, define subjects of human rights as 'all humans,' mention only 'citizens,'[518] when it comes to political rights.[519] This has long been the reason for the interpretation that the scope of human rights of foreigners defended under them did not include political rights.

---

[517] Lillich, R. B., *The Human Rights of Aliens in Contemporary International Law*(Manchester University Press, 1984), p.45.

[518] The term 'national,' a cousin concept of 'nationality,' is used as an 'external' designation of the status of an individual belonging to a certain state or nation. On the other hand, the term 'citizen,' from which derives the word 'citizenship,' expresses the internal facet of the same status, implying the rights and duties associated with this status, in addition to the national appurtenance of an individual. Hence, the term 'citizen' is used to designate particularly those nationals who have full political rights under domestic law(see Kim, D. S., *op. cit.*, pp.419-420). This is also what undermines the argument by certain ethnic Korean organizations in Japan, involved in the local political rights movement, resting on an extended interpretation of the term 'citizens' in Article 25 of the Appendix B of 「the International Covenant on Civil and Political Rights」, as meaning also 'residents.' For further reading on this subject, see Hosaka, Y., *op. cit.*, p.8.

[519] Article 25 of Appendix B; 「International Covenant on Civil and Political Rights」 and 「the Declaration on the Elimination of All Forms of Intolerance and of Discrimination Based on Religion or Belief」: "Every citizen shall have the right and the opportunity, without any of the distinctions mentioned in article 2 and without unreasonable restrictions: (a) To take part in the conduct of public affairs, directly or through freely chosen representatives; (b) To vote and to be elected at genuine periodic elections which shall be by universal and equal suffrage and shall be held by secret ballot, guaranteeing the free expression of the will of the electors; (c) To have access, on general terms of equality, to public service in his country."

However, the mere absence of an explicit mention of the term 'nationality' cannot be construed to mean that nationality—based discriminatory treatment of foreigners is a permissible practice in any active sense. All rights, save those accompanied by express statements in the text of a treaty reserving them exclusively for nationals or citizens, should be interpreted as applying also to foreigners. Concerning political rights, unlike the International Covenant on Civil and Political Rights, the Universal Declaration of Human Rights stipulates that 'everyone' shall enjoy rights of political participation 'in his country.'[520]

Nothing in this provision warrants the equation of the term 'country' used here with a 'national State.'[521] The phrase 'in his country' can very well be understood as a country to which an individual has substantial real connections such as family ties, continuous or lasting residence and economic activities, and not just his country of nationality. In other words, the provision can be construed to recognize rights of political participation to all individuals residing in a country with such substantial connections to this country.[522]

---

520 Article 21 (1): "Everyone has the right to take part in the government of his country, directly or through freely chosen representatives."

521 See Lee, Ho Yong(hereinafter 'Lee, H. Y.') ed., *Toward Legislation Granting Voting Rights to Permanent Residents*(Ministry of Justice Office of Legal Counsel, 2000), p.16.

522 Lillich, R. B., *op. cit.*; Concerning the right of diplomatic protection, whose exercise was traditionally considered as pertaining solely to the country of nationality of the victim, in recent years, the argument has been gaining ground that the determination of the connection between

Furthermore, even when a treaty mentions 'citizens' as the subjects of political rights, as is the case with the International Covenant on Civil and Political Rights, this does not imply that these rights are necessarily to be denied to 'foreigners.' It only means that a State must guarantee the right to participate in the affairs of the government at least to its citizens. Hence, in the absence of an express and explicit provision giving countries the right to deny political rights to foreigners, granting rights of political participation to foreigners is a matter within the discretion of individual States.[523]

### 2) Universality of Human Rights — Residents and Non Citizens Are the Subjects of Basic Human Rights?

Amidst accelerating globalization and localization, an increasing number of legal scholars have been pointing out just how outdated is the practice of defining the legal status and treatment of an individual according to an abstract criterion such as 'nationality.'

---

a state and the victim should not be based only on 'nationality,' but should also consider another factor: 'habitual residence.' The underlying idea is that today, many people reside in countries other than their country of origin, and that they may form an effective connection with their host nation, which may oftentimes be as substantial as the connection through nationality. 'Residence,' therefore, must not be considered an accessory factor, but an actual linking factor. For further reading on this topic, see Kim, B. C., "The Right of Diplomatic Protection"(Research Report to Ministry of Foreign Affairs and Trade), 2001, pp.42–43.

[523] Lillich, R. B., *op. cit.*, p.46.

For all countries or regions, it is more natural as well as rational, they argue, to assign a legal status to its members on the basis of 'residence,' rather than 'nationality.'[524]

Japanese legal scholar Onuma, for instance, notes that the dominant and exclusive position of 'nation' and 'nationals' as means to explain or justify legal relationships is gradually being eroded, in favor of the concept of human rights, based on the notion of 'humanity,' increasingly perceived as a more legitimate basis for bestowing rights. Citing how growing numbers of foreigners make up communities around the world today, and how the notion of 'residents' has been extended to include both nationals and permanent resident aliens, Onuma calls into question the validity of the practice of equating residents with nationals or citizens, qualifying it as narrow and formalistic, and argues that the use of such a premise for imparting rights and benefits is unjustifiable, both at an ideological and a practical level. This position, according to Onuma, is hardly sustainable, whether at an ideological level, since foreigners are human beings with the same rights as nationals, or at a practical level, since permanent resident aliens are as fully fledged residents as any others.[525]

Seeing foreigners' social appurtenance or community member-

---

524 Onuma, Y., "Rethinking the Rights of Foreigners in Japan," *International Law Issues*(special publication for the 70th birthday of Dr. Lee Hangi), 1986, p.417.

525 *Ibid.*, p.420.

ship as the prime criterion of their eligibility for basic rights in a host State is an idea stemming from the concept of 'equity,' whose fundamental tenet is that where there are the same contributions and burdens, there are the same rights and benefits. This view has powerful implications for the under-standing of international human rights law, especially as there is a growing consensus that 'nationality' can no longer be perceived as a 'rational basis of discrimination' and must be recognized to be as wrongful a basis for discrimination as are race, sex, religion or ethnic or social origin.

Ideas like the right to equality and non-discrimination have fast gained ground in recent years, lending support to minority rights movements around the globe, fighting discrimination on the basis of sex, language or nationality.[526] It is therefore only natural to reflect human rights principles espoused by today's society, when interpreting the Constitution or any other laws. Concerning especially the rights of foreigners, the interpretation should be open to considering social appurtenance as a factor just as important as nationality in the determination of the legal status of an individual.[527]

It is high time now to make 'social appurtenance' the fundamental criterion for determining rights relations within a community. Unless a law expressly posits citizenship as a

---

[526] *Ibid.*, pp. 420–421.
[527] *Ibid.*, p. 422.

condition, social appurtenance should be the overriding principle in deciding rights and eligibility to other privileges and benefits. Even when nationality is specifically mentioned as a condition, a growing number of cases require an open interpretation of the term 'nationals' or 'citizens,' to give it the broader meaning of 'residents.' The right to equality and non—discrimination, serving as the underlying principles for national Constitutions and human rights—related international treaties, rests on the idea of the universality of human rights. Hence, any legal interpretation concerning the status or rights of foreigners must be attentive to the universal applicability of basic human rights.[528]

### 3) Doctrine of the Sovereignty of Nation and Foreigners' Political Rights Extending the Concept of Nationals

Voting rights and rights of political participation, both under international law and national laws, stem from the doctrine of the sovereignty of the nation, and, for this reason, have been traditionally regarded as privileges exclusively guaranteed to the 'nationals' having the sovereign power over a nation State. Meanwhile, 'nationals' in this context mean those who possess the nationality of the country concerned. The doctrine of the sovereignty of the nation, therefore, has been one of the biggest theoretical obstacles to recognizing political rights to foreigners. Legal scholars favorable to the idea of recognizing rights of

---

[528] *Ibid.*, p.431.

political participation to foreigners, at times, argue that the term 'the nation's sovereignty' should be understood more broadly, as including permanent foreign residents.

Japanese legal scholar Noriho Urabe, a proponent of this view, brought up three arguments in support of his position:[529]

First, the doctrine of the sovereignty of the nation is an idea that emerged during the era of bourgeois revolution to oppose that of the sovereignty of the monarch, and was in no way meant to exclude foreign nationals from the affairs of the government. Second, the doctrine of the sovereignty of the nation signifies the essential oneness of the governors and the governed. Democratic governance is the people's self-governance, and all those composing a given political society are its sovereigns. Third, when determining the subjects of sovereignty in a country, it is wrong to equate those who possess its nationality with the people. The people should be, instead, those who are sovereigns. Under such definition of citizens, Urabe maintains, foreign residents under the same living conditions as the nationals and who are for this reason subject to political decisions in this country 'are' effectively its citizens, and should, therefore, be guaranteed political rights (right to vote in national elections).

---

[529] Urabe, N., "The Japanese Constitution and Foreigners' Right to Vote," Suh, Y. D. ed., *Permanent Residents' Right to Participate in Local Politics*(Nippon Hyoronsa, 1992), pp.55—57(requoted from Lee, Y. H., "Permanent Resident Aliens' Right to Vote in Local Elections According to the Japanese Constitution," *International Human Rights Law*, No.4, 2001, p.72).

In Germany, concerning the interpretation of 'Volk' under its Basic Law(*Grundgesetz*), some legal scholars are advancing the view that the term should not be understood to designate exclusively '*Staatsvolk*,' in other words, German nationals, but to include all permanent resident aliens, having the same living conditions as the nationals, insofar as this term is to be primarily determined by the existence of a community of life and fate within the territory of the Federal Republic of Germany.[530] Hence, there is a steadily growing trend toward a more open interpretation of the 'nation' in the context of the doctrine of the sovereignty of the nation as a constitutional principle, to include permanent resident aliens, and not just those who possess citizenship. This interpretative trend has been prompted both by the new social context and new constitutional theories.[531]

### 4) The Purpose of Local Self-Government and Subjects of Local Political Rights

The view that the right to participate in local politics should be granted to permanent resident aliens, if not to all foreign residents, is enjoying growing support from even those who are, otherwise, reticent to the idea of recognizing foreigners' political rights at a national level. Onuma, for instance, defines 'permanent foreign residents' in Japan as "people who do not own Japanese

---

530 See Lee, Y. H., *op. cit.*, pp.72–74.
531 *Ibid.*, pp.75–76; Kim, H. G., *op. cit.*, p.298.

citizenship, but who live and work in Japan and whose tie to Japanese society is stronger than that to any other countries including his own country of citizenship and who are integrated to this society to such a degree that they do not differ from Japanese nationals in any concrete and essential aspects touching their daily existence."[532] Permanent foreign residents, according to Onuma, are integral members of Japanese society having the same lifestyle as Japanese citizens, and therefore meet all requisites for participating in the process of formation of a political wills within this society.

There is no obvious reason *a priori*, still according to Onuma, to believe that granting rights of political participation to permanent resident aliens at the local government level would run counter to the principle of the sovereignty of the people. Meanwhile, if the principal purpose of local self-government is to bestow on the residents of local regions the power to decide on the affairs of their home towns, excluding permanent resident aliens from 'residents' with rights of self-governance seems to be totally at odds with this purpose.

In today's regional communities, the subjects of self-government are their residents. Permanent resident aliens are taxpayers like any other members of regional communities, and nothing really distinguishes them from nationals in real and practical terms

---

532 Onuma, Y., *Overcoming the Myth of an Ethnically-Homogeneous Nation - Ethnic Koreans in Japan and the Japanese Immigration Control System*(Tosindo, 1986), p.204.(requoted from Lee, Y. H. *op. cit.*, p.81).

touching their everyday life. Hence, discriminating against permanent resident aliens on the basis of their 'foreignness,' whether in practical matters or legal relations, would be unambiguously counter to the fundamental purpose of local self–government.[533]

## 3. Current Status of Political Rights of Foreign Residents Worldwide

The increasing cross–border movement of humans, goods and information and active international exchange in today's globalized world have brought about some major changes in the traditional notion of nation–State, that have repercussions at multiple levels of society. While changes in the official stance of countries toward political rights have been comparatively minor, there have been, nevertheless, substantial and profound shifts at the level of perception and practice. Many countries are moving toward greater compliance with international human rights law, a discipline that came of age after the conclusion of the Second World War, either by reducing or completely eliminating nationality–based discrimination against foreigners in accordance with the principle of national treatment of foreigners.[534]

---

533 Yun, Yong Taek(hereinafter 'Yun, Y. T.'), "The Legal Status of Ethnic Koreans in Japan," *Journal of Legal Studies*, Vol.22, Chonbuk National University, 2001, p.18.

534 Choi, Y. H., *op. cit.*(*supra* note 497), pp.4–5.

## 1) Europe

In spite of the growing trend toward non—discriminatory treatment of foreigners and protection of their basic rights, and the increasing popularity of the notion of 'residents' as an alternative to 'citizens' for the era of globalization and regionali— zation, there has been thus far no instance where a country recognized full political rights equal to those enjoyed by nationals, concerning both national and local politics, to its foreign residents. However, several European countries are already according partial rights of political participation at a national or/and local level, to their foreign residents.

The first example is the U.K. and other Commonwealth countries. Nationals of a Commonwealth country, residing in another Commonwealth country, have the right to vote in both national and local elections in the host State.[535] Second, in Sweden, Norway, Denmark, Iceland, Finland and the Netherlands, permanent resident aliens are granted the right to vote in local elections and the right to be elected into local offices.[536] Third, all EU States are required to grant the right to vote in local elections to foreign nationals from another E.U. State, residing on their soil for 6 weeks or more, in accordance with the principle of reciprocity. Fourth, Portugal has a reciprocity arrangement

---

[535] This type of practice is seen outside Europe as well, in countries like Canada, Australia and New Zealand. For more information on this subject, see Chung, I. S., *op. cit.*, pp.406—409.

[536] *Ibid.*

with Portuguese-speaking countries like Brazil and Peru, allowing the nationals of the latter countries to vote in local elections.[537] Fifth, in former Soviet-bloc countries or Eastern European countries like Lithuania, Estonia, Slovakia, Slovenia and Hungary, foreign nationals with permanent residency or quasi-permanent residency have the right to vote in local elections.[538] Sixth and lastly, there are countries like Switzerland where local governments have the discretion to bestow voting rights on foreign residents satisfying a certain set of requirements.[539]

Already back in 1992, member States of the Council of Europe and other European countries signed 「the Convention on the Participation of Foreigners in Public Life at Local Level」 and motioned to make the granting of local voting rights to permanently residing foreign nationals a practice prescribed by international law.[540] In accordance with Article 8 b, Paragraph 1

---

537 *Ibid*, p.409; Kim, Hee Jeong(hereinafter 'Kim, H. J.'), "Voting Rights for Permanent Resident Aliens: Its Validity and Current Practice," (http://www.missionmagazine. com) pp.3-5.

538 *Ibid*.

539 Refer to Chung, I. S., *op. cit.*, p.407.

540 This convention, signed by 11 countries and ratified by eight, entered into effect on May 1, 1995 when it was ratified by four countries. The convention demands that the right to vote in local elections as well as the right to be elected to office be guaranteed to all lawful and habitual foreign residents, in addition to traditional rights such as the right to organize and right to the freedom of press, assembly and association. The grounds cited for granting the right to participate in public life at a local level in this convention are as follows: first, the right to

of the Treaty on the EU, better known as the Maastricht Treaty, and Article I-10, Paragraph 2 of the Treaty Establishing a Constitution for Europe, European countries are acknowledging 'European citizenship' to nationals of member States and guarantee them the right to participate in local politics, putting into practice the idea of the Council of Europe and taking its effort to the next level. Today, citizens of all EU member States enjoy the full right to participate in public life at the local level in any other member States, to the same extent as the nationals.

Although EU citizenship is something that serves the specific purpose of political integration and shared prosperity of European countries through the union, it remains nevertheless a progressive move having highly positive repercussions for the protection of human rights of foreigners worldwide. Even if examples of countries where permanent resident aliens are granted the right

---

participate in public life is a basic and universal human right. Second, in modern societies, immigration and settlement in a foreign country is not a transitory or exceptional phenomenon, but a continuously recurring and widespread phenomenon. Third, given that resident aliens have virtually the same duties as citizens, they are also entitled to political rights enjoyed by the latter. Fourth, granting political rights to resident aliens, as it incites them to participate in the public sphere of life, helps toward a more active integration into the host society. Fifth, when a country accords rights of political participation to resident aliens, this helps broaden, through the mechanism of reciprocity, the opportunity for its own nationals residing in foreign countries to take part in the politics of their host nations and weigh in on policy-making. On this topic, see the "Explanatory Report of the Convention on the Participation of Foreigners in Public Life at the Local Level" and "Summary of the Treaty" (http://conventions.coe.int/Treaty); Kim, H. J., *op. cit.*, pp.1-7.

to take part in local public life, are still rare, at a global level, these European precedents have certainly begun a 'worldwide trend,' undeniably creating a favorable disposition toward extending such a right to resident non-nationals.[541]

## 2) Korea

Korean constitutional scholars frequently distinguish basic rights prescribed by the Korean Constitution into 'human rights' and 'rights of citizens(or nationals).' Under this reasoning, whilst basic rights are recognized for foreigners, insofar as they pertain to 'human rights,' other basic rights, pertaining to the 'rights of citizens,' are to be denied to them, or to be recognized only if a reciprocity agreement exists between Korea and their country of citizenship(or nationality).[542] Hence, basic rights, deemed to fall into the category of 'human rights,' are recognized for foreigners, including stateless persons, even when the provisions specifically designate the subjects of these rights as 'all citizens.'[543]

---

541 Lee, Y. H., *op. cit.*, p.107.

542 Hur, Y., *op. cit.*, pp.234–237; Kwon, Y. S., *op. cit.*, p.580.

543 This type of interpretation is underpinned by precepts of natural law, which lays strong emphasis on human rights, and reflects also commitment to international cooperation and world peace. See Lee Y. H., *ibid.*, p.61. For other legal scholars with positivistic inclination, however, basic rights are not natural rights, but positive rights, whose subjects are limited to citizens composing a nation–state, not inclusive of foreign residents. They further hold the view that the Korean Constitution does not guarantee the rights laid down under Chapter II for foreigners, based on the formulation of its very title: "Rights and Duties of Citizens." See Park,

While most of the basic rights guaranteed under the Korean Constitution are considered to pertain to the category of human rights, some of them are deemed as the 'rights of citizens,' and as such are acknowledged only for Korean nationals. Freedom to enter the country, basic social rights and political rights are generally regarded as belonging to the category of 'rights of citizens.'[544] Articles 24 and 25 of the Korean Constitution stipulate that the subjects of the right to vote and the right to be elected into public office are 'citizens.'[545] This is the principal reason why the vast majority of Korean constitutional scholars used to subscribe to the view that 'political rights' are the 'rights of citizens,' which may not be granted to non-nationals.[546]

Furthermore, Articles 15 and 16 of 「the Act on the Election of Public Officials and Prevention of Election Malpractices」 also set forth that the 'citizens' can cast a vote in the presidential and parliamentary election, and the election of local council and the head of a local government. 'Citizens' in these provisions have been long understood as automatically designating those who own Korean nationality.

---

Il Kyeong(hereinafter 'Park, I. K.'), *A New Constitution*(Bopkyong Publishing, 1990), p.199.

544 *Ibid.*

545 Article 24; "All citizens shall have the right to vote under the conditions as prescribed by law."
Article 25; "All citizens shall have the right to hold public office under the conditions as prescribed by law."

546 See Kwon, Y. S., *op. cit.*

However, some constitutional scholars have voiced a less inflexible position with regard to the political rights of foreign residents, in recognition of the recent international trend whereby a growing number of countries grant voting rights at the local government level to their permanent resident aliens.[547] Some even advance very progressive views to the effect, for instance, that "given that the right to engage in political life is a right deriving from natural law(predating nation–States), incorporated into the Constitution, granting voting rights to long–term foreign residents, by progressively extending the scope of rights, would be both more sensible and in greater compliance with international practice."[548]

Meanwhile, ┌the Local Autonomy Act┘, the law laying down the system and rules of local self–government, also adopts an equally progressive outlook, by keeping out nationality from the concept of residents. Article 12 of the Local Autonomy Act stipulates: "Any individuals domiciled within the jurisdiction of a local government shall be considered its residents." Article 13, Paragraph 1 and Article 14 which follow simply set forth the rights and duties of residents without adding any further conditions for qualification as residents.

---

547 Legislation indeed is another way of conferring political rights to foreign residents. See Kim, Cheol Su(hereinafter 'Kim, C. S.'), *Introduction to Constitutional Law*(Pakyoungsa, 2001), p.279.

548 See Hong, Seong Bang(hereinafter 'Hong, S. B.'), *Constitutional Law* (Hyeonamsa, 2003), p.603.

The definition of local self-government by the Constitutional Tribunal of Korea is based on a likewise presupposition that all residents of a region qualify as subjects of its local government:

> "Local self-government is a system whereby people residing within a certain geographical unit take charge of affairs related to the welfare of local residents; affairs related to the management of property; and other affairs mandated by law, by handling them through offices to which they elect officials, created to increase the democracy of local governance and the efficiency of local administration and ultimately contribute to the balanced national development and democratic rule of the nation as a whole."[549]

Meanwhile, a legislative initiative by the national government is already under way to grant local voting rights to foreign nationals residing in Korea on a long-term basis. On September 8, 1999, the Ministry of Government Administration and Home Affairs announced that it and other government agencies had begun joint studies in view of conferring to foreign nationals who resided in Korea for five years or longer, and are aged twenty and older, the right to vote in the election of local council members and heads of local governing bodies, starting from the

---

549 See Oh, Dong Seok(hereinafter 'Oh, D. S.'), "The Political Rights of Foreign Residents in Korea: A Constitutional Perspective,"(Seoul National University School of Law Center for Public Interest and Human Rights Law; http:// jus.snu.ac.kr/~bk21) pp.11-12.

year 2002.[550] In 2006, ⌈the Act on the Election of Public Officials and Prevention of Election Malpractices⌋ was amended to allow permanent resident aliens in Korea, aged 19 or older, satisfying a certain set of conditions, to vote in local elections.[551] Further, the Residents' Voting Act, passed on December 29, 2003, grants foreign nationals with long-term residency status, meeting conditions set out in the ordinance of the relevant local government the so-called 'residents' voting rights.'[552]

The Korean decision to give local voting rights to resident aliens, including 'residents' voting rights,' is a move unprecedented outside Europe, and is an important turning point in its internationalization and opening-up policy. This will furthermore give substantial leverage to Korea in its negotiations with Japan toward granting local voting rights to Koreans residing in the latter's territory, allowing it to demand reciprocity on this account.[553]

---

550 See *Hankook Ilbo*, Sep. 9, 1999.

551 Article 15 of this Act accords the right to vote in local elections to foreign nationals aged 19 and older, who is a permanent resident in Korea, pursuant to the Immigration Control Act, since at least three years.

552 Article 5, Paragraph 2 of the Residents' Voting Act confers 'residents' voting rights' to foreign nationals aged 20 and older, authorized by immigration law to continuously reside in Korea, meeting conditions prescribed by the ordinance of a relevant local government.

553 Some legal experts have expressed their skepticism about the idea that granting local voting rights to foreigners residing in Korea could be an effective basis to demand reciprocity to Japan. This skepticism derives from the fact that, due to the special historical circumstances surrounding the origin of the ethnic Korean community in Japan, it is difficult to consider the Korean government's decision to give local voting rights to its foreign residents as a move on an equal footing with

# Ⅲ. Legal Issues Surrounding Political Rights of Koreans in Japan

## 1. Local Political Rights Movement by Koreans in Japan

### 1) The Origin and Development of the Local Political Rights Movement[554]

The political rights movement by Korean residents in Japan has its origin in the movement by the 'Federation of Korean Residents in Japan,' dating back to the years immediately following Japan's

---

the Japanese government recognizing the same rights to the former. Yet, it remains that setting an example for Japan of guaranteeing basic human rights for all by allowing foreigners residing on Korean soil to vote was an important step to be made, before demanding the former to allow, in its turn, Korean residents to vote in its local elections. Meanwhile, in the context of the Overseas Korean Act, lawmakers discussed the possibility of giving voting rights to Koreans living in Japan. However, related provisions were removed from the final bill, in fear that granting them political rights in Korea at this juncture may interfere, if not hurt, their cause of winning voting rights in Japan. For further reading on this subject, see To, Hoe Geun(hereinafter 'To, H. G.'), "The Legal Status of Koreans in Japan," *Social Science Papers*, Vol.11, No.1, Ulsan University, 2001, p.175. In my opinion, however, it is rather problematic for the Korean government to completely deny the right to participate in the political process in Korea, whether at a national or local level, to Koreans in Japan, while demanding Japan to give them local voting rights. The best course of action, therefore, would be to guarantee all Koreans with Korean nationality, including those residing in Japan, the right to take part in the political process at a national level and ensure that they be given the same rights at a local level in their countries of residence. See Oh, D. S., *op. cit*, p.10; Kim, K. D., *op. cit.*(*supra* note 497), p.7.

554 See Chung, I. S., *op. cit.*, pp.410–414.

defeat and surrender in August 1945, which demanded voting rights and citizenship for ethnic Koreans remained on its soil after the conclusion of the war. The Japanese government forcibly broke up the organization, bringing the movement to a halt for a time. The resurgence came in the form of a movement to abolish racial discrimination against Koreans in Japan. The anti racial discrimination movement aimed principally at putting an end to administrative discrimination by the government, and the greatest bone of contention was the many nationality-based restrictions barring Korean nationals from certain professions and benefits. On the front of political rights, the ultimate goal was obtaining the right to vote in local elections and be elected into local office.[555]

The movement specifically aimed at winning the right to participate in local politics was revived in the mid-1970s, by a group of Korean intellectuals living in Japan. In September 1975, a grassroots organization based in Kitakyusu submitted an open letter addressing this issue. Less than a year later, in July 1976, in a conference by the Osaka Korean Junior Chamber of Commerce, held on the occasion of its 5th anniversary, Suh, Yong Dal delivered a speech proposing the basic ideas of the local political rights movement as we know of today. In September 1976, Reverend Choi Chang Hwa of Fukuoka addressed a letter

---

[555] See Kim, K. D., "The Amendment of Nationality Law and Koreans in Japan," *Seoul International Law Journal*, Vol.4, No.2, 1997, pp.58-59.

demanding that Korean residents in Japan be given the right to participate in local politics to the governor of the prefectural governor. The issue of voting rights resurfaced again in the mid–1980s. In 1986, a group of Koreans residing in Osaka submitted a petition demanding the right to vote in local elections. In January 1987, the subject was broached in the national representatives' convention of the Council Against Racial Discrimination. The Council Against Racial Discrimination finalized in November 1988, in its 14th national conference, a legislative proposal entitled "Bill for the Postwar Compensation of Nationals of Former Occupied Territories Residing in Japan and the Protection of Their Rights," which includes a clause demanding the granting of the right to participate in local politics to foreign nationals having resided in Japan for five years or more.

During the negotiations on a Korea–Japan treaty concluded in January 1991, concerning the legal status of 3rd and later–generation Koreans in Japan, the Korean government put forth the same demand for local political rights for its nationals residing in the Japanese territory. Several years earlier, at a senior officials' talk between the two countries, which began in December 1988, granting Korean residents in Japan the right to vote in local elections was one of the key issues on the table. Since then, demands related to the enhancement of the legal status of Korean residents in Japan, including allowing them to participate in local political processes, have been routinely issued at bilateral meetings of foreign ministers, senior officials, and at summits between the two countries.

## 2) The Positions of Mindan and Jochongnyeon

The Korean Residents Union in Japan(hereinafter 'Mindan') is an organization actively involved in the effort to win local political rights for Koreans based in Japan. Its regional headquarters launch petition drives, and the main headquarters makes legislative demands to the Japanese government.[556] Reasons cited by Mindan as to why Korean residents in Japan should be entitled to take part in local political processes are as follows: ( i ) Korean residents in Japan are people having their principal residence in Japan and taxpaying members of society; (ii) Article 93, Paragraph 2 of the Japanese Constitution guarantees the right to vote in local elections to all 'residents,' and nowhere mentions 'citizens' as the subjects of this right; and (iii) most Koreans in Japan are people who consider Japan a home not just for themselves, but for all their children and future descendants.[557]

Mindan regards the political rights of permanent resident aliens including Koreans as an issue with grave consequences for Japan's internationalization and democracy. For Mindan, this is

---

[556] The content of these legislative demands is eliminating nationality restrictions either through the amendment of Japan's Local Government Law and Public Office Election Law or by legislating a special law to this effect.

[557] See Onuma, Y., *op. cit.*

both a question related to the basic rights of resident aliens, as prescribed by 「the International Covenant on Civil and Political Rights」 and other international human rights treaties, in the context of protection of rights of minority members and in accordance with the principle of equality of treatment of nationals and non-nationals, and one that has to do with the Korean minority's freedom to preserve their culture and ethnic identity.

Mindan's position is, further, that the Japanese government needs to make more efforts to protect the rights of Koreans in Japan, also as part of the postwar reparations process, and that authorizing local voting rights is an especially important step forward in the integration of these Koreans into Japanese society, to which it should give serious consideration.[558]

The position of the pro-Pyongyang Federation of Korean Residents in Japan(hereinafter 'Jochongnyeon'), the other major ethnic Korean organization, is quite distinct from Mindan's. The pro-Pyongyang organization condemns initiatives related to granting political rights to Koreans in Japan as going along with the South Korean government's tacit policy of 'abandoning' its people for whom the only viable choice it believes is assimilation to the Japanese society. According to Jochongnyeon, the urgent priority for the community of Koreans in Japan is restoring loyalty to their fatherland and a strong sense of national identity.

---

[558] See the Korean Residents Union in Japan, "The Local Political Rights Movement"(http://www.mindan.org).

The right to participate in public life in Japan would, they argue, only accelerate assimilation and encourage naturalization among Koreans. Seeking political rights would be a crime against Korean people, as this will disintegrate the fabric of the ethnic Korean community in Japan, ultimately threatening its very existence.[559]

This difference of opinion between the two Korean organizations mainly stems from the difference in the future they envision for Koreans in Japan. Unlike Mindan, which envisions for Koreans in Japan continuous residence on Japanese soil, Jochongnyeon's position is that their ultimate goal should be returning home to Korea some day.[560] Jochongnyeon's adamant opposition to the Korean participation in Japanese domestic politics also owes to the fact that this may interfere with its own organizational goal, which is to foster a strong affiliation to North Korea among ethnic Koreans, putting, in the worst case

---

559 See the Federation of Korean Residents in Japan, "The Issue of Local Political Rights," Joseon Sinbo Publishing, 1996.

560 (Young) Koreans in Japan may be classified into four principal categories, according to their attitude toward Japanese society: those who view their own local community as a community of fate with which they must seek harmonious co-existence, those for whom Korea remains the only true home, those for whom individual self-determination has precedence over social appurtenance, and those who consider eventual naturalization. Of these four types, those who seek co-existence with their local community generally favor the idea of acquiring local voting rights, whilst those who consider Korea as their only real home tend to oppose it on the basis that this will result in complete assimilation with the Japanese society. See Kim, C. G., "Toward An Identity for Koreans in Japan," *Journal of Northeast Asian Studies*, Vol.33, 2004, pp.272–274.

scenario, its continued existence at risk.[561] An opinion survey, however, revealed that the vast majority of Koreans in Japans, regardless of their affiliation to these two organizations, supported the local political rights movement.[562]

## 2. The Japanese Government's Position on Korean Residents' Demand for Local Political Rights

The Memorandum signed between Korea and Japan in 1991 contains no conclusive statement concerning the local political rights of Korean residents in Japan. The agreement contains a mere mention that reads: "the Government of Korea expressed the wish to see local political rights granted to Korean nationals residing in Japan." The Japanese position at the time of the MOU was that authorizing the right to participate in local political processes for Korean residents in Japan would violate Article 15 of the Japanese Constitution.

---

561 Chung, I. S., *op. cit.*, pp. 411–412.

562 A survey conducted on the residents of Kanagawa Prefecture with Korean origin in September 1984 found that 82.4% of respondents with Korean nationality and 79% of those with Joseon nationality indicated an interest in or desire for local political rights. Meanwhile, according to a November 1994 survey by the Embassy of Korea in Japan, 84.3% of all respondents desired to obtain local political rights(See the Korean Residents Union, "The Local Political Rights Movement" (http://www.mindan.org)).

## 1) Theoretical Debate: Legal Examination

Concerning the political rights of permanent resident aliens, Japanese legal scholarship is divided into three different currents: ( i ) the first group opposes granting political rights to foreign residents, both at a local and national level;[563] (ii) The second group believes that while granting political rights at a national level would be unconstitutional under the current Japanese Constitutiona, local political rights may be bestowed on foreign residents, with minor amendments to relevant laws;[564] (iii) The third group unites scholars who see no constitutional or legal obstacle in allowing foreign residents to vote in both national and local elections.[565] Traditionally, the prevailing view among Japanese legal scholars has been that most basic rights under the Constitution should be extended to foreigners, except political rights and social rights that they deem reserved for citizens. Hence, the widespread view was that permanent resident aliens including Koreans in Japan were not entitled to political rights.[566]

---

563 Sato, K., "The Subjects of Basic Rights," Abe, T. ed., *Constitutional Theories and Precedents I*, 1976, p.67(requoted from Chung, I. S., *op. cit.*, p.418); Hashimoto, C., *The Japanese Constitution*(Yuhikaku, 1990), p.130; Itoh, M., *The Constitution*(Kobundo, 1990), p.197.

564 Onuma, Y., "A Study on the Legal Status of Koreans in Japan(Part II)," *Journal of the Japanese Society of Law*, Vol.97, No.4, p.498(requoted from Chung, I. S., *op. cit.*, p.419).

565 Okuda, K., "The Legal Status of Foreigners in Japan," *Journal of Social Science Studies*, Vol.27, No.2, p.77(requoted from Chung, I. S., *op. cit.*, p.419).

566 Cho, S. G., *op. cit.*, pp.381−382.

More recently, however, discussions on the local political rights of permanent residents in Japan is taking a less rigid tone, with many new takes on the issue and progressive approaches joining this debate.

To begin with the disagreement among Japanese legal scholars concerning the constitutionality of allowing foreign residents to vote in local elections or to be elected into local office, the rationale of those who see it as unconstitutional is as follows: the right to vote in parliamentary elections (Article 15 of the Constitution) and the right to vote in local elections (Article 93, Paragraph 2) are both rights derivative of the doctrine of the sovereignty of the people. Hence, 'citizens' that are the subjects of these rights, should be understood as 'Japanese citizens.' Even if the Constitution specifies the subjects of local political rights as 'residents,' the term 'citizens' under Article 15, Paragraph 1 and the term 'residents' under Article 93, Paragraph 2 form a 'whole-part relationship' and designate the same subjects within a national and regional context, respectively. Hence, it would be wrong to interpret 'residents' under the provisions relating to local self-government as including foreign residents.[567]

Meanwhile, the position of those who consider it constitutional to grant local political rights to permanent resident aliens is based on the following interpretation of the same Constitution: even if the term 'residents' used in Article 93, Paragraph 2 of the

---

[567] Chung, I. S., *op. cit.*, p.419.

Constitution were to designate 'Japanese citizens,' the intended meaning is that Japanese citizens are guaranteed the right to take part in local political processes, without implying that foreign residents are necessarily denied the same right. As the Constitution neither denies nor explicitly acknowledges the local political rights of foreign residents, deciding whether to grant such rights to the latter is within the legislative discretion of the Parliament.

The third take on the issue has it that the term 'residents,' the subjects of local self-government under Article 93 of the Japanese Constitution, designates "all those composing the local administrative unit, in other words all those who are domiciled within its jurisdiction," and a literal interpretation of the same Article does not exclude foreign residents. Further, if the provision on parliamentary elections under Article 15, Paragraph 1 derives from the doctrine of the sovereignty of the people, Article 93, Paragraph 2, in its turn, derives from Article 92 on local government. Hence, 'residents' under Article 93, Paragraph 2 must be interpreted in a manner appropriate to the purpose of local government. Unilaterally excluding over 700,000 permanent resident aliens from the affairs of their local governments runs against the fundamental purpose of the local self-government system. In conclusion, foreign residents, they argue, are guaranteed the right to vote in local elections pursuant to Article 93, Paragraph 2 of the current Japanese Constitution.[568]

## 2) The Position of the Japanese Judiciary

Since 1989, several lawsuits related to the political rights of foreign residents have been filed with Japanese courts. The position of the judicial branch on this issue has been noteworthy, even if there has been thus far no ruling clearly in favor of plaintiffs. The text of ruling in the case of *Kim Jeong Gyu, a Korean resident in Japan, vs. Japanese Government*, issued by the Supreme Court on February 28, 1995, contains the following passage:

"The provisions related to local self—government under Chapter Ⅷ of the Constitution appear to be intended as an acknowledgement of the governing system whereby local public agencies handle public affairs closely related to the day—to—day existence in the local community, according to the wish of its residents, as a constitutional system, in appreciation of the importance of local self—government in a democratic society. As, of foreign nationals residing in our country(Japan), those residing here on a permanent basis maintain a particularly close relationship to the local government in their place of residence, this Court deems that the Constitution does not prohibit legislative initiatives seeking to allow them to vote in the elections of local council members or the head of the local government, as a means to make it possible to reflect their opinion in the way businesses closely touching their daily existence are handled by their local

---

**568** *Ibid.*, pp.419—420.

authorities. However, whether or not to undertake such initiatives belongs solely to the legislative branch of the Government. Therefore, the absence of such initiatives cannot as such be considered unconstitutional."

This interpretation of the Supreme Court of Japan clearly departs from the position long—held by its government and some of its legal scholars that the Constitution bans the conferral of local voting rights to foreign nationals, as it treats the issue as pertaining to legislative policy; in other words, suggesting that no constitutional obstacle exists and that the amendment of election—related laws suffices to allow foreign residents to vote in local elections. This ruling gave a major boost to the local political rights movement by Koreans in Japan, as it significantly undermined the government's unconstitutionality argument.[569] The ruling, furthermore, triggered a shift in perception of the issue, from a legal and ideological issue having to do with the very foundation of Japanese democracy, to a simple political and policy issue chiefly dependent on legislative decisions.[570]

---

[569] *Ibid.*, p.423; In a lawsuit by Kim, Myeong Seok *et al.*, demanding the right to be elected into public office, the District Court of Osaka also ruled, on May 28, 1997, that the conferral of such right falls into the domain of legislative discretion.

[570] Kim, Seong Ho(hereinafter 'Kim, S. H.'), "The Local Political Rights of Korean Residents in Japan: Current Status and Outlook," *Journal of Peace Studies*, Vol.8, No.1, Korea University, 2000, p.38.

### 3) The Stance of Political Leadership and Local Governments (Councils)

Following this ruling by the Supreme Court, Murayama, Japanese Premier of that time and a member of the Social Democratic Party, expressed his support for the local political rights of foreign residents. Meanwhile, Nonaka, Minister of the Interior and Local Government, indicated that he is willing to reflect the opinion of the Supreme Court in future local self-government policies and review the issue of foreign residents' rights from a more progressive angle.[571] The cause of foreign residents, otherwise, has been receiving growing support from Japanese society.

Since late 1993, an increasing number of local councils have adopted a resolution demanding that voting rights be extended to permanent resident aliens. These resolutions condemn the exclusion of taxpaying permanent resident aliens from the public life of their local community as wrongful, and propose to open the door to local political processes for them, on the basis that they are integral and contributing members of their communities. According to a study by the International Division of Mindan, as of February 2003, 1511 of 3302 total local governments in 47 prefectures in Japan, corresponding to 45.76% of them, adopted a favorable opinion on granting local political rights to permanent resident aliens.[572]

---

[571] Chung, I. S., *op. cit.*, p.423.

The political rights of foreign residents in Japan also earned support from the Japanese Diet(Lower House). In 1998, the Komeito ('Clean Government Party,' formerly New Peace/Reformist Party) and the Democratic Party, two of the opposition parties, made an unprecedented move of jointly proposing a legislative bill to allow permanent resident aliens in Japan to vote in elections of local councils and the head of local government. Around the same time, the Communist Party also submitted a legislative proposal to authorize permanent resident aliens to vote in local public office elections and elections of heads of local government and be elected to public office.[573] While these legislative activities stirred up interest in the issue of local political rights for foreign residents, both bills failed to reach the stage of deliberation by the Election Law Committee of the Lower House.

The local political rights of foreign residents ceased to be the exclusive concern of opposition party lawmakers, when in 1999, the Komeito party took part in the coalition government. In October of the same year, the Liberal Democratic Party, Liberal Party and the Komeito party, the three members of the coalition government, agreed on a new legislation extending local political rights to permanent resident aliens in Japan.

---

572  Refer to the Korean Residents Union In Japan, "The Local Political Rights Movement" (http://www.mindan.org/kr).

573  This progressive legislative bill, extending voting rights and the right to be elected at a local level to all permanent residents including special−category permanent residents, conceives political rights in the so−called Nordic−style. See Choi, Y. H., *op. cit.*(*supra* note 497), p.7.

However, the Liberal Democratic Party desisted from pursuing the project, yielding to pressure from its own more moderate wing. In January 2000, the Komeito and Liberal parties went ahead without the latter to submit the 'Bill on Granting the Right to Vote in Elections of Local Council and Head of Local Government to Permanent Resident Aliens.' On July 4 of the same year, the Komeito party and the Conservative party, created by former members of the Liberal party, re-submitted the same legislative bill.[574] On May 9, 2001, it was decided that the bill was to be carried to the next session, due to the strong opposition from the Liberal Democratic Party, causing delay in deliberation and vote.

Meanwhile, seen from examples like the 'Highlights of the Legislative Bill on Facilitating the Naturalization of Special Permanent Resident Aliens,' summarizing a legislative proposal to ease rules related to acquiring Japanese citizenship, issued by the 'Nationality Project Team' on April 19, 2001, the tide seems to be turning in Japan's political circle, toward absorbing and assimilating foreigners, rather than extending them the right to participate in political processes as foreign residents.[575] This atmosphere makes it unlikely, some political watchers believe, that a new law guaranteeing any meaningful political rights such as the right to vote in local elections for foreign residents be

---

574 *Ibid.*, pp.7–10; Kim, S. H., *op. cit.*, pp.41–47.

575 See the Korean Residents Union in Japan, "The Local Political Rights Movement" (http://www.mindan.org).

passed in Japan anytime soon.[576]

Notwithstanding, even though not equivalent to the right to vote or to be elected into office, quite a few local governments passed ordinances allowing permanent resident aliens meeting certain eligibility requirements, to participate in 'residents' referendums.' Takahama of Aichi Prefecture enacted one such ordinance, and Iwakicho of Akita Prefecture held a residents' referendum, on September 29, 2002, on the merger of two towns, authorizing "permanent resident aliens, aged 18 or older, having resided in either of the towns for at least three months in a continuous fashion" to cast a ballot.

As of July 30, 2003, there are as many as 52 local self-governing bodies which either enacted a new ordinance on residents' referendum or amended an existing one to allow permanent resident aliens to participate in city governance.[577] Such political rights, exclusive of the right to elect public officials and to be elected into public offices, however, remain imperfect compromises, certainly not at the level of the expectations held by the Korean community in Japan.

---

576 Lee, Suk Jong(hereinafter 'Lee, S. J.'), "Local Political Rights for Koreans in Japan: Current Status and Outlook," *Political Trends and Policies*, July 2001, p.10.

577 See *Mindan Sinmun*, Jul. 30, 2003(requoted from Hosaka, Y., "The Japanese Permanent Resident Aliens Policy and Koreans in Japan," *Journal of Korean Studies*, No.11, 2003, p.63).

# IV. Summary and Future Directions

A dual trend toward globalization and localization characterizes the 21st century. Globalization or internationalization is a process that requires respect for oneself as well as others. Most countries in today's world proclaim to be democratic communities. A democratic community, to fully deserve the name, must guarantee all its members the right to participate in the collective decision−making process and policy−making.[578]

International human rights law, a discipline emerged in the mid 20th century, urges national societies to protect the basic human rights of all members residing within their physical boundaries, as much as possible. Meanwhile, the accelerating trend toward localization has brought to the fore the importance of effectively upholding the rights of foreigners within local communities in host nation−States, of which they are residents and members. In other words, the subjects of rights in the era of localization are no longer 'citizens,' but 'residents,' as place of residence and actual community of life become more legitimate sources of rights than nationality.

---

[578] In a democratic community where decisions are made by majority votes, all members of community must be guaranteed the participation in the decision−making process, in order to justify the legitimacy of majority decisions and demands resulting from such decisions. In other words, stripping minorities of political freedom and rights is tantamount to the abandonment by the democratic majority of its claim to be a legitimate majority. See Kim, B. C., *op. cit.*(*supra* note 491), p.5.

The Japanese government's basic ethnic Korean policy has thus far tended toward assimilation.[579] During its occupation of Korea, Japan forcibly imposed Japanese nationality on all Koreans, on the grounds of the former being an annexed country. In post war years, its government unilaterally revoked the Japanese nationality of Koreans in Japan and discriminated against them, treating them as 'general–category foreigners.'

By continuing its discriminatory treatment of Koreans, the Japanese government is in reality forcing them to choose between repatriation to Korea and naturalization. In recent years, its policy has been more overtly pro assimilation. The amendment of the Nationality Law and loosening of naturalization–related restrictions have made the acquisition of Japanese nationality easier.[580] As a result, the Korean community in Japan has been fast shrinking in size and may even end up diminishing to a more negligible quantity.

---

579 Kim, K. D., *op. cit.*(*supra* note 555), p.57.

580 Article 6 of 「The Japanese Nationality Law」 recognizes the right to become naturalized citizens to foreign nationals born in Japan who continuously resided there for three years or longer or have an established residence there, or whose father or mother(excluding adoptive parents) were born in Japan; and foreign nationals who have maintained a continuous residence in the country for 10 years or more. This amended provision overrides Article 5 of the same law requiring a minimum of five years of continuous residence for access to naturalization. As of January 2001, the vast majority of Koreans residing in Japan on a permanent basis satisfied this condition. Thus, this amendment basically removed all formal obstacles to Korean permanent residents' access to Japanese citizenship. For further reading on this subject, see Hosaka, Y., *op. cit.*, p.11.

The Korean community, the largest ethnic minority in Japan, has the right to maintain its cultural identity, both based on the special historic circumstances which gave rise to it and as guaranteed by international human rights law. It is entitled to demand of the Japanese government, the representation of the ethnic minority of Japan, equal treatment and acceptance.[581] In the age of globalization and localization, Japan as a self-proclaimed democratic society, must step up to guarantee the basic rights of Koreans both as human beings and as 'residents' of their respective local communities, as required by international law.

Living in a country other than one's country of citizenship is today a usual way of life, not an exceptional circumstance, and foreign residents in all parts of the world are making tremendous economic, social and cultural contributions to their host countries. It therefore behooves the Japanese government to look into extending political rights to its permanent resident aliens, to manifest its commitment to human rights as well as to affirm human autonomy and dignity.[582]

Giving permanent resident aliens the right to participate in

---

[581] 「International Covenant on Civil and Political Rights」, Article 27: "In those States in which ethnic, religious or linguistic minorities exist, persons belonging to such minorities shall not be denied the right, in community with the other members of their group, to enjoy their own culture, to profess and practice their own religion, or to use their own language."

[582] Hagino, Y., "Permanent Resident Aliens and Their Political Rights," Suh, Y. D. ed., *op. cit.*, pp.205-240.

local political processes and treating them equally will enable them to become more active members of Japanese society with the same rights and duties as nationals, which will also help it create the kind of social fabric needed for the 'symbiotic and cooperative society' it aspires to be.

Given the special historical background of the issue of Koreans in Japan and the fact that Japan was primarily responsible for bringing this ethnic minority to its soil, the obligation of finding a solution to enable them to live with dignity and lead a socially fulfilling existence befalls on its government as well. Yet, the government of Japan has never actively sought to enhance the legal status of its Korean residents and their human rights conditions.

Coming from a country which sees itself today as a leader in the international community, this is a surprising degree of obliviousness to responsibility and deficit of human rights. The government of Japan must make more active efforts toward improving the legal status of ethnic Koreans whom it once forced to become citizens of the Japanese Empire, also as part of reparations for the historical injustices these people suffered.[583]

As for the government of Korea, at the same time as reminding Japanese government of the special historical background to the issue of Koreans in Japan and urging the latter to rise to its responsibilities, it must also tackle this issue as a broader human

---

[583] Hagino, Y., *op. cit.*, pp.13-14.

rights issue and an occasion to affirm the principle of the equal treatment of nationals and non nationals. Most importantly, the Korean government must more actively look for ways to prevail on the Japanese government for a legislation authorizing the right to take part in local political processes for Koreans in Japan. The fact that the Japanese government, at a time where ideological or constitutional obstacles to granting local political rights to permanent resident aliens have already been proven non-existent, is still balking at legislative efforts may be seen as an indication of the diplomatic incompetency on the part of Seoul.

The Japanese government is dealing with the problem of ethnic Koreans currently through a pro-assimilation policy and refuses to see it as a human rights issue or an issue touching its responsibility on the historical injustices committed by it. If abandoning its citizens abroad to the fate of complete assimilation to the host country's culture and letting, for instance, the Korean community in Japan disintegrate and disappear is indeed not what the Korean government envisions for them, and if it sees some sense in, and respects, their struggle against the Japanese government's assimilation policy and discriminatory treatment to preserve their own ethnic identity and defend their basic human rights, it must show their support by coming up with a more fundamental solution to their plight.

The Korean government, in a move affirming of the basic rights of foreigners and universality of human rights, has granted local voting rights to permanent resident aliens. This has given it a diplomatic high ground *vis-à-vis* Japan on the issue of local political rights for Koreans residing in Japan. Korea may not even need to evoke the historical origin of the Korean community in Japan, according to some international relations experts, to press its case, since it just added a new weapon to its arsenal of arguments, the principle of reciprocity.

On the other hand, the restrictions, in former days, as to the participation of Koreans residing in Japan and elsewhere in the world in political processes at home in Korea could be a factor weakening the Korean position in the negotiations with Japan. True, there are a lot of practical and technical difficulties involved in allowing Korean expatriates to exercise their political rights at home. Also, this may give some Koreans overseas political rights in two countries, their country of residence and country of citizenship. However, demanding the Japanese government that political rights be granted to Koreans in Japan, while not guaranteeing them the same rights at home in Korea seems like an unsustainable posture.

Indeed, for a long time, Koreans in Japan had been stripped of political rights both at home in Korea and in Japan, at a national as well as local level. Because there is no doubt that the Korean government should hold Japan responsible for the displacement suffered by Koreans in Japan and continue to press its demand to grant the right to participate in local politics, recently, it took a step by amending its own laws, especially the Public Position

Election Act, to grant Koreans in Japan and elsewhere in the world the right to weigh in on public and policy issues in Korea.

Such a proactive move will make the Korean stance toward the local political rights of Koreans residing in Japan more coherent, strengthen its position in bilateral negotiations with the Japanese government, and give it more bargaining power.

# CHAPTER 10

# Global Governance and Maritime Cooperation

— focusing on Jeju Waters and Northeast Asian Seas —

## I. Introduction

Having entered the globalized 21st century, ensuring the safety and protection of sea lanes have become a major concern among littoral states of the northeast Asian seas from both military and non-military perspectives. The economic development strategies of these states are highly dependent upon foreign trade, which are mostly conducted over sea. The strategic interests of the United States, Russia, China and Japan, as well as that of the divided States of North and South Korea, in Northeast Asia have become more sensitive and more focused than in any of the other region of the world. Competition and confrontation among the states in the region have often been heightened by the issues of sea lane protection and safety. The semi-enclosed nature of the

Northeast Asian seas have further pushed the relationship among these states into a more acute tension, in particular concerning the expansion of maritime jurisdiction and the continuing sovereignty dispute over islands, especially following the entry into effect of the UN Convention on the Law of the Sea(UNCLOS) in 1994.[584]

Today, it is difficult for any single state to independently secure the oceans and sea lanes as they cover a very extensive area. Thus, securing the safety of oceans and sea lanes through cooperation is becoming an increasingly important item on the state agenda not only at the global level but also at the regional level. While regionalism is spreading around the world there remain, however, visible disparate and divergent factors among states in the Northeast Asian region, from which confrontations and conflicts still continue to arise.[585]

Based upon this background, this paper first evaluates the importance of protecting Northeast Asian sea lanes and the strategic value of the Jeju Sea around the Jeju Strait and Ieodo waters. This chapter then proposes the formation of a regional marine cooperation system at the maritime governance level for sea lane security.

---

[584] United Nations Law of the Sea Treaty, 10 December1982, 1833 U.N.T.S. 3.

[585] Young-Koo Cha, "A Korean Perspective on the Security of the Sea Lanes in East Asia," in Lau Teik Soon & Lee Lai To, eds., *The Security Of The Sea Lanes In The Asia-Pacific Region*(Heinemann Asia, 1988), pp.195-196.

# II. Significance of the Northeast Asian Seas and Sea Lanes

## 1. Definition of the Northeast Asian Seas

Northeast Asia refers to the region of Asia that includes Korea, Japan and China while a broader definition includes the Northeastern region of China, Mongolia and far eastern Russia. The 'Northeast Asian Seas' refer to the waters where these Northeast Asian states are coastal states. The China Sea is generally referred to as the waters surrounded by the eastern coast of the Asian continent beginning at the Korean Peninsula extending to Singapore in the South, and the group of islands in the Japanese archipelago, the Ryukyu Islands, Taiwan, the Philippines, to Borneo and Sumatra. This area is divided by the Taiwan Strait, serving as a boundary, the northern side known as the East China Sea and on the southern side as the South China Sea. The East China Sea is generally referred to as the Northeast Asian Sea. More specifically, drawing a line drawn from the southern point of the Korean Peninsula to the Yangtze River as a reference point, the Northeast Asian Seas can be divided into the Yellow Sea(West Sea) located between the Korean Peninsula and the Eastern coast of China; the East China Sea between Taiwan and the Korean Peninsula; the East Sea between the Korean Peninsula and Japan; and the Sea of Okhotsk between Eastern Sakhalin of Russia and Kamchatka Peninsula. Among these four seas included in the Northeast Asian Seas, the Sea of Okhotsk has been considered an inland sea of Russia; but the other three seas have been at the center of major activities and interests of the surrounding states.[586]

With the Northeast Asian waters at the center, Korea lies both adjacent to and opposite major powers such as Japan, China, Taiwan, and Russia, while maintaining a distinctive relationship with North Korea, as a divided state. The United States is not a state in the Northeast Asian seas *per se*, but due to the cooperative military relationships with Korea and Japan, established through the "Mutual Defense Treaty between the Republic of Korea and the United States of America"[587] and the "Security Treaty between Japan and the United States of America,"[588] it has become an indirect marginal state with very important political and military interests in Northeast Asian waters. Thus, it can be said that there are seven states, which include Korea, Japan, North Korea, China, Russia, Taiwan and the United States, surrounding the Northeast Asian seas region.

The Northeast Asian seas have been utilized as major sea lanes

---

586  Sangwoo Lee, "Increase of Soviet Navy and the Safety of Northeast Asian Sea Lane," in Dal—Choong Kim ed., *Korea and Sea Lane Security* (Beopmunsa, 1988), pp.228—231 (in Korean).

587  Mutual Defense Treaty between The Republic of Korea and the United States of America, 1 October 1953, available at ⟨ http://www.usfk.mil/usfk/sofa.1953.mutual.defense.treaty.76 ⟩ (last visited on 2013—06—17)

588  Treaty of Mutual Cooperation and Security Between Japan and the United States, 19 January 1960, available at ⟨ http://www.mofa.go.jp/region/n—america/us/q&a/ref/1.html⟩ (last visited on 2013—06—17).

for trade and military purposes by the littoral states and major maritime powers, and they have long received much international political and economic attention. The East China Sea is an important body of water situated at the intersection of sea lanes of communication connecting the East Sea and the Yellow Sea to the north, the South China Sea and the Philippine Sea to the south, and the Pacific Ocean to the east. And because it is surrounded by states with competitive or hostile relations with each other, *i.e.* Korea, China, Taiwan, Japan, Russia and the US, conflict can arise at any time.

The Northeast Asian seas have become a major stage of activity for the US and Russian navies, as well as China and Japan. From the American perspective, the Northeast Asian seas are recognized for their strategic importance not only in maintaining a maritime military presence but also in safeguarding sea lanes to hold the southward advance of the Russian navy in check. For Japan, China and Korea that are oriented towards ocean−going navies, the Northeast Asian seas are recognized for their strategic importance for state security.[589] There are also many choke−points, which include the Jeju Strait, the Straits of Korea, Tsushima Strait, Taiwan Strait, Tsugaru Strait, Soya Strait and Tatar Strait, the strategic value of which have received attention for their location in the Northeast Asian sea lanes.

---

[589] Sangwoo Lee, *supra* note 586, pp.238−242.

## 2. Current Northeast Asian Sea Lanes and their Significance

### 1) Current Status of the Northeast Asian Sea Lanes

Strictly speaking, the Sea Lines of Communication(SLOC), referred to the concept of supply lines or munitions vessel, as "the maritime routes which connected operation forces and the base of operations, along which supplies and augmentation forces would be transported." The same definition was often utilized in a non-military context, thus causing confusion with Sea Lanes of Communication. SLOC today, or sea lanes, encompass "lanes of marine transport for commercial and military purposes."[590]

With regard to economic development, the importance of sea lanes has long been recognized. As Sir Walter Raleigh, during the reign of Queen Elizabeth of England in the 16th century, stated, "For whosoever commands the sea commands the trade; whosoever commands the trade of the world commands the riches of the world, and consequently the world itself."[591] It has been historically proven that a state which has control over the sea or had the power to effectively rule the oceans became a rich and powerful state that prospered. Admiral Mahan emphasized principles of maritime strategies early on as a foundation for

---

590 Dal-Choong Kim, "Maritime Strategy of the Four Powers surrounding Northeast Asian SLOCs," in Dal-Choong Kim ed., *supra* note 586, p.147 (in Korean).

591 Sir Walter Raleigh, "A Discourse of the Invention of Ships, Anchors, Compass, etc.," in *The Works of Sir Walter Raleigh, Kt.*, Vol.8, 1829, p.325.

national development; and based on this strategy, England and the US have built great maritime military strength to become maritime states which lead the world.

Maritime military strength, or sea power having this as a core element, has become the foundation for national development and a basic factor for measuring national power today.[592] States that possess sea power, for the safety of their own sea routes, passively utilize the vast SLOCs while more actively attempting to focus and demonstrate their sea power in the oceans in order to support their allies, eliminate opposing forces within the region and to neutralize the interventions of other states.[593]

No state today can be self-sufficient, self-supporting, and independent economically; rather we live in a system of an international division of labor and cooperation where resources and products must be traded. In particular, the explosive increase of the world population today and the increase in the demand for resources, as well as the accompanying rise in the exchange of goods and services, make the usage of sea lanes for maritime trade

---

592 Traditionally, 'sea power' referred to the control of the oceans using military vessels, or power projection. Today, it is recognized as an aggregate of national powers regarding the use of the oceans — ultimately the power to utilize the oceans in order to maximize a state's powers. Jin-Hyun Paik, "Development of Korea's Maritime Policy and Sea Power," in *21$^{st}$ Century and Korea's Maritime Security*(conference proceedings) (1994), pp.214-215 (in Korean).

593 Hyun-Gi Kim, "Korea's Sea Lane Safety and Sea Power," in Hyun-Gi Kim ed., *State Economy and Maritime Security*(Korea Institute for Maritime Strategy('KIMS'), 1999), p.175 (in Korean).

inevitable. In order to safely transport goods necessary for survival, e.g., oil, food, raw materials or military goods to one's own country, not only during peaceful times but also in times of emergency, there arises the need to protect sea lanes.[594] The oceans also bear important economic value as a treasure trove of biological and mineral resources. It would not be an overstatement to say that together with maritime trade, securing the safety of sea lanes for the exploration and exploitation of marine resources is now becoming an important agenda not only for individual states but for the international community as well.

There are varying different explanations regarding the distribution of the sea lanes in the Northeast Asian Seas. One view provides that among the regular line of traffic[595] utilized by foreign trade vessels of Korean nationality, there are eight sea lanes, which are the Korea-Japan route, Southeast Asian route, North American route, Middle Eastern route, European route, Australian route, African route, and Middle and South American route.[596] Another view posits that there are three Korea-Japan

---

594 Yeon-Won Hwang, "Study on the Maritime Security Policy of Korea" (Master's Thesis, Donguk University Graduate School of Administration, 1989), p.90 (in Korean).

595 Line of traffic utilized by foreign trade vessels refer to routes connecting to foreign trade ports from major ports e.g. Busan, Gwangyang, Ulsan, Incheon, etc.

596 Among these, the African route and South American routes not only have low participation rates of state vessels but even the operation of state vessels are mostly lump sum-partial charter or joint ventures. Realistically, therefore, major lines of traffic can be seen as the other

routes and four Korea — Southeast Asia — Middle East route for a total of seven sea lanes.[597] A third view notes the Northern route connecting the North American region and the Siberian region, the Korea–Japan route connecting Japan, the Korea–China route connecting China, and a Southern route connecting Southeast Asia — Middle East — Europe, for a total of four sea lanes.[598] Lastly, there is a view that describes a Korea–China route passing through the West Sea directly to the East Coast of China; a southwestern route passing through the East China Sea and

---

six. *See* Dal–Choong Kim, "Study of the Korean Sea Lane Safety," *Academic Journal on National Defense*, Vol.2, 1989, p.78 (in Korean).

[597] The sea lane between Korea and Japan can be largely divided into three parts. The first goes from various ports of the west and south coast of Korea to Japan, mainly passing through the Jeju Strait and the Tsushima Strait, then the Shimonoseki Strait between Honshu and Kyushu of Japan to arrive at Japanese ports along the Pacific coast. The second goes from ports of the east and southeast coast of Korea, passing through the Korea Strait or the Tsushima Strait to arrive in Japan. The third goes from ports on the east coast of Korea, passing through the waters adjacent to Dokdo and arriving at ports along the west coast of Japan. Among routes leading from Korea, the Korea–Southeast Asia–Middle East route passing through the East China Sea and the Indian Ocean to arrive at the Persian Gulf, there are four routes: 1) Korea — Bashi Strait — Malacca Strait — Indian Ocean — Persian Gulf, 2) Korea — Bashi Strait — Karimata Strait — Sunda Strait — Indian Ocean — Persian Gulf, 3) Korea — Bashi Strait — Balabac Strait — Makassar Strait — Lombok Strait — Indian Ocean — Persian Gulf, 4) Korea — the Philippines — Banda Strait — Ombai Wetar Strait — Indian Ocean — Persian Gulf. Traveling from Korea to the Persian Gulf at 20 knots, under good weather conditions, takes between 22 days at least up to 28 days. *See* Hyun–Gi Kim, *supra* note 593, pp.183–184.

[598] Jong–Min Kim, "Issue of Korea's Sea Lane Protection," in *Maritime Strategy*, Vol.85, 1994, pp.55–57 (in Korean).

leading to Southeast Asia, the Middle East, Europe and Africa; a southeastern route passing around the Japanese archipelago or the strait and leading to North, Middle and South America; and a Korea–Japan route passing through the East Sea and the Korea Strait and leading to Japan, for a total of four major sea lanes.[599]

The strategic significance of the North American route has been highly evaluated not only from an economic perspective but also from that of the Korea–US alliance and military cooperation. The Korea–China route has had significant growth in trade volume since the establishment of Korea–China relations. The Middle East route is one that has been receiving much attention because of its instability due to oil transport and conflicts in the region. The Korea–Japan route, besides its significance in itself, is important because Korea transports oil from the Persian Gulf along the same route up to the East China Sea. Considering that it must pass through the Japanese sea lane, there certainly is a close connection. Furthermore, the Korea–Japan route is more important as any disruption of the Japanese route can directly affect the safety of Korean routes.[600] The Southeast Asian route connecting Korea to Southeast Asia passes southeast of Jeju Island and the Ryukyu Islands of Japan, through the Bashi Strait between the Philippines and Taiwan, or the Taiwan Strait between

---

599 Hyeong–Soo Bae, "Development of National Sea Power and the Protection of SLOCs," in *Maritime Policy Symposium Proceedings*(2006), pp.5–6 (in Korean).

600 Hyun–Gi Kim, *supra* note 593, p.184

China and Taiwan, finally arriving at the South China Sea. In order to enter the Indian Ocean from the South China Sea, vessels must pass by the wide spread of islands of the five ASEAN (Association of Southeast Asian Nations) states — the Philippines, Indonesia, Malaysia, Thailand and Singapore.[601]

## 2) Significance of the Northeast Asian Sea Lanes[602]

Geographically, Korean foreign trade is inherently dependent upon air and sea lanes, especially because maritime trade accounts for almost all of Korea's foreign trade. Thus, securing the safety of sea lanes is an absolute necessity for national development. It is also an absolute requisite for state survival, not only in times of peace but also in national emergencies. Nearly the entire trade volume of Korea is dependent upon trade coming through the Northeast Asian Sea Lanes. Having followed an export-oriented development strategy from the 1960s, Korea has emphasized foreign trade as a mechanism for economic development. Korea's achievement as a maritime power — the world's 11th largest economy, 10th in maritime trade volume, foremost in shipbuilding capabilities, and 5th in handling containers — was attributable to the sea lanes connecting Korea to the world. Seventy-three percent of Korea's GDP is dependent upon foreign trade, and 99.7% of the entire trade volume is being

---

601 *Ibid.*
602 *Ibid.*, pp.193–195.

transported over the sea.[603] With the scale-up in transport volume and extended distances, in addition to lower transport costs, the importance of shipping and ports and the need for sea lane safety will be greatly emphasized in the future.

As a littoral state of the East Sea, the Yellow Sea and the East China Sea, and being situated where it can control the Korea Strait (a critical route for Russia's entry into East China Sea); and the Jeju Strait (a traffic point connecting the Yellow Sea and the East China Sea); as well as the outer sea lanes, Korea has historically been subject to attacks by great maritime powers with an interest in these sea lanes. Korea is surrounded by seas in which the navies of the major maritime powers co-exist despite the fact that these powers have in the past engaged in intense confrontations. The Russian Pacific Fleet, the US 7th Fleet, as well as the Japanese and the North Korean Fleets have a constant presence in the East Sea. The Chinese, North Korean and US Fleets are also in the Yellow Sea, and in the south, the US, Russian, Chinese, Japanese and Taiwanese Fleets are in the East China Sea. Trade and military supplies are transported through these sea lanes with these fleets present. Thus, the Northeast Asian sea lanes have great significance for Korea from a military, strategic and economic perspective. More recently, with a change in the maritime strategic order and the heightening of regional conflict

---

603 Ho-Seob Jeong, "Korea's Sea Lane Security Strategy," in *Sea Lane Security of East Asia*(Korea Institute for Maritime Strategy('KIMS'), 2007), p.197 (in Korean).

over maritime jurisdiction claims and access to marine resources, the importance of safety and defense of sea lanes have gained more attention.

# III. Strategic Value of the Northeast Asian Sea Lanes and the Jeju Sea

## 1. Northeast Asian Sea Lanes and the Jeju Sea

Jeju Island[604] is situated at the southernmost point of the Korean Peninsula. It is not only at the center of the triangle connecting the Chinese mainland, the Korean Peninsula and the Japanese archipelago, but it is also located at the center of the Northeast Asian sea lanes that are surrounded by these states.[605] The waters around Jeju Island, often called the Jeju Sea, includes the Jeju Strait and the East China Sea while what is called the 'Ieodo Waters' south of the Jeju Island is part of the East China Sea. From a geographical perspective, the Jeju Island and Strait lie at a strategic area of the sea lane through which Korean

---

604 Jeju Island consists of eight inhabited islands of Biyangdo, Woodo, Sangchujado, Hachujado, Hwenggando, Gapado, Marado and fifty-four uninhabited islands.

605 Geographically, it lies 141.6 km away from Mokpo in the north, 286.5 km from Busan in the northeast, 255 km from Tsushima of Japan on the east, 352 km from Fukuoka, 528 km from Shanghai of China on the west, 796 km from Okinawa on the southeast.

vessels travel not only to the Korea–Japan and Korea–China routes but also to Southeast Asia, the Middle East, Europe and other regions. Because of its geopolitical location, Jeju Island has long been evaluated among states of the Northeast Asian Sea region as bearing strategic value for peace, security, economic, and other cooperation.[606]

The Jeju Strait is a strait[607] situated between the southern mainland and Jeju Island. The distance from the northernmost point of Jeju Island at 34° N (Chuja–myun Daeseo–ri) to Haenam of Jeolla–namdo is 47 nm (87 km), and to Mokpo is 76.5 nm (141.6 km) and from Jeju's main island to its Isle of Chuja is 25 nm (48 km). There are many small islets scattered throughout the Jeju Strait with depth averages around 70m with its deepest point at 140m[608] With straight baselines connecting the surrounding islands of Geomundo, Yeoseodo, Jangsoodo, Jeolmyungseodo, and Soheuksando as the starting point, the waters towards the mainland constitute internal waters, while the waters towards Jeju Island constitute the territorial sea. The Jeju Strait is often used for international navigation between one part of the high seas to an exclusive economic zone and another part of the high

---

606 The planning of the strategies of 'Island of World Peace' and 'International Free City' were progressed based on these backgrounds.

607 The Oxford English Dictionary defines a strait as "a comparatively narrow water–way or passage connecting two large bodies of water" as cited in D.H.N. Johnson, 'Straits,' in R. Bernhardt(ed.), *Encyclopedia of Public International Law*, Vol. IV(2000), p.693.

608 Chi Young Pak, *The Korea Strait*(Martinus Nijhof Publishers, 1983), p.3.

seas to an exclusive economic zone.

## 2. Legal Status and Strategic Significance of the Jeju Strait

### 1) Definition and Types of 'International Straits'

Examination of the legal status of the Jeju Strait under international law, and in particular the nature of the applicable passage regime, begins with examining the relevant provisions of the United Nations Convention on the Law of the Sea(UNCLOS)[609] concerning the conditions and categories of straits. UNCLOS, also referred to as the Constitution of the Oceans, adopted in 1982 and entering into effect in 1994, categorizes such straits with regard to the passage regime into the following six types:[610]

① Article 37: "[S]traits which are used for international

---

[609] United Nations Law of the Sea Treaty, 10 December 1982, 1833 U.N.T.S. 3(hereinafter 'UNCLOS').

[610] Chan-Ho Park, Chae-Hyung Kim, Hyun-Soo Kim, Seok-Yong Lee and Chang-Wee Lee, *Handbook to the UNCLOS I*(Ji-in Books, 2009), pp.126-128 (in Korean); William L. Schachte, Jr. and J. Peter A. Bernhardt, "International Straits and Navigational Freedoms," *Virginia Journal of International Law*, Vol.33, 1993, pp.538-547. According to Schachte, Jr. & Bernhardt, this important category of international straits is treated slightly differently from straits in which transit passage applies. These straits are located in whole or in part within the archipelagic waters of mid-oceanic archipelagic states. These were excluded because of geographical and international legal differences with 'straits.'

navigation between one part of the high seas or an exclusive economic zone and another part of the high seas or an exclusive economic zone" in which 'transit passage' shall not be impeded;

② Article 38(1): "[A] strait [that] is formed by an island of a State bordering the strait and its mainland, [where] there exists seaward of the island a route through the high seas or through an exclusive economic zone of similar con-venience with respect to navigational and hydrographical characteristics" in which nonsuspendable 'innocent passage' applies;

③ Article 45(1)(b): "[S]traits used for international navigation between a part of the high seas or an exclusive economic zone and the territorial sea of a foreign State" in which nonsuspendable 'innocent passage' applies;

④ Article 36: "[S]trait [where] there exists through the strait a route through the high seas or through an exclusive economic zone of similar convenience with respect to navigational and hydrographical characteristics;"[611]

⑤ Article 35(c): "[S]traits in which passage is regulated in whole or in part by long-standing international conventions in force specifically relating to such straits;"[612]

---

[611] In this situation, 'innocent passage' regime applies within the territorial waters of the littoral state, but freedom of navigation applies in the high seas or EEZ(UNCLOS Art. 36).

[612] UNCLOS Art. 35: "Nothing in this Part affects ⋯ (c) the legal regime

⑥ Article 311(2): Straits whose passage regime is regulated by
"other agreements compatible with this Convention and
which do not affect the enjoyment by other States Parties
of their rights or the performance of their obligations under
this Convention" though not long—standing.[613]

---

in straits in which passage is regulated in whole or in part by
long—standing international conventions in force specifically relating
to such straits."

[613] UNCLOS Art. 311 (2): "This Convention shall not alter the rights and
obligations of States Parties which arise from other agreements
compatible with this Convention and which do not affect the enjoyment
by other States Parties of their rights or the performance of their
obligations under this Convention." The Istanbul (Bosphorus) Strait and
Çanakkale (Dardanelles) Strait are examples of such straits, to which
a special regime pursuant to the 1936 Convention regarding the Regime
of the Straits, signed at Montreux on 20 July 1936, entered into force
9 November 1936(173 *League of Nations Treaty Series* 213), applies to
the passage through these straits and takes precedence over the UNCLOS
passage regime. These straits, which connect the Black Sea and the
Mediterranean Sea, are also called the Turkish Straits. According to the
Treaty, in times of peace, passage of all ships through the strait is
guaranteed, while passage of military vessels is allowed during the day
time with prior notice to the Turkish Government. The passage of
submarines are permitted for only for Black Sea coastal states in the
limited cases of allowing submarines purchased, constructed or repaired
outside of the Black Sea to rejoin their base in the Black Sea, but prior
notice must be given to the Turkish Government, after which it must
navigate on the surface during day time only. Aircrafts are limited to
civilian aircrafts, which must pass over designated air routes after
giving prior notice to the Turkish Government. And passage during times
of war is more strictly regulated. *Generally refer* to Nihan Ünlü, *The
Turkish Straits*(Martinus Nijhoff Publishers, 2002).

## 2) Evaluation of the Passage Regime for Straits Used for International Navigation

The 12 provisions regulating straits in UNCLOS, Articles 34 to 45, greatly differ from the provisions of the 1958 Convention on the Territorial Sea and Contiguous Zone[hereinafter 'Territorial Sea Convention'].[614] The Territorial Sea Convention only provided for a single regime for straits found in the territorial sea of a coastal State, which was nonsuspendable innocent passage.[615] UNCLOS, on the other hand, not only provides for nonsuspendable innocent passage in the territorial sea and in archipelagic waters[616] but

---

614  The 1958 Geneva Conventions on the Territorial Sea and the Contiguous Zone, 29 April 1958, 516 U.N.T.S. 205.

615  UNCLOS provides that "Passage is innocent so long as it is not prejudicial to the peace, good order or security of the coastal State." (Art. 19(1)). Then it provides, "Passage of a foreign ship shall be considered to be prejudicial to the peace, good order or security of the coastal State if in the territorial sea it engages in any of the following activities: (a) any threat or use of force against the sovereignty, territorial integrity or political independence of the coastal State, or in any other manner in violation of the principles of international law embodied in the Charter of the United Nations; (b) any exercise or practice with weapons of any kind; (c) any act aimed at collecting information to the prejudice of the defence or security of the coastal State; (d) any act of propaganda aimed at affecting the defence or security of the coastal State; (e) … ; (f) … ; (g) … ; (h) … ; (i) any fishing activities; (j) the carrying out of research or survey activities; (k) … ; (l) any other activity not having a direct bearing on passage." (Art. 19(2)).

616  "[S]hips of all States enjoy the right of innocent passage through archipelagic waters." (UNCLOS Art. 52(1)). "An archipelagic State may designate sea lanes and air routes thereabove, suitable for the continuous and expeditious passage of foreign ships and aircraft through or over its archipelagic waters and the adjacent territorial sea. All ships and aircraft enjoy the right of archipelagic sea lanes passage in such

also introduced the regime of transit passage applicable to certain types of straits.[617]

The transit passage regime was the product of a compromise made between the major maritime powers and the coastal States. The former group, in particular the US and the former Soviet Union, demanded to maintain absolute freedom of navigation in the waters of international straits which would become part of the territorial seas of the littoral states if the breadth of the territorial sea was extended to 12 nautical mile (nm). The latter group, on the other hand, referred to as the Strait States, demanded the application of the traditional innocent passage regime for territorial waters. The US, Soviet Union, and other maritime powers that desired to secure freedom of navigation and naval mobility sought a separate strait passage regime rather than that of innocent passage. The littoral states who continued to expand their maritime jurisdiction by extending their territorial waters and establishing economic zones, however, supported to have innocent passage regime apply to territorial waters.

---

sea lanes and air routes. (Art. 53(1)−(2)). The right of archipelagic sea lanes passage refers to "the exercise in accordance with this Convention of the rights of navigation and overflight in the normal mode solely for the purpose of continuous, expeditious and unobstructed transit between one part of the high seas or an exclusive economic zone and another part of the high seas or an exclusive economic zone." (Art. 53(3)) "If an archipelagic State does not designate sea lanes or air routes, the right of archipelagic sea lanes passage may be exercised through the routes normally used for international navigation." (Art. 53(12))

**617** UNCLOS Arts. 37−44.

Ultimately, both sides compromised and agreed to acknowledge the increased ocean jurisdiction of the littoral states, while implementing the new 'transit passage' regime guaranteeing the 'free passage and normal navigation' of ships and aircrafts for certain types of international straits.[618]

UNCLOS, in implementing 'transit passage' as a passage regime limits its application to certain types of straits. According to the Convention, transit passage applies to straits used for international navigation between a part of the high seas or an exclusive economic zone and the territorial sea of a foreign State. Seas where such passages are freely conducted, or in straits connecting two seas where the law of the high seas are applicable, the right of transit passage is guaranteed for military vessels and other non-commercial government vessels.[619] Additionally, transit passage refers to "the exercise of ⋯ the freedom of navigation and overflight solely for the purpose of continuous and expeditious transit of the strait" through the zones where transit passage is recognized. With regard to submarines, which under the innocent passage regime are required to navigate on the surface and to show their flag, there are different views as to whether submerged passage is permissible.[620]

---

618 Seok-Yong Lee, "Territorial Violation of North Korean Vessels and State Security," *Military Forum*, Vol.29, 2001, pp.143-145 (in Korean).

619 UNCLOS Arts. 37-38.

620 The reasoning behind the denial is as follows: 1) UNCLOS Art. 38(2) 'Freedom of navigation' does not absolutely include the right of underwater passage; 2) Article 39(1) (c) "normal mode of ⋯ transit" in

## 3) Legal Status of the Jeju Strait and the Passage Regime

Because of their strategic significance, Jeju and the Korea Straits raise a number of issues concerning the passage of foreign, especially military vessels. With a width of only 23.5 nm, Korea and Japan have both limited their territorial seas to three nm in the Korea Strait[621] thereby leaving a route for high seas passage in their respective exclusive economic zones(EEZ). For this reason the Korea Strait is not a strait to which transit passage, pursuant to Article 36 of UNCLOS, would apply. Instead, the traditional regime of innocent passage applies within the territorial waters of the two states; and freedom of passage for

---

itself cannot guarantee the underwater passage of submarines; 3) Provisions of Article 20 regarding territorial waters also apply to international straits that are part of territorial waters; 4) There are no provisions that clearly provide for 'underwater passage.' Young-Koo Kim, *Korea and International Law of the Sea*(1999), p.240 (in Korean). On the other hand, the basis for permitting this is as follows: 1) UNCLOS Art. 38(2) 'Freedom of navigation' certainly includes the right of underwater passage; 2) Article 39(1)(c) provides for restraint "from any activities other than those incident to their normal modes of continuous and expeditious transit unless rendered necessary by *force majeure* or by distress," in which case "normal mode of ⋯ transit" would be understood to be underwater for submarines; 3) It needs to be taken into consideration that Article 20, which provides for the passage on the surface for submarines, is included in Part II regarding territorial waters to which 'innocent passage' applies, and not Part III regulating international straits. *Id.*

621 Japan set its territorial sea width at 12 nm in May 1977 when legislating its Territorial Sea Law, but the width of the Korea Strait was limited to 3 nm just like the other four major straits. Korea similarly set the territorial sea width at 12 nm at the end of 1977 when legislating the Territorial Sea Law, but limited that of the Korea Strait to 3 nm.

the high seas or EEZ, applies for vessels and aircraft.

By contrast, the Jeju Strait, as stated earlier, is a strait formed by the Korean mainland and Jeju Island, falling entirely within the territorial waters of Korea. The geographical and hydro-graphical characteristic of the Jeju Strait give it a different international legal status.

Geographically, the Jeju Strait lies between the Korean mainland and the island of Jeju. The distance from Jeju's northernmost point to Haenam of Jeollanamdo on the Korean mainland is 47 nm. However, due to the straight baselines formed by the islets in between, the distance between Jeju's baselines and these straight baselines is less than 24 nm. Thus, the Jeju Strait in its entirety is included within the territorial waters of Korea. If the Jeju Strait had no other characteristic but was used for international navigation between one part of the high seas or EEZ to another part of the high seas or EEZ in the Yellow Sea, the East China Sea or the East Sea, it would be a strait in which transit passage would apply. However, because there is "a route through the high seas or through an EEZ of similar convenience," transit passage would not be applicable to the Jeju Strait.

In truth, there is no clear guideline as to what this "route through the high seas or through an EEZ of similar convenience" means or who determines the existence of such a route; therefore, there is much debate — and potential for dispute — regarding this issue.[622] The general opinion is that the Jeju Strait is a strait used for international navigation but has the navigational, hydrographical characteristic of "a route through the high seas or through an EEZ of similar convenience" at the same time.[623] Therefore, it is the regime of nonsuspendable innocent passage that applies in the Jeju Strait and not the transit passage regime of UNCLOS. It follows that in the Jeju Strait innocent passage applies only to vessels but not to the passage of aircraft in the airspace above the strait or to "submarines and other underwater vehicles [that] are required to navigate on the surface and to show their flag."[624] Further, as stated in UNCLOS "[t]here shall be no suspension of innocent passage through such straits."[625] The authors are of the opinion that this fact — that the regime of nonsuspendable innocent passage applies in the Jeju Strait and not transit passage — should be clearly indicated in the 1995 Law on Territorial & Adjacent Waters ('Territorial Sea Laws') of Korea[626] and their Enforcement Decree[627] in order to prevent unnecessary

---

622  Young–Hoon Kang, "Issues and Solutions to the Right of Innocent Passage," in Dal–Choong Kim ed., *supra* note 586, p.491 (in Korean); Young–Koo Kim, *supra* note 620, pp.232–233. Reference should be made to the Messina Straits, which is the basis of this provision.

623  Boo–Chan Kim, "Maritime Order in Northeast Asia and International Law," 1 *Journal of East Asia Studies*(1990), pp.43–45 (in Korean); Chan–Ho Park, *et al.*, *supra* note 610, p.165; Kang, *ibid.*, pp.482–491; Kim, *supra* note 620, pp.232–233. However, Japan is of the position that such 'passage of convenience' does not exist on the outer coast of Jeju Island and therefore the Jeju Strait is an international strait to which transit passage under UNCLOS applies. Kim, *supra* note 620.

624  UNCLOS Art. 20.

625  UNCLOS Art. 1(b).

626  Territorial Sea and Contiguous Zone Act, Act No. 3037(Dec. 31, 1977), Amended by Act No. 4986(Dec. 6, 1995).

debate or dispute.[628]

If the Jeju Strait is not subject to the transit passage regime, Korea must therefore guarantee the rights of nonsuspendable innocent passage for all foreign vessels, including the passage of foreign military vessels or non-commercial government vessels, pursuant to UNCLOS. However, this would give rise to discrepancies in the application of Article 5 of Korea's 1995 Territorial Sea Laws and Article 4 of the Enforcement Decree. According to UNCLOS all vessels, including military vessels, must be guaranteed innocent passage rights through the territorial waters of litttoral states. However, Article 5(1) of Korea's Territorial Sea Act requires foreign military vessels or government vessels of non-commercial purposes seeking to pass through its territorial waters, to give prior notice to the proper authorities in accordance with a Presidential Decree. Article 4 of the Enforcement Decree further provides that pursuant to Article 5(1), prior notice must be given to the Minister of Foreign Affairs three business days prior to its passage.

Innocent passage of foreign government vessels in the territorial waters of a State, including military vessels, is a right guaranteed by UNCLOS. The legality of a requiring prior notification or authorization can be assessed by the effect on the

---

627 Enforcement Decree of Territorial Sea and Contiguous Zone Act, Presidential Decree No. 9162(Sept. 20, 1978), Amended by Presidential Decree No. 17803(Dec. 18, 2002).

628 Kang, *supra* note 622, p.494.

right of passage of foreign vessels. The requirement of prior 'authorization' is based on the premise that passage can be denied, which is not the case under UNCLOS or customary international law. Prior 'notification,' on the other hand, seeks to allow passage on the condition of providing prior notification to the littoral State. Therefore, as long as the request for prior notification does not contradict international law, a state may regulate the activities of foreign vessels within its territorial waters, which includes the rights of littoral states to take actions to prevent non-innocent passage. As such, prior notification appears to be consistent with UNCLOS passage regimes.[629] There are other views, however, arguing that, Korea's Territorial Sea Act could be interpreted as placing Korea in the category of a state 'regulating' the passage of foreign vessels within its territorial waters. There would be no practical benefit to such categorization.[630]

Because the Jeju Strait is included in Korea's territorial waters, the very requirement of prior notification under Article 5 may be problematic. However, Article 4 of the Implementation Order, with regard to the passage of foreign military vessels, recognizes an exception to the prior notification requirement in cases where there is no area of high sea in the strait used for international navigation. Therefore, the effect of Article 4 that essentially

---

629 Kang, *ibid.*, pp.482–488.
630 Kim, *supra* note 620, pp.128–129.

eliminates prior notification in most cases in the Jeju Strait avoids any controversy regarding the implementation of the prior notification system.

### 4) Passage of North Korean Vessels through the Jeju Strait

Article 5 of Korea's Territorial Sea Act provides that foreign vessels that do not threaten the peace and order of the Republic of Korea(ROK) or its national security may pass through its territorial waters. This gives rise to the issue of whether North Korean vessels — military or non-commercial government vessels — have a right of innocent passage through ROK waters since North Korea is currently in a state of armistice with South Korea and would presumably constitute a threat to South Korea's national security. Furthermore, whether South Korea, on these same grounds, can refuse the innocent passage of any and all North Korean vessels?

This situation occurred in June 2001 when four North Korean merchant vessels entered the Jeju Strait. At the time, South Korea did not allow any North Korean vessels to enter its territorial and adjacent waters; thus, a South Korean naval corvette and patrol killer medium(PKM) demanded the immediate exit of these vessels. As the first attempt of such passage through the Jeju Strait since the armistice, this incident generated much debate regarding the legal status of the Jeju Strait and the adequacy of the government response.[631] South Korea had permitted innocent passage of other foreign vessels over the years but had prohibited North Korea from doing so pursuant to its rules of operation.[632] This practice lead to the view that innocent passage cannot apply to North Korea because the two countries are maintaining a ceasefire and technically are still at war.[633] However, there still has been much debate as to whether the ceasefire relationship should be interpreted to constitute a state of war rather than being at peace, and whether prohibition of passage should continue for both government and civilian vessels even though the ceasefire has continued since 1953.[634]

Since then, North and South Korea, with the purpose of materializing the spirit behind the June 15 Declaration,[635] agreed

---

[631] Seok-Yong Lee, *supra* note 618, pp.124-125.

[632] Hyun-Soo Kim, "Legal Analysis of the Issue of Passage in the Jeju Strait" (Paper presented at the 2003 Korean Society on Marine Environment & Safety Fall Conference) (2003), pp.40-44(On File with the Author) (in Korean); Jong-Pil Ha and Jong-Sam Park, "Study of the Territorial Sea Law for Rights & Interests in the Oceans and Logistics Cooperation" *Logistics Journal*, Vol.18, 2008, pp.258-267 (in Korean). On the other hand, there are views stating that because a ship's passage through the territorial sea or international strait of a foreign state is indispensable to international trade, even if North and South Korea were in the state of armistice, South Korea must guarantee innocent passage of the other state's vessels. If the 'innocence' could not be recognized with regard to a passage, it could only separately restrict the passage at issue. Stephen Kong, "The Right of Innocent Passage: a Case Study on Two Koreas," *Minnesota Journal of Global Trade*, Vol.11, 2002, pp.373-394.

[633] Seok-Yong Lee, *supra* note 618, p.150.

[634] *Ibid.*, p.151.

[635] The June 15 Declaration was a pronouncement of the agreement reached at the North-South Korean Summit on June 15, 2000 in the form of

to the 「Agreement on Maritime Transportation between North and South Koreas」 and its annexes at the 14th Ministerial Meeting in 2004, that would guarantee the operation of vessels in sea routes connecting Incheon, Gunsan, Yeosu, Busan, Ulsan, Pohang and Sokcho ports in the South and Nampo, Haeju, Goseong, Wonsan, Heungnam, Cheongjin and Najin ports of the North.[636] At the 15th Ministerial Meeting in June 2005, it was agreed that civilian vessels of the North could pass through the Jeju Strait; and in August, an 「Amendment and Supplement Agreement to implement and comply with the North and South Koreas Agreement on Maritime Transportation」 was reached that would add the Jeju Strait sea route to the previous Agreement on Maritime Transportation annexes.[637] In one sense, this shows that there has been a change in the perception of North Korea from that of an enemy state to a partner in cooperation and exchange.[638] Even so,

---

Joint Declaration. It included agreements on various issues i.e. autonomous unification between South and North, agreement concerning common ideas for unification, resolution of humanitarian issues such as reunion of separated families, economic cooperation and various exchanges, further talks between the two states, etc. *See* Keun-Sik Kim, "South-North Korean Summit and the June 15 Declaration; Analysis and Evaluation," *The Korean Association of North Korean Studies Bulletin*, Vol.10, 2006, pp.39-56 (in Korean).

[636] The agreement was concluded on 28 May 2004 and came into force on 1 August 2005.

[637] The agreement was concluded on 10 August 2005 and came into effect on 24 April 2006.

[638] Jong-Pil Ha and Jong-Sam Park, *supra* note 632, p.259. After the Agreement on Maritime Transportation between North and South Koreas entered in to effect, North Korean ships sailed through the South Korean

the exclusion of the issue of passage of North Korean military vessels and non-commercial government vessels show that the fundamental attitude has not changed.

As part of its May 24 response to North Korea's attack on the South Korean corvette Cheonan on March 26,[639] South Korea prohibited the entry of North Korean vessels into South Korean territorial and adjacent waters,[640] thereby returning to the pre-August 2005 situation prohibiting the operation of North Korean vessels.[641] As such, the Jeju Strait is an area where North-South Korean relations can easily and clearly be observed,

---

seas 2,165 times until June 2010. Among these, sail between South and North numbered 1,477 times, while passage of South Korean seas numbered 688 times. Ministry of Unification, Korea, *White Paper on Korean Unification*(2010), pp.92-93.

[639] On March 26, 2010, the South Korean corvette, Cheonan, tragically sank near the Northern Limit Line(NLL), the disputed maritime border between North and South Korea in the Yellow Sea on the South Korean side killing 46 sailors. Calling for a thorough investigation, the South Korean government commissioned the Joint Civilian-Military Investigation Group comprised of investigators from South Korea, the United States, Australia, the United Kingdom and the Kingdom of Sweden. On May 20, 2010 the group issued its final report and laid responsibility for the attack on Cheonan solely with North Korea. It concluded that the "'Cheonan' was sunk as the result of an external underwater explosion caused by a torpedo made in North Korea." *See* Investigation Result on the Sinking of ROKS 'Cheonan,' Ministry of Nat'l Def. (May 20, 2010), available at http://www.mnd.go.kr/web module/htsboard/template/read/engbdread.jsp?typeID=16&boardid=88&seqno=871&c=TITLE&t=&pagenum=3&tableName=ENGBASIC&pc=undefined&dc=&wc=&lu=&vu=&iu=&du=&st=. (last visited on 2013-06-17)

[640] *Chosun Ilbo*, May 24, 2010 ("Reason for Continued Shipping Agreement in the Midst of 'Prohibition of Passage'") (in Korean)

[641] *Ibid.*

playing an important role in South Korea's national security.

### 3. Legal Status and Significance of the Ieodo Waters[642]

#### 1) Location and Legal Status of Ieodo

Ieodo is situated at the center of the East China Sea, precisely at 125 degrees 10 minutes 57 seconds east longitude and 32 degrees 07 minutes 23 seconds north latitude. It is a 'submerged rock or reef,' the peak of which is 4.6 m below sea level, and lies 149 km (81 nm) southwest of Korea's Marado, 276 km (149 nm) west of Japan's Torishima and 245 km (133 nm) northeast of China's Tongdao.[643]

Ieodo is a major fishing ground in East China Sea. The convergence of the north bound Kuroshio current with the south bound cold current of the Yellow Sea, and the coastal waters of the Chinese mainland, has resulted in an rich habitat for various types of fish (e.g. mackerel, croacker, anchovy, bream, pollack, etc.).[644]

---

[642] *See* Boo-Chan Kim, "Maritime Jurisdiction in Northeast Asia and the Issue of Ieodo," in *Globalization Strategy of Jeju*(Onnuri, 2007), pp.318-350 (in Korean).

[643] Sang-Bok Han, "The Value of Parangdo from Oceanography Perspective," *Ocean Policy Research*, Vol.6, 1991, pp.461-463 (in Korean). Recently, China has changed its starting point from Tongdao to Sheshando in measuring its distance to Ieodo, thereby extending the distance to 155 nm(287 km). *Voice of Jeju*, September 16, 2008.

[644] Hong-Gil Noh, "Properties of the Waters Surrounding Socotra Reef in Terms of Fisheries," *Ocean Policy Research*, Vol.6, 1991, pp.475-492.

The ocean floor around Ieodo, furthermore, forms part of the continental shelf that is presumed to contain valuable mineral resources. Above sea level, it lies in the pathway of major typhoons, making it a key location for marine scientific research and meteorological observation *i. e.* changes in marine environment, as well as the establishment of bases for rescue operations and fisheries support. Lastly, the waters surrounding Ieodo have been recognized by states around the Northeast Asian seas not only as a major SLOC but also as a primary maritime zone for military and strategic activities.[645]

Ieodo is not an island as defined under Artcile 121(1) UNCLOS but a mere underwater reef. However, because the name Ieodo, early known as Parangdo, includes the Korean word 'do' or island, it is highly likely that those who do not know its reality can misconstrue it to be an actual island. Ieodo is marked as Socotra 'Rock' in international charts; however, even the word 'rock' under UNCLOS refers to a very small island which is always lying above sea level.[646] Thus, even the name Socotra Rock can lead to misconceptions regarding its true nature. Ieodo does not bear the

---

[645] Jae−Seol Shim, Gwang−Soon Park, and Dong−Yeong Lee, "Construction Analysis of the Ieodo Ocean Research Station," *Ocean Policy Research*, Vol.11, 1996, pp.408−413.

[646] Article 121 (1) of UNCLOS, to which Korea and China are both state parties, defines an 'island' as "a naturally formed area of land, surrounded by water, which is above water at high tide." Article 121 (3) of UNCLOS also provides that "Rocks which cannot sustain human habitation or economic life of their own shall have no exclusive economic zone or continental shelf."

status of an island or a rock under provisions of the UNCLOS. Therefore, any claim of sovereignty over Ieodo or efforts to make it a base point for establishing maritime jurisdiction zones i.e. territorial seas, EEZ and continental shelf, including expanding maritime jurisdiction, are without legal effect.[647]

## 2) Significance of the Ieodo Waters and the 'Ieodo Issue'

The Korean Government recognized the significance of Ieodo and the surrounding waters by constructing an Ocean Research Station which has been in operation since 2003.[648] The Ieodo Ocean Research Station is a fixed structure in Jacket form, located about 700 m south from Ieodo, and 41 m in depth. Its

---

[647] UNCLOS Art. 60(8). Lighthouses and other similar facilities installed at low-tide elevation are recognized as base points for drawing straight base lines. If the maritime facilities form an indivisible part of port facilities, it is no longer a separate maritime facility but rather a component of the coast affecting maritime delimitations. Thus, even if maritime facilities were to be installed on Ieodo, an underwater reef, it cannot be utilized as a base point for maritime boundary delimitation.

[648] The Ieodo Ocean Research Station was completed in 2003 and was first operated by the Korea Ocean Research & Development Institute(KORDI) due to concern for diplomatic friction with China and Japan. Jeju Maritime Management Division of the Busan Regional Maritime Affairs and Fisheries Office acquired various navigational aids installed at the station, e.g., visual aids(lighthouse), audible aids(horn), radio beacon, etc. and requisite power facilities and spare supplies from KORDI to begin operation on January 1, 2007. For the first time in four years following the construction of the Ocean Research Station, the Korean government was officially in charge of its management and operation. *Newsis*, November 28, 2006.

upper portion is approximately 1320 square meters, consisting of a cellar deck for equipment and facility installations, a main deck for living quarters and laboratories, and a helideck for rescue operations equipment and human transport.[649]

The Chinese Government in the years 2000 and 2002, raised objections through diplomatic channels concerning Korea's construction of the Ocean Research Station. And on September 14, 2006, during a Foreign Ministry briefing the Chinese Government stated that 'Suyanzao' (the Chinese name for Ieodo) was a reef situated where Korean and Chinese EEZs overlap and that any unilateral act of Korea on Ieodo would have no legal effect.[650] While on the one hand the Chinese representative stated that as an underwater reef there was no territorial sovereignty dispute between Korea and China over Ieodo, at the same time he also expressed the view that China wanted to settle maritime jurisdiction issues through dialogue.[651] Recently, in June and July 2011, China, in addition to making unreasonable demands for

---

649  Jae-Seol Shim, "Treasure Trove for Ocean Science: Ieodo," in *Ieodo: What Is It to Us Now?*(Proceedings for Policy Debate of Congressman Chang-Il Kang, 2007), pp.43-44(On File with the Author) (in Korean)

650  *The Hankyoreh*, Sept. 14, 2006 (in Korean).

651  Recently, China published in its official China Oceanic Information Network that Ieodo(Suyan Rock), which cannot be subject to the exercise of sovereignty, was part of its territory but soon withdrew its position. China appears to consider the Ieodo issue one concerning sovereignty, while a civic group by the name of Suyanzao Conservation Union claimed that Ieodo had traditionally been considered part of Chinese territory. *Yonhap News*, Aug. 7, 2008 (in Korean).

Korea to stop salvage activities undertaken by two Korean vessels southwest of Ieodo last April, also sent Chinese state vessels to the area.[652]

The authors are of the opinion that the 'Ieodo Problem' is not a 'sovereignty issue' under international law of the sea, nor is it a simple 'maritime jurisdiction issue.' China's actions in raising the Ieodo issue is a visible example of China's movement towards expanding its maritime jurisdiction in the East China Sea[653] In that sense, the Ieodo issue is not simply an international legal issue related to the law of the sea, but is also a complex international issue with international political implications in which China is unreasonably asserting its views in order to expand its influence in the Northeast Asian Seas. It is a potential issue that may possibly lead to acute confrontations and conflicts between Korea and China regarding the maritime order and security in the region.

---

652 Chang—Ryeol Lee, "Ieodo EEZ: Firm Action against China Necessary," *Dokdo Research Journal*, Vol.16, 2011, p.84 (in Korean).

653 Hyo—Baek Kang, "Maritime Boundary Delimitation Issue between Korea and China, with Focus on Ieodo," *Journal East Asian Affairs*, Vol.50, 2009, p.102; *Newsis*, in reporting the formation of Suyanzao Conservation Union in China as well as China's activities regarding Ieodo, has termed this movement the 'South Sea Project' following the 'Northeast Project,' *Newsis*, Nov. 28, 2006 (in Korean).

# IV. Peace and Marine Cooperation in Northeast Asia

## 1. Order in the Northeast Asian Seas and Changes in Marine Security Policy

### 1) Changes in the Order in the Northeast Asian Seas

The entry into effect of UNCLOS in 1994 brought many changes to the maritime legal order. UNCLOS allows the extension of territorial seas and adjacent zones up to 12 and 24 nm respectively, the continental shelf up to 350 nm, and extension of the EEZ up to 200 nm. In this manner, UNCLOS guarantees the quantitative and qualitative expansion of the maritime jurisdiction of littoral states. Maintaining the traditional principle of "freedom of the high seas" for the development and exploitation of high sea resources, the management and exploitation of the seabed and its minerals in the Area under Part XI is subject to the regime of the common heritage of mankind, and placed under the international management of the International Seabed Authority.[654] UNCLOS further created a maritime order with a compulsory dispute resolution system. The UNCLOS system, by expanding the jurisdictional reach of coastal States gave them greater access to marine resources.

Today, under UNCLOS, freedom of navigation of ships and

---

[654] UNCLOS Arts. 156-158.

aircraft in air space above in the high seas and EEZ is guaranteed. However, issues concerning freedom of military activities of foreign vessels in the EEZ of littoral states,[655] non-military issues such as the development and exploitation of marine resources, marine scientific research, and protection of the marine environment, are becoming sources of international maritime disputes. Furthermore, in the Northeast Asian Seas, there are many islands over which there are sovereignty disputes such as Japan's 'Four Northern Islands' (Etorohu, Kunashiri, Habomai, Shikotan), Diaoyutai (also known as the Senkaku Islands), and Dokdo, which in turn is causing an increase in diplomatic and military confrontations among the interested states.[656] The sovereignty issue over these islands alone has significant negative effects, not only on the peace and stability of Northeast Asia, but also in the creation of a stable maritime order and for the settlement of relevant disputes. Recently, there have been

---

655 Because there is no specific provision in the UNCLOS regarding military activities in the EEZ, the possibility or the legitimacy of military activities, e.g., naval mobilization drill, aircraft operations, military training, patrol acts, intelligence gathering, weapons test or launch, without the permission of the littoral states came under much debate. *See also* Hyun—Soo Kim, "Military Activities in the EEZ under Law of the Sea," *Ocean Law Research*, Vol.15, No.2, 2003, pp.225—240 (in Korean).

656 Kyu—Deok Hong, "Regional Disputes in East Asia," in Tae—Hyeon Kim ed., *Security Order in the New East Asia*(The Sejong Institute, 1997), p.93 (in Korean). As mentioned earlier, China's continuous raising of the issue and keeping watch over Ieodo — which is not an island but is highly valued for its significance — and the Ocean Research Station have been evidence of tensions between Korea and China.

many disputes in the Northeast Asian Seas regarding EEZ delimitation and fisheries jurisdiction, while confrontations regarding marine pollution and environmental conservation have also been emerging.[657]

## 2) Changes in Marine Security Policy of Northeast Asian States

Recently, threats to the maritime security of states around the Northeast Asian Seas that had been dormant are resurfacing. Amidst the continuing confrontation between Japan and China that has been continuing concerning the Senkaku Islands and the sinking of the Corvette Cheonan,[658] and the shelling of Yeonpyeong Island in 2010 between the two Koreas,[659] there has been a movement among states around the Korean Peninsula and the Northeast Asian Seas to establish strategies for strengthening national maritime security against actual and potential threats. There is an urgent need to form an international cooperation system and a regional common security system that would also secure the safety of SLOC.

---

657  *See also* Boo-Chan Kim, Jin-Ho Kim, and Seong-Joon Koh, "Dispute Resolution in the Northeast Asian Seas and Formation of Cooperative System," *New Asia*, Vol.8, No.2, 2001, pp.99-107 (in Korean).

658  *See, supra* note 639.

659  "North Korean Artillery Hits South Korean Island," *BBC*, Nov. 23, 2010, available at http://www.bbc.co.uk/news/world-asia-pacific-11818005 (last visited on 2013-06-17)

Meanwhile, in addition to the Proliferation Security Initiative (PSI) which seeks to prevent the proliferation of nuclear weapons and weapons of mass destruction(WMD),[660] the Container Security Initiative(CSI)[661] was implemented at the initiative of the U.S. Customs and Border Protection following the attack that took place on September 11, 2001 in the United States. In addition, the Convention for the Suppression of Unlawful Acts Against the Safety of Maritime Navigation(SUA Convention) of 1988 and 2005 was strengthened with a new Protocol, adopted in 2005,[662] that

---

[660] U.S. Department of State, Bureau of International Security and Nonproliferation, "Proliferation Security Initiative," available at www.state.gov/t/isn/c10390.htm. (last visited on 2013-06-17)

[661] CSI aims to protect world trade order and to secure the safety of the routes between the US and CSI ports by stationing teams of US officers from both CBP and Immigration and Customs Enforcement(ICE) in the major ports around the world to ensure all containers that pose a potential risk for terrorism are identified and inspected at foreign ports before they are placed on vessels destined for the United States. As of December 2010, CSI operates in 58 ports worldwide, in regions including North, Central, and South America; the Caribbean, Europe, Africa, the Middle East; and throughout Asia. Northeast states of Korea, China and Japan that are highly dependent upon trade with the US have been actively involved in CSI since its first implementation. Suk-kyoon Kim, "CSI & PSI," in Sea Lanes of Communication Study Group-Korea [SLOC-Korea] ed., *International Law of the Sea and Politics*(Oreum Publishers, 2011), pp.105-113 (in Korean).

[662] 'SUA Convention Regime' refers to a set of treaties adopted by the International Maritime Organization for the purpose of suppressing unlawful acts against the safety of maritime navigation and ensuring that appropriate action is taken against persons committing unlawful acts against ships. The regime includes the SUA Convention above, Protocol for the Suppression of Unlawful Acts against the Safety of Fixed Platforms Located on the Continental Shelf(hereinafter '1988 SUA Protocol'), and the 2005 SUA Convention and Protocol amending the 1988

is aimed to suppress acts of maritime terror threatening the safety of maritime navigation.[663]

Undoubtedly, the increasing sea power of the Northeast Asian states is a factor that has contributed to the current disputes over maritime jurisdiction and access to resources. One particular feature that stands out is while the sea power of the US, Russia, and other former maritime powers have been diminishing, those of regional powers such as China and Japan, as well as Korea and Taiwan, are becoming stronger. China, in particular, has been actively modernizing its navy to build an ocean-going navy.[664] The indicia of the strengthening of Northeast Asian sea power in China, Japan and other states in the region are: 1) emphasis in large scale and cutting edge technology as reflected in the 'Military Revolution Project;' 2) improvement and expansion of submarine powers; 3) expansion of fleet building by the states within the region.[665] Such increase in the sea power of Northeast Asian states is reflective of 'a shift in defense priorities'

---

Convention and Protocol. Yong-Hee Lee, "SUA Convention Regime," in SLOC-Korea ed., *id.*, pp.93-94 (in Korean). Korea became party to the 1988 SUA Convention and Protocol in 2003, but it has yet to become party to the 2005 SUA Convention and Protocol.

663  *Ibid.*, pp.93-103; Suk-Kyoon Kim, *supra* note 661, pp.105-113.

664  *See also* Soo-Jeong Choi, "Can the Modernization of the Chinese Navy Guarantee the Peace of East Asian Seas?," *Dokdo Research Journal*, Vol.16, 2011, pp.57-60 (in Korean).

665  Seo-Hang Lee, "Changes in the Northeast Asian Maritime Security and Future Development of the Korean Navy," *Military Forum*, Vol.29, 2001, pp.53-54 (in Korean).

emphasizing the importance of sea power at the global scale in the aftermath of the end of the Cold War.

The strengthening of sea power of Northeast Asian states reflects their awareness of the need to secure maritime deterrence and the attempt to limit the maritime activities of other states. For this reason competition for increased sea power is expected to become more conspicuous in relation to securing the safety of major international straits. Since the states in the region are highly dependent upon sea-borne trade, securing the safety of sea lanes is directly related to the transportation of goods, which is also directly connected to national economies and survival. Thus, as long as this interdependence is recognized, the states in the region will continue to strength of their sea power and maritime police force. However, if this heightened sea power capacity were to be mobilized within a limited area, this would increase the possibility of accidental confrontations resulting from misunderstandings or misjudgments. Furthermore, the expansion of naval activity for securing islands that are under dispute and for EEZ surveillance will also likely increase the probability of confrontation.[666]

---

[666] *Ibid.*, pp.55–56; *see also ibid.*, pp.47–53 for specific information regarding the increase of sea power.

## 2. Northeast Asian Sea Lanes Security and Marine Cooperation System/Regime

### 1) Introduction

Fundamentally, all states need adequate police and military power to protect their peace and security. The security of major Northeast Asian sea lanes, including the Jeju Strait, also requires adequate safety and security capacities.[667] Such sea power is absolutely necessary not only to secure the safety of straits and sea lanes and protect maritime sovereignty in times of war or crises, but also to effectively maintain maritime safety and prevent unlawful acts, such as piracy or illegal fishing. Only when a state can provide for its own maritime security can it then actively participate in multilateral cooperative systems.

An effective Northeast Asian maritime cooperative system must meet certain criteria in order to advance security and peaceful cooperation in the region. The need to construct a cooperation framework for maritime security in the region lies in the change in the international order since the post−Cold War era.[668] Unlike the Cold−War period, which was shaped by the confrontation of

---

667 The construction of the Jeju naval base has been progressing based on such a theory, but there currently is an aggressive, ongoing debate regarding its legitimacy and progress.

668 Young−Seon Ha, "New Northeast Asian Order and Formation of a Peaceful Regime," in Tae−Hyeon Kim ed., *supra* note 656, pp.187−210 (in Korean); Hyeok−Seob Lee, "Multilateral Security Agreement of Northeast Asia and Its Realization in the 21st Century," *Korean Journal of International Relations*, Vol.36, No.3, 1997, pp.194−197 (in Korean).

the two Super Powers with ideological differences, the post–Cold War international order is based on entirely different political dynamics. Other new issues and concerns have also emerged that have reduced the role of traditional military security in international politics. For example, the increase in transboundary issues such as the protection of the marine environment, since the collapse of the Cold War, have created the need for comprehensive transnational maritime cooperation rather than inter–State competition and confrontation.[669]

The concept that is gaining more attention today over 'joint security' is 'cooperative security.' Cooperative security refers to ending the confrontational relationship among the military regimes of each state and reaching security objectives through a cooperative relationship. The main thrust is in inducing a cooperative intervention of interested states not by physical threats or coercion but by an institutionalized process through consent. 'Cooperative security' differs from 'joint security' in that it actively pursues, for the prevention of war, institutionalized measures that have been consented to by all parties.[670]

Those emphasizing opportunistic factors assert that such a

---

669 Jin–Young Jeong, "Economic Cooperation and Regional Security in East Asia – Criticism of Insecurity of East Asia," in Tae–Hyeon Kim ed., *supra* note 656, pp.153–186 (in Korean); Suk–Joon Yoon, "National Sea Power and Maritime Strategy," in SLOC–Korea ed., *supra* note 661, pp.27–37 (in Korean).

670 Hyun–Gi Kim, "Possibility and Future of Maritime Cooperation in Northeast Asia," *Military Forum*, Vol.29, 2001, p.26 (in Korean).

change in the international order is also appearing in Northeast Asia — that military confrontation in the region has also weakened due to the end of the Cold War, replaced instead by economic and environmental factors. However, though the international environment in the post−Cold War era may have these positive impacts, there also are new sources of international conflict, together with uncertainties for the future. There are more complicated geopolitical factors at play in the Northeast Asian region compared to other regions. The competitive relationship among the four major powers surrounding Northeast Asia — the US, China, Japan, and Russia — is still very fierce and complicated; thus even the formation of mutual trust is difficult prior to an institutionalization of cooperation. Ironically, it is these very issues that have heightened the need for a maritime security cooperative regime.

## 2) Building a Northeast Asian Maritime Cooperation Regime

Clearly, to effectively protect and to secure maritime security in the sea lanes surrounding the Jeju Strait and Ieodo waters, Korea above all must be equipped with a sufficient level of sea power and an adequate maritime police force. Furthermore, a system allowing close, joint operations between the navy and the coast guard needs to be built.[671] As mentioned above, realizing

---

671 Ho−Seob Jeong, *supra* note 603, pp.219−220; Hyun−Gi Kim, "Korean Sea Power and the Changing Maritime Security," in Chun−Keun Lee ed.,

sea lane protection and maritime security by building a cooperative regime among the states of the Northeast Asian Seas is one viable approach.[672] In this regard, Korea should strengthen its cooperative activities not only with North Korea, Japan, China, and Russia but also with the coastal states of the Pacific, (*i.e.*, US and Canada), and be able to actively respond to changes in the international maritime order in order to elevate its stature as a maritime power.

The first step necessary in achieving the goal of sea lane security and maritime cooperation through such a regional, multilateral cooperative regime, is building mutual political and military trust among the states in the region.[673] However, diplomatic relations have yet to be established between North and South Korea, the US and North Korea, and Japan and North Korea. The formation of a relationship of trust between Korea and China through improving mutual understanding is also urgently needed. Ultimately, based on such a foundation can trust in military relations be possible upon which maritime cooperation can be built, transforming the Northeast Asian Seas, long known

---

*Maritime Disputes and Increasing Sea Power in East Asia*(KIMS, 1998), p.217 (in Korean).

672 Ho-Seob Jeong stated, "The Korean Navy must actively promote mutually beneficial exchange and cooperation with all the other navies in the region. In other words, it must cooperate with other navies in order to form 'a partnership for regional maritime security' that will effectively respond to various unlawful acts on the seas including terrorism, piracy, drug and weapons dealing." Jeong, *id.*, p.221.

673 Young-Seon Ha, *supra* note 668, pp.197-203.

as 'Sea of the Cold War,' into a 'Sea of Peace.'[674]

There is also a need to strengthen the regional cooperative regime regarding fisheries and other uses of the oceans in the East Sea, East China Sea, and the Yellow Sea that is surrounded by Korea, Japan, Taiwan, Russia, and North Korea. This area bears the characteristics of semi-enclosed seas and requires close regional cooperation in the management and distribution of resources, including biological resources.[675] Thus, there is an urgent need to further efforts toward establishing a system of regional cooperation in regard to baselines, maritime delimitation, marine scientific research, continental shelf, management of fishery resources, prevention of marine pollution and environmental protection, sea lane safety and protection, and maritime policy and dispute resolution.

The existing framework for fisheries in the Northeast Asian Seas is regulated by fishery agreements concluded between Korea,

---

674  *Ibid.*, p.201.

675  Hee-Chul Yang, "Current Issues with China," in SLOC-Korea, ed., *supra* note 661, p.324. With regard to this, the UNCLOS provided for the cooperation among states bordering enclosed or semi-enclosed seas, calling for their efforts to: (a) to coordinate the management, conservation, exploration, and exploitation of living resources of the sea; (b) to coordinate the implementation of their rights and duties with respect to the protection and preservation of the marine environment; (c) to coordinate their scientific research policies and undertake where appropriate joint programmes of scientific research in the area; (d) to invite, as appropriate, other interested States or international organizations to cooperate with them in furtherance of the provisions of this article. Art. 123.

China, and Japan. As a result, there are instances in which the establishment of areas, such as the waters south of the Jeju Island, overlaps with three independently concluded agreements, e.g., Korea—Japan Fisheries Agreement, Korea—China Fisheries Agreement, and the China—Japan Fisheries Agreement. There is also an urgent need to establish a joint management and regulatory framework among these three states.[676] Located at the center of the Northeast Asian Seas, Korea is greatly concerned with securing sea lane safety because of the variety of maritime challenges it faces. Therefore, it is important that Korean government fully appreciates the security and economic facets of maritime issues so that will not only seek to improve the maritime security environment, but also actively participate in the discussions to form a more secure maritime order in the region.

There are a number of a matters giving rise to potential conflict in the Northeast Asian Seas in relation to sovereignty over islands and securing sea lane safety. Thus, institutionalized options for peaceful mediation or resolution of maritime disputes and cooperation are necessary through regional dialogue among governments, such as through the ASEAN Regional Forum, the

---

[676] Moon—Sang Kwon, Yong—Hee Lee, and Seong—Wook Park, "Study of the EEZ Fisheries Management System among Korea, China and Japan and the New Fisheries Agreement," *Korean Journal of International Law*, Vol. 44, No. 1, 1999, pp. 1–17 (in Korean); Chan—Kyu Kim, Myung—Joon Noh, and Chang—Wee Lee, "Management of the Northeast Asian Fisheries Order following the Conclusion of Korea—Japan and Korea—China Fisheries Agreements," *Korean Journal of International Law*, Vol. 44, No. 1, 1999, p. 109 (in Korean).

Council for Security Cooperation in the Asia Pacific,[677] and the JEJU Forum[678] at the civilian level.[679]

# V. Conclusion

For Korea, which is surrounded by the sea on three sides, sea lane safety and the securing of passageways are necessary tasks for building economic power through foreign trade and securing sea power for national security. Situated at the center of the Northeast Asian Seas, the sea lane connecting Korea to the world is of very important value from an economic, military, and strategic perspective. More recently, intensified competition for maritime jurisdiction and marine resources among the Northeast Asian states together with island sovereignty disputes have made

---

677 The Council for Security Cooperation in the Asia Pacific(CSCAP) provides an informal mechanism for scholars, officials and others in their private capacities to discuss political and security issues and challenges facing the region. http://www.cscap.org (last visited on 2013-06-17)

678 Boo-Chan Kim, "Protection of Northeast Asian Sea Lanes and Jeju 'Island of Peace' Strategy," in *Globalization Strategy of Jeju, supra* note 642, pp.285-287 (in Korean).

679 Kyu-Deok Hong, *supra* note 656, pp.128-129; Jin-Hyun Paik, "Asia-Pacific Maritime Security Cooperation Challenge and Its Future," *International Area Studies*, Vol.8, No.3, 1999, pp.58-59 (in Korean); Gareth Evans and Paul Dibb, *Australian Paper on Political Proposals for Security Cooperation in the Asia-Pacific Region*(Department of Foreign Affairs and Trade and Strategic Studies Centre in Canberra, 1984), p.10.

the issues of maritime order and safety of sea lanes a vital concern, directly relevant to state survival, as well as to the peace and safety of the region.

With regard to the safety of Northeast Asian sea lanes, Korea has two straits — Korea Strait and Jeju Strait — that can be recognized for their strategic value. While the width of the Korea Strait is a mere 23.5 nm, Korea and Japan have both limited their territorial seas to 3 nm. Therefore, these waters include a passage route through the high seas or an EEZ and thus the potential for issues concerning the passage of military vessels or submarines is not very high. In contrast, the Jeju Strait can be distinguished geographically and hydrographically in that it is entirely included within the territorial waters of Korea, thereby having a different international legal status. Though the Jeju Strait itself is part of Korea's territorial waters, it connects parts of the high seas or EEZ, thereby giving it the status of an international strait. However, opinions are divided as to which passage regime is applicable to it under the law of the sea.

If the Jeju Strait is a 'normal' international strait utilized for international navigation between one part of the high seas or EEZ to another part of the high seas or EEZ in the Yellow Sea, the East China Sea or the East Sea, it would be an international strait to which transit passage would apply, which would significantly limit the scope of regulation and jurisdiction that could be exercised by Korea as its littoral state. Korea would also have to bear the burden of permitting right of flight over the area by foreign aircrafts. However, many agree that there exists "a route through the high seas or through an EEZ of similar convenience" beyond Jeju Island, making it an international strait to which 'innocent passage' rather than 'transit passage' which applies pursuant to Article 38(1) of the UNCLOS.

Thus, there is a need to clearly indicate this as such to prevent unnecessary conflict in the Territorial Sea Act and the Enforcement Decree, through specific provisions applicable to military vessels and submarines, that the Jeju Strait is a strait to which continuous, 'innocent passage' of ships is applicable. Passage of North Korean vessels is another issue requiring thorough evaluation, but there is a need to distinguish between military and non-commercial government vessels from civilian ships and to determine policies regarding their passage through Korean territorial waters such as the Jeju Strait based on clear theoretical foundations.

As for the Ieodo waters, if a hypothetical 'median line' is drawn between Korea and Japan, Ieodo lies much closer to Korea than China. Because there is no particular reason to rule out the 'median line' standard, Ieodo and its surrounding waters can be seen as belonging to the EEZ of Korea even before finalizing the boundary delimitation between Korea and China. Thus, Ieodo and the seabed of its surrounding waters become part of the Korean continental shelf or EEZ seabed which Korea can freely develop and exploit. China, however, is seeking to exercise rights equal to Korea in Korea's EEZ jurisdiction by claiming that the Ieodo waters are located in an area where both states can freely operate pursuant to the current Korea–China Fisheries Agreement. China is particularly interested, not only in the fishing issue but also in resource development in the EEZ and continental shelf; therefore, it has been continuously raising issues with Korea's installation and operation of the Ocean Research Station on Ieodo. In order to establish Korea's jurisdiction over Ieodo waters, as well as maritime security and order, there is a need to strengthen its international legal arguments against China and to devote its efforts to building a maritime cooperation system based on mutual benefits for both states.

The authors are of the opinion that in order for Korea to effectively protect the Northeast Asian SLOCs including the Jeju Strait and Ieodo waters, it must first of all secure a sufficient level of sea power and maintain an adequate maritime police force. At the same time, it ought to actively search out options to realize maritime security and sea lane protection issues through international maritime cooperation through strengthened exchange and cooperation with other states surrounding the Northeast Asian Seas such as Japan and China. It must strengthen international cooperation not only with Japan, China, Taiwan, and Russia, but also with the coastal states of the Pacific such as the US and Canada in order to prevent an escalation of sea power. It also needs to improve its diplomatic efforts and national power to actively participate in the establishment of a cooperative maritime security system in Northeast Asia.

# References

## Books

Amnesty International, *The International Criminal Court: Fundamental Principles Concerning the Elements of Genocide* (Amnesty International, 1999).

Anand, R. P., *Origin and Development of the Law of the Sea* (Martinus Nijhoff Publishers, 1983).

Barnett, Michael and Raymond Duvall, eds., *Power in Global Governance*(Cambridge: Cambridge University Press, 2008).

Broomhall, Bruce, *International Justice and the International Criminal Court* (Oxford University Press, 2003).

Bassiouni, M. Cherif, *Crimes Against Humanity under International Law* (Martinus Nijhoff, 1992).

Bennett, A. LeRoy & Oliver, James K., *International Organizations ― Principles and Issues ―*, 7th ed. (Prentice Hall, 2002).

Bertrand, Maurice & Warner, Daniel eds., *A New Charter for a Worldwide Organization* (Kluwer Law International, 1997).

Breau, Susan, *The Responsibility to Protect in International Law: An Emerging Parddigm Shift*(London & New York: Routledge, 2016).

Brown, Chris, *Sovereignty, Rights and Justice: International Political Theory Today* (Polity Press, 2002).

Brown, E. D., *The Area Beyond the Limits of National Jurisdiction* (Graham & Trotman, 1986).

Brownlie, Ian, *Principles of Public International Law, 5th ed.* (Oxford University Press, 1999.

Brus, M., Muller, S. & Wiemers, Serv eds., *The United Nations Decade of International Law* (Martinus Nijhoff Publishers, 1991).

Bryant, Robert D., *A World Rule of Law, A Way to Peace* (R & E Research Associates, Inc., 1977).

Buchholz, Hanns J., *Law of the Sea Zones in the Pacific Ocean* (the Southeast Asian Studies, 1987).

Buergenthal, Thomas & Maier, Harold G., *Public International Law* (West Publishing Co., 1990).

Byers M. ed., *The Role of Law in International Politics* (Oxford University Press, 2001).

Cassese, Antonio, *International Law in a Divided World* (Clarendon Press, 1986).

_____, *International Law*, 2$^{nd}$ ed, (Oxford: Oxford University Press, 2005).

Chanrney, Jonathan I., *The New Nationalism and the Use of Common Spaces* (Osmun Publishers, 1982).

Chen, Lung-chu, *An Introduction to Contemporary International Law* (Yale University Press, 1989).

Childers, Erskine with Urquhart, Brian, *Renewing the United Nations System* (Ford Foundation & Dag Hammarskjold Foundation, 1994).

Chung, In Seop, *The Legal Status of Ethnic Koreans in Japan* (Seoul National University Press, 1996).

Churchill, R. R., & Lowe, A. V., *The Law of the Sea* (Manchester University Press, 1983).

Collier, John & Lowe, Vaughan, *The Settlement of Disputes in International Law — Institutions and Procedures —*(Oxford University Press, 1999).

Cunningham, Robert L. ed., *Liberty and the Rule of Law* (Texas A&M University Press, 1979).

De Hoogh, Andre, *Obligations Erga Omnes and International Crimes: A Theoretical Inquiry into the Implementation and Enforcement of the International Responsibility of States* (Springer, 1996).

De Waart, Paul, Peters & Denters, Erik, *International Law and Development* (Martinus Nijhoff Publishers, 1988).

De Lupis, Ingrid Detter, *The Concept of International Law* (Norstedts Verlag, 1987).

Dixon, Martin, *Text on International Law* (Blackstone Press Ltd., 1990).

Eriksen, Christoffer C. and Marius Emberland eds., *The New International Law: An Anthology*(Leiden · Boston: Martinus Nijhoff publishers, 2010).

Evans, Gareth and Paul Dibb, *Australian Paper on Political Proposals for Security Cooperation in the Asia—Pacific Region* (Department of Foreign Affairs and Trade and Strategic Studies Centre in Canberra, 1984).

_____, *The Responsibility to Protect: Ending Mass Atrocity Crimes Once and For All*(Washington, D.C.: Brookings Institution Press, 2008).

Falk, Richard, *Revitalizing International Law*(Ames: Iowa State University Press, 1989).

Fisas, Vicence, *Blue Geopolitics — the United Nations Reform and the Future of the Blue Helmets —*(Pluto Press with Transnational

Institute(TNI), 1995).

Fox Gregory H. & Roth, Brad R. eds., *Democratic Governance and International Law* (Cambridge University Press, 2000).

Friedmann, Wolfgang, *The Changing Structure of International Law*(New York: Columbia University Press, 1964).

Grewe, Wilhelm G., transl. and rev. by Michael Byers, *The Epochs of International Law*(Berin · New York: Walter de Gruyter, 2000).

Hall, R. Bruce & Biersteker, Thomas J. eds., *The Emergence of Private Authority in Global Governance* (Cambridge University Press, 2002).

Hashimoto, C., *The Japanese Constitution* (Yuhikaku, 1990).

Hayek, Friedrich A., *The Road to Serfdom* (University of Chicago Press, 1944).

Hays, Michael & Morgante, Amy, eds., *A People's Response To OUR GLOBAL NEIGHBORHOOD: Dialogues on the Report of the Commission on Global Governance* (Boston Research Center for the 21st Century, 1995).

Henderson, Conway W., *Understanding International Law*(Chichester: John Willey & Sons, 2010).

Henkin, Louis, *How Nations Behave: Law and Foreign Policy*, 2nd ed.(Columbia University Press, 1979).

_____ *et al., Human Rights* (Foundation Press, 1999).

Higgins, Rosalyn, *Problems and Process: International Law and How We Use It* (Oxford University Press, 1994).

Hong, Seong Bang, *Constitutional Law* (Hyeonamsa, 2003).

Hur, Yeong, *Korean Constitution* (Pakyoungsa, 1999).

Hutchinson, Allan C. & Monahan, Patrick eds., *The Rule of Law —*

*Ideal or Ideology* ─(Carswell, 1987).

International Commission of Jurists, *The Rule of Law and Human Rights ─ Principles and Definitions* ─(Geneva, 1966).

Iriye, Akira, *Global Community ─ The Role of International Organizations in the Making of the Contemporary World* ─(University of California Press, 2002).

Itoh, M., *The Constitution* (Kobundo, 1990).

Jakubowski, Andrzej and Karolina Wierczyńska, eds., *Fragmentation vs the Constitutionalization of International Law: A Practical Inquiry*(London and New York: Routledge, 2016).

Jasentuliyana, Nandasiri, ed., *Perspectives on International law* (London · The Hague · Boston: Kluwer Law International, 1995).

Joyner, Christopher C. ed., *The United Nations and International Law* (Cambridge University Press, 1997).

Kamminga, Menno T. & Martin Scheinen, eds., *The Impact of Human Rights Law on General International Law*(Oxford: Oxford University Press, 2009).

Karen, Margaret P. & Mingst, Karen A., *International Organizations: The Politics and Processes of Global Governance* (Lynne Rienner Publishers, 2004).

Kim, Boo Chan, *Special Lectures on International Law*(BoGoSa, 2014).

_____, *Special Lectures on International Law*, revised edition(BoGoSa, 2018).

_____, *Global Governance and International Law: Some Global and Regional Issues*(BoGoSa, 2011).

Kim, Cheong Geon, *International Law* (Pakyoungsa, 1998).

Kim, Cheol Su, *Introduction to Constitutional Law* (Pakyoungsa,

2001).

Kim, Dae Sun, *International Law*, 11th ed. (Samyoungsa, 2006).

Klabbers, Jan, *International Law*(Cambridge: Cambridge University Press, 2013).

Klabbers, Jan, Anne Peters, and Geir Ulfstein, *The Constitutionalization of International Law*(Oxford: Oxford University Press, 2011).

Köchler, Hans, *Democracy and the International Rule of Law* (Springer-Verlag, 1995).

Krasner, Stephen D., *Sovereignty ― Organized Hypocrisy ―* (Princeton and New York: Princeton University Press, 1999).

Ku, Charlotte & Weiss, Thomas G. eds., *Toward Understanding Global Governance: The International Law and International Relations Toolbox ― ACUNS Reports and Papers, 1998 No.2―* (ACUNS, 1998).

Ku, Charlotte, *International law, International Relations and Global Governance*(London and New York: Routledge, 2012).

Kuhn, Thomas, *The Structure of Scientific Revolutions*, 2nd. ed.(Chicago: University of Chicago Press, 1970).

_____, *The Structure of Scientific Revolutions with An Introductory Essay by Ian Hacking*, 50th Anniversary Edition(Chicago and London: The University of Chicago Press, 2012).

Kunugi, T., Iokibe, M., Shinyo, T. & Hashimoto, K., *Towards a More Effective UN* (PHP Research Institute, 1996).

Kwon, Yeong Seong, *Introduction to the Study of Constitutional Law* (Bobmunsa, 2006).

Larson, Arthur, *The International Rule of Law* (Institute for International Order, 1961).

Lee, Chang Hee ed., *International Law Issues Between Korea and Japan* (Asayeon, 1998).

Lee, Ho Yong, ed., *Toward Legislation Granting Voting Rights to Permanent Residents* (Ministry of Justice Office of Legal Counsel, 2000).

Lee, Kwang Gyu, *Koreans in Japan* (Iljogak, 1993).

Levi, Werner, *Contemporary International Law: A Concise Introduction* (Westview Press, 1979).

Lillich, R. B., *The Human Rights of Aliens in Contemporary International Law* (Manchester University Press, 1984).

Luard, Evan, rev. by Heater, Derek, *The United Nations: How It Works and What It Does?* (St. Martin's Press, 1979).

Lyons, Gene M. and Michael Mastanduno, eds., *Beyond Westphalia? — State Sovereignty and International Intervention*(Baltimore and london: The Johns Hopkins University Press, 1995).

Malanczuk, Peter, *Akehurst's Modern Introduction to International Law*, 7th ed. (Routledge, 1997).

Merrills, J. G., *International Dispute Settlement* (Sweet & Maxwell, 1984).

Meron, Thedor, *The Humanization of International Law*(Leiden and Boston: Martinus Nijhoff Publishers, 2006).

Miller, Joachim W., *The Reform of the United Nations*(Oceana, 1992).

Ministry of Unification, Korea, *White Paper on Korean Unification*, 2010.

Mosler, Hermann, *The International Society as a Legal Community* (Alphen aan Rijn and Germantown: Sijthoff & Noordhoff, 1980).

Nardin, Terry, *Law, Morality, and the Relations of States*(Princeton

University Press, 1983).

Neumann, Franz, *The Rule of Law* (Berg Publishers, 1986).

Neumann, Michael, *The Rule of Law* (Ashgate Pub. Ltd., 2002).

Onuma, Y., *Overcoming the Myth of an Ethnically Homogeneous Nation: Ethnic Koreans in Japan and the Japanese Immigration Control System* (Tosindo, 1986).

Osmañczyk, Edmand J., *Encyclopedia of the United Nations and International Agreements* (Taylor & Francis Inc., 1985).

Ott, David H., *Public International Law in the Modern World* (Pitman Publishing, 1987).

Pak, Chi Young, *The Korea Strait* (Martinus Nijhof Publishers, 1983).

Parlett, Kate, *The Individual in the International Legal System: Continuity and Changd in International Law*(Cambridge: Cambridge University Press, 2011).

Park, Choon-ho, *East Asia and the Law of the Sea* (Seoul National University Press, 1983).

Park, Il Kyeong, *A New Constitution* (Beokyeong Publishing, 1990).

Proukaki, Elena Katselli, *The Problem of Enforcement of International Law: Counter-measures, the non-injured state and the idea of international community*(London and New York: Routledge, 2010).

Reid, John Phillip, *Rule of Law* (Northern Illinois University Press, 2004).

Rosenau, James N. & Czempiel, Ernst-Otto eds., *Governance Without Government: Order and Change in World Politics* (Cambridge University Press, 1995).

Sanger, Clyde, *Ordering the Oceans — the Making of the Law of the*

*Sea* ─(University of Toronto Press, 1987).

Schabas, William A., *An Introduction to the International Criminal Court*, 2nd ed. (Cambridge University Press, 2004).

Shapiro, Ian ed., *The Rule of Law* (New York University Press, 1994).

Simai, Mihaly, *The Future of Global Governance* (United States Institute of Peace Press, 1994).

Slaughter, Anne-Marie, *A New World Order*(Princeton and Oxford: Princeton University Press, 2009).

Slomanson, William R., *Fundamental Perspectives on International Law*, 3rd. ed. (Wadsworth/Thomson Learning, 2000).

Smith, Rhona K. M., *Textbook on International Human Rights*, 3rd ed. (Oxford University Press, 2007).

Sohn, Louis B. & Kristen Gustafson, *The Law of the Sea* (West Publishing Co., 1984).

South Centre, *For a Strong and Democratic United Nations: a South Perspective on UN Reform* (South Centre, 1996).

Stassen, Harold, *United Nations ─ A Working Paper for Restructuring* ─(Lerner Publications Company, 1994).

Sunga, Lyal S., *Individual Responsibility in International Law for Serious Human Rights Violations* (Springer, 1992).

Tabata, M., *Lectures on International Law I* (Yushindo, 1984).

Tamanaha, Brian Z., *On the Rule of Law: History, Politics, Theory* (Cmabridge: Cambridge University Press, 2004).

The Commission on Global Governance, *Our Global Neighborhood* (Oxford University Press, 1995).

_____, *Issues in Global Governance: Papers written for the Commission on Global*

*Governance* (Kluwer Law International, 1995).

The United Nations, *Basic Facts about the United Nations* (The United Nations, 1995).

The United Nations Commission on Improving the Effectiveness of the United Nations, *Defining Purpose: the U.N. and the Health of Nations* (US Commission, 1993).

The UN Non-Governmental Liaison Service(NGLS), *The United Nations, NGOs and Global Governance: Challenges for the 21st Century* (NGLS, 1996).

Thomas G. Weiss and Ramesh Thakur, *Global Governance and the UN: Unfinished Journey*(Bloomington and Indianapolis: Indiana University Press, 2010).

Trachtman, Joel. P., *The Future of International Law — Global Government* —(Cambridge University Press, 2013).

Tung, William L., *International Law in an Organizing World* (Thomas Y. Crowell Company, 1968).

Walker, Geoffrey de Q., *The Rule of Law* (Melbourne University Press, 1988).

Weiss, Thomas G. *et al.*, *The United Nations and Changing World Politics* (Westview Press, 1994).

Yee, Sienho and Wang Tieya, eds., *International Law in the Post-Cold War World: Essays in Memory of Li Haopei*(London and New York: Routledge, 2001).

Yi, Taejin *et al.*, *International Legal Issues in Korea-Japan Relations* (Northeast Asian History Foundation, 2008).

## Articles

Adede, A. O., "Settlement of Disputes Arising Under the Law of the Sea Convention," *American Journal of International Law*, Vol.69, 1975.

Akaha, Tsuneo, "From Conflict to Cooperation: Fishery Relations in the Sea of Japan," *Pacific Lim Law and Policy Journal*, Vol.1, Summer, 1992.

Allot, Philip, "The Emerging Universal Legal System," *International law Forum du Droit International*, Vol.3, 2001.

Altwicker, Tilmann and Oliver Diggelmann, "How is Progress Constructed in International Legal Scholarship?," *The European Journal of International Law*, Vol.25, No.2.

Bae, Hyeong Soo, "Development of National Sea Power and the Protection of SLOCs," in *Maritime Policy Symposium Proceedings*, 2006.

Barnett, Michael and Raymond Duvall, "Power in Global Governance," in Michael Barnett and Raymond Duvall, eds., *Power in Global Governance*(Cambridge: Cambridge University Press, 2008).

Bassiouni, M. Cherif, "Universal Jurisdiction for International Crimes: Historical Perspectives and Contemporary Practice," *Vanderbilt Journal of Int'l Law*, Vol.42, 2001.

Bernhardt, Rudolf, "Law of the Sea, Settlement of Disputes," Bernhardt R. ed., *Encyclopedia of Public International Law*, Installment 1, 1981.

Bishop, William W., "The International Rule of Law," *Michigan Law Review*, Vol.59, 1961.

Bottini, Gabriel, "Universal Jurisdiction After the Creation of the International Criminal Court," *N.Y.U. Journal of Int'l Law & Policy*, Vol.36, 2004.

Brand, Ronald A., "The Role of International Law in the Twenty-First Century: External Sovereignty and International Law," *Fordham International Law Journal*, Vol.18, 1995.

Cha, Young-Koo, "A Korean Perspective on the Security of the Sea Lanes in East Asia," in Lau Teik Soon & Lee Lai To, eds., *The Security of The Sea Lanes In The Asia-Pacific Region*(Heinemann Asia, 1988).

Charney, Jonathan I., "Universal International Law," *American Journal of International Law*, Vol.87, 1993.

_____, "Entry into Force of the 1982 Convention on the Law of the Sea," *Virginia Journal of International Law*, Vol.35, Winter, 1995.

_____, "The Role of IGOs in Global Governance," Ku, Charlotte & Weiss, Thomas G. eds., *Toward Understanding Global Governance* (Academic Council on the UN System, 1998).

Chesterman, Simon, "An International Rule of Law?," *American Journal of Comparative Law*, Vol.56, 2008.

Chinkin, Christine, "Human Rights and the Politics of Presentation: Is there a Role for International Law," Byers M. ed., *The Role of Law in International Politics* (Oxford University Press, 2001).

Cho, Sang Gyun, "The Legal Status of Ethnic Koreans in Japan," *Korea Journal of Northeast Asian Studies*, Vol.33, 2004.

Choi, Soo Jeong, "Can the Modernization of the Chinese Navy Guarantee the Peace of East Asian Seas?," *Dokdo Research Journal*, Vol. 16, 2011.

Choi, Yeong Ho, "Ethnic Koreans In Japan and Their Response to the Changing Landscape of Right of Political Participation in Post War Japan," *Journal of Korea Political Science Association*, Vol.34, No.1, 2000.

Choi, Yeong Ho, "Ethnic Koreans' Rights of Participation in Local Politics: The Korean and Japanese Views," *Yongsan Collective Paper Series*, Vol.7, Youngsan University, 2001.

Choi, Tae-Hyun, "An Analysis on the Nature and Function of the International Rule of Law," *Dong-A Law Review*, No.43, 2009.

Claude, Inis L., Jr., "Peace and Security: Prospective Roles for the Two United Nations," *Global Governance*, Vol.2, No.3, 1996.

Colangelo, Anthony J., "The New Universal Jurisdiction: In Absentia Signaling Over Clearly Defined Crime," *Georgia Journal of Int'l Law*, Vol.36, 2005.

Coquia, Jorge R., "Settlement of Disputes in the UN Convention on the Law of the Sea," *Indian Journal of International Law*, Vol.25, No.2, 1985.

D'Amato, Anthony, "Is International Law Really 'Law'?," *Northwestern University Law Review*, Vol.79, 1984.

Delbruck, Jost, "A More Effective International Law or a New 'World Law'? — Some of the Development of International Law in a Changing International System," *Indiana Law Journal*, Vol.68, 1993.

Ettari, Samantha V., "A Foundation of Granite or Sand? The International Criminal Court and United States Bilateral Immunity Agreement," *Brooklyn Journal of Int'l Law*, Vol.30, 2004.

Evans, Gareth, "The Responsibility to Protect: Rethinking Humanitarian Intervention," *American Journal of International Law*, Vol.98, No.1, 2004.

Falk, Richard A., "The United Nations and the Rule of Law," *Transnational Law & Contemporary Problems*, Vol.4, 1994.

Feller, S. Z., "Jurisdiction over Offenses with a Foreign Element,"

Bassiouni, M. Cherif & Nanda, Ved P., eds., *A Treatise on International Criminal Law: Jurisdiction and Cooperations* (Thomas, 1973).

Fox, Gregory H., "New Approaches to International Human Rights," Hashmi, Sohail H. & Hashmi, Schail H. eds., *State Sovereignty: Change and Persistence in International Relations* (Pennsylvania State University Press, 1997).

Frakes, Jennifer, "The Common Heritage of Mankind Principle and the Deep Seabed, Outer Space, and the Antarctica: Will Developed and Developing Nations Reach a compromise?," *Wisconsin International Law Journal*, Vol.21.

Frank, Thomas M. & El−Baradei, Mohamed, "Current Development: The Codification and Progressive Development of International Law: A UNITAR Study of the Role and Use of the International Law Commission," *American Journal of International Law*, Vol.76, 1982.

Gamble, John King, Jr., "The 1982 UN Convention on the Law of the Sea: Binding Dispute Settlement?," *Boston University International Law Journal*, Vol.9, Spring, 1991.

Glen, P., "Paradigm Shifts in International Justice and the Duty to Protect: in Search of an Action Principle," *University of Botswana Law Journal*, Vol. 11, 2010.

Ha, Jong Pil and Jong Sam Park, "Study of the Territorial Sea Law for Rights & Interests in the Oceans and Logistics Cooperation," *Logistics Journal*, Vol. 18, 2008.

Han, Sang Bok, "The Value of Parangdo from Oceanography Perspective," *Ocean Policy Research*, Vol 6, 1991.

Held, David, "Democracy and Globalization," *Global Governance*, Vol.3, No.3, 1997.

Hernandez-Truyol, Berta Esperanza, "The Rule of Law and Human Right," *Florida Journal of Int'l Law*, Vol.16, 2004.

Higgins, R., "The General International Law of Terrorism and International Law," Higgins, R. & Flory, M. eds., *Terrorism and International Law* (Routledge, 1997).

Hirssh, Joachim, "The Democratic Potential of Non-Governmental Organizations," Cho, Hee-Yeon & Hirsch, Joachim eds., *The State and NGOs in the Context of Globalization* (Hanul Publishing Co., 20021).

Hong, Kyu Deok, "Regional Disputes in East Asia," in Tae-Hyeon Kim, ed., *Security Order in the New East Asia*(The Sejong Institute, 1997).

Horowitz, Jodi, "Regina v. Bartle and the Commissioner of Police for the Metropolis and Others *Ex Parte* Pinochet: Universal Jurisdiction and Sovereign Immunity for *Jus Cogens* Violations," *Fordham Int'l Law Journal*, Vol.23, 1999.

Hosaka, Y., "The Japanese Permanent Resident Aliens Policy and Koreans in Japan," *Journal of Korean Studies*, No.11, 2003.

_____, "The Legal Status of Koreans Residing in Japan: Review of Recent Amendments to the Nationality Law and Immigration Law," *Journal of Peace Studies*, Vol.8, No.1, Korea University, 2000.

Jackson, Schuyler W., "The Rule of Law Among Nations," MacDonald, H. Malcolm *et al.* eds., *The Rule of Law* (Southern Methodist University Press, 1961).

Janis, Mark W., "Dispute Settlement in the Law of the Sea Convention: The Military Activities Exception," *Ocean Development and International Law Journal*, Vol.4, No.1, 1977.

Jeong, Ho Seob, "Korea's Sea Lane Security Strategy," in *Sea Lane*

*Security of East Asia* (Korea Institute for Maritime Strategy(KIMS), 2007).

Jhe, Seong Ho, "Some Delimitation Issues in the Maritime Areas Surrounding the Korean Peninsular," *Ocean Policy Research*, Vol.11, No.1, Summer, 1996.

Johansen, Robert C., "Reforming the United Nations to Eliminate War," *Transnational Law & Contemporary Problems*, Vol.4, 1994.

Johnson, "Straits," in R. Bernhardt(ed.), *Encyclopedia of Public International Law*, Vol. Ⅳ, 2000.

Jordan, Jon B., "Universal Jurisdiction in a Dangerous World: A Weapon for All Nations Against International Crime," *MSU-DCL Journal of Int'l Law*, Vol.9, 2000.

Kamminga, Menno T., "Final Report on the Impact of Internatioanl Human Rights Law on General International Law," in Menno T. Kamminga & Martin Scheinen, eds., *The Impact of Human Rights Law on General International Law*(Oxford: Oxford University Press, 2009).

Kang, Hyo Baek, "Maritime Boundary Delimitation Issue between Korea and China with Focus on Ieodo," *Journal of East Asian Affairs*, Vol. 50, 2009.

Kim, Boo Chan, "Maritime Order in Northeast Asia and International Law," *Journal of East Asia Studies*, Vol. 1, 1990.

＿＿＿＿＿＿, "New Trends in International Law and the Common Heritage of Mankind," *Korean Journal of International Law*, Vol.40, No.1, 1995.

＿＿＿＿＿＿, "The United Nations and the International Rule of Law," *Korean Yearbook of International Law*, Vol.1, 1997.

＿＿＿＿＿＿, "The Rights of Minority under International Law," *Journal of East Asian Studies*, Vol.8, Jeju National University,

1997.

Kim, Boo Chan, "The System for Dispute Settlement in the Law of the Sea and Korean Perspective," *Korean Yearbook of International Law*, Vol.2, 1998.

_____, "Global Governance and the International Rule of Law," *Korean Journal of International Law*, Vol.45, No.2, 2000.

_____, "The Right of Diplomatic Protection," *Ministry of Foreign Affairs and Trade Research Report*, 2001.

_____, "The Legal Status of Korean Residents in Japan — focusing on Political Rights at a local level —," *Local Government Law Journal*, Vol.2, No.2, 2002.

_____, "Global Governance and International Non-Governmental Organizations," *Korean International Law Review*, Vol.20, 2004.

_____, "Maritime Jurisdiction in Northeast Asia and the Issue of Ieodo," in *Globalization Strategy of Jeju*(Onnuri, 2007).

_____, "Political Rights of Koreans in Japan at a Local Level," *International Legal Issues in Korea-Japan Relations* (Northeast Asian History Foundation, 2008).

_____, "An Introduction to the Study on the Humanization of International Law: Focusing on its Background and Trend," *Korean Journal of International Law*, Vol.59, No.4, 2014.

_____, "The Evolution of International Community and the Role of the United Nations," *Ajou Law Review*, Vol.10, No.2, 2016.

_____, "The Changing Structure and Paradigm Shift in International Law," *The Korean Journal of International Law*, Vol.63, No.4, 2018.

Kim, Boo Chan, Jin-Ho Kim and Seong-Joon Koh, "Dispute Resolution in the Northeast Asian Seas and Formation of Cooperative System," *New Asia,* Vol.8, No.2, 2001.

_____ and Seung Jin Oh, "The International Rule of Law and Universal Jurisdiction," *Korean Journal of International Law,* Vol.51, No.1, 2006.

_____ and Seok Woo Lee, "Protection of the Sea Lanes in the Jeju Waters and Maritime Cooperation in Northeast Asia," David D. Caron and Nilufer Oral eds., *Navigating Straits: Challenges for International Law*(Brill/Nijhoff,2014).

Kim, Chan Kyu, Myung Joon Noh, and Chang Wee Lee, "Management of the Northeast Asian Fisheries Order following the Conclusion of Korea-Japan and Korea-China Fisheries Agreements," *Korean Journal of International Law,* Vol.44, No.1, 1999.

Kim, Cheong Geon, "Toward An Identity for Koreans in Japan," *Journal of Northeast Asian Studies,* Vol.33, 2004.

Kim, Dal Choong, "Study of the Korean Sea Lane Safety," *Academic Journal of National Defense,* Vol. 2, 1989.

Kim, Hee Gon, "Foreign Residents' Rights to Participate in Local Politics," *Journal of Public Land Law Studies,* Vol.7, 1999.

Kim, Hee Jeong, "Voting Rights for Permanent Resident Aliens: Its Validity and Current Practice,"(http://www.mission-magazine. com)

Kim, Hyun Gi, "Korea's Sea Lane Safety and Sea Power," in Hyun-Gi Kim, ed., *State Economy and Maritime Security*(Korea Institute for Maritime Strategy(KIMS), 1999).

_____, "Korean Sea Power and the Changing Maritime Security," in Chun-Keun Lee, ed., *Maritime Disputes and Increasing Sea Power in East Asia*(KIMS, 1998).

Kim, Suk Kyoon, "CSI & PSI," in Sea Lanes of Communication Study Group—Korea [SLOC—Korea, ed., *International Law of the Sea and Politics*(Oreum Publishers, 2011).

Kim, Jong Min, "Issue of Korea's Sea Lane Protection," in *Maritime Strategy*, Vol. 85, 1994.

Kim, Keun Sik, "South—North Korean Summit and the June 15 Declaration: Analysis and Evaluation," *The Korean Association of North Korean Studies Bulletin*, Vol. 10, 2006.

Kim, Kyeong Deuk, "The Amendment of Nationality Law and Koreans in Japan," *Seoul International Law Journal*, Vol.4, No.2, 1997.

Kim, Kyeong Deuk, "The Overseas Koreans Act From the Perspective of Koreans in Japan and Future Directions," *Korea—Japan Ethnic Studies*, No.5, 2003.

_____, "The Question of Citizenship for Ethnic Koreans in Japan and Their Right of Participation in Local Politics," (*Seoul National University School of Law Center for Public Interest and Human Rights Law*; http://jus.snu.ac.kr/~bk21).

Kim, Seong Ho, "The Local Political Rights of Korean Residents in Japan: Current Status and Outlook," *Journal of Peace Studies*, Vol.8, No.1, Korea University, 2000.

Kim, Seok Hyun, "Erga Omnes Character of the Obligations of Human Rights Protection in International Law," *Korean Journal of International Law*, Vol.59, No.4, 2014.

Kim, Seong Won, "A Review on the Constitutionalization of International Law," *Korean Journal of International Law*, Vol.58, No.4, 2013.

Kim, Eung Ryeol, "The Refugee Convention and Treatment of Koreans in Japan," *Journal of Asian Studies*, No.88, 1992.

Kim, Hyun Gi, "Possibility and Future of Maritime cooperation in

Northeast Asia," *Military Forum*, Vol. 29, 2001.

Kim, Hyun Soo, "Legal Analysis of the Issue of Passage in the Jeju Strait"(Paper Presented at the 2003 Korean Society on Marine Environment & Safety Fall Conference, 2003).

_____, "Military Activities in the EEZ under Law of the Sea," *Ocean Law Research*, Vol. 15, 2003.

Kong, Stephen, "The Right of Innocent Passage: a Case Study on Two Koreas," *Minnesota Journal of Global Trade*, Vol. 11, 2002.

Kontorovich, Eugene, "The Piracy Analogy: Modern Universal Jurisdiction's Hollow Foundation," *Harvard Int'l Law Journal*, Vol. 45, 2004.

Krahmann, Elke, "National, Regional, and Global Governance: One Phenomenon or Many?" *Global Governance*, Vol. 9, No. 3, 2003.

Kumm, Mattias, "International Law in National Courts: The International Rule of Law and the Limits of the Internationalist Model," *Vanderbilt Journal of Int'l Law*, Vol. 44, 2003.

_____, "The Legitimacy of International Law: A Constitutionalist Framework of Analysis," *European Journal of International Law*, Vol. 15, 2004.

Kwon, Moon Sang, Yong Hee Lee, and Seong Wook Park, "Study of the EEZ Fisheries Management System among Korea, China and Japan and the New Fisheries Agreement," *Korean Journal of International Law*, Vol. 44, No. 1, 1999.

Lee, Chang-Ryeol, "Ieodo EEZ: Firm Action against China Necessary," *Dokdo Research Journal*, Vol 16, 2011.

Lee, Ho Yong, "Permanent Resident Aliens' Right to Vote in Local Elections According to the Japanese Constitution," *International Human Rights Law*, No. 4, 2001.

Lee, Hyeok Seob, "Multilateral Security Agreement of Northeast Asia and Its Realization in the 21$^{st}$ Century," *Korean Journal of International Relations*, Vol 36, No. 3, 1997.

Lee, Sang Woo, "Increase of Soviet Navy and the Safety of Northeast Asian Sea lane," in Dal-choong Kim, ed., *Korea and Sea Lane Security*(Beopmunsa, 1988).

Lee, Seo Hang, "Changes in the Northeast Asian Maritime Security and Future Development of the Korean Navy," *Military Forum*, Vol. 29, 2001.

Lee, Seok Yong, "Territorial Violation of North Korean Vessels and State Security," *Military Forum*, Vol. 29, 2001.

Lee, Suk Jong, "Local Political Rights for Koreans in Japan: Current Status and Outlook," *Political Trends and Policies*, July 2001.

Lee, Wei-chin, "Troubles under the Water: Sino-Japanese Conflict of Sovereignty on the Continental Shelf in the East China Sea," *Ocean Development and International Law*, Vol.18 No.5, 1987.

Ma, Young Sam, "International Legal Personality of NGOs," *Korean Yearbook of International Law*, Vol.4, 2004.

Mangone, Gerard J., "The Dynamics of International Law for the Next Century"(unpublished paper) presented at Jeju National University on 21 November, 1994.

Mann, F. A., "The Doctrine of Jurisdiction in International Law," *Recueil des Cours* (1964, I).

McWhinney, Edward, "Shifting Paradigms of International Law and World Order in an Era of Historical Transition," in Sienho Yee and Wang Tieya, eds., *International Law in the Post-Cold War World: Essays in Memory of Li Haopei*(London and New York: Routledge, 2001).

Menon, P. K., "The International Personality of Individuals in International Law: A Broadening of the Traditional Doctrine." *Journal of Transnational Law and Policy*, Vol.1, 1992.

Meron, Theodor, "International Criminalization of Internal Atrocities," *American Journal of International Law*, Vol.89, 1995.

Meyer, William H. & Stefanova, Boyka, "Human Rights, the UN Global Compact and Global Governance," *Cornell Int'l Law Journal*, Vol.34, 2001.

Milewicz, Karolina, "Emerging Patterns of Global Constitutionalization: Toward a Conceptual Framework," *Indiana Journal of International Law*, Vol.16, Issue 2, 2014.

Moon, Kyoung Su, "The Origin of the Ethnic Korean Community in Japan," *Journal of East Asian Studies*, Vol.9, Jeju National University, 1998.

Morais, Herbert V., "The Globalization of Human Rights Law and the Role of International financial Institutions in Promoting Human Right." *George Washington Int'l Law Review (A Festschrift Honoring Professor Louis B. Sohn* (April 8, 2000), Vol.33, 2000.

Morris, Virgina & M.-Christiane Bourloyannis-Vrailas, "The Work of the Sixth Committee at the Fiftieth Session of the UN General Assembly," *American Journal of International Law*, Vol.90, pp.491-500.

Mutharika, Peter, "The Role of the United Nations Security Council in African Peace Management: Some Proposals," *Michigan Journal of International Law*, Vol.17, 1996.

Moyo, Monica P., "The International Rule of Law: An Analysis," *Minnesota International Law Journal*, Vol.23, 2014.

Nagan, Winston P., "Global Governance: A New Paradigm for the Rule of Law," *Cadmus*, Vol.2, Issue 1, 2013.

Nanda, V. P., "International Law in the Twenty-first Century," in

Nandasiri Jasentuliyana ed., *Perspectives on International law* (London · The Hague · Boston: Kluwer Law International, 1995).

Noh, Hong Gil, "Properties of the Waters Surrounding Socotra Reef in Terms of Fisheries," *Ocean Policy*, Vol.6, 1991.

Nowrot, Karsten, "Legal Consequences of Globalization: The Status of Non-Governmental Organizations under International Law," *Indiana Journal of Global Legal Studies*, Vol.6, Spring, 1999.

O'Connor, Sandra Day, "Vindicating the Rule of Law: Balancing Competing Demands for Justice." Dorsen, Norman & Gifford, Prosser, *Democracy and the Rule of Law* (CQ Press, 2001).

Oh, Tong Seok, "The Political Rights of Foreign Residents in Korea: A Constitutional Perspective," (Seoul National University School of Law Center for Public Interest and Human Rights Law; http://jus.snu.ac.kr/~bk21).

Okuda, K., "The Legal Status of Foreigners in Japan," *Journal of Social Science Studies*, Vol.27, No.2.

Ong, David M., "The Dispute Settlement Mechanism of the 1982 UN Convention on the Law of the Sea: Implications for East Asia," Kim, Dal-choong et al. eds., *Convention on the Law of the Sea and East Asia* (Institute of East and West Studies, 1996).

Onuma, Y., "A Study on the Legal Status of Koreans in Japan (Part II)," *Journal of the Japanese Society of Law*, Vol.97, No.4.

_____, "Rethinking the Rights of Foreigners in Japan," *International Law Issues* (special publication for the 70th birthday of Dr. Lee, Han-gi), 1986.

Oxman, Bernard H., "The 1994 Agreement and the Convention," *American Journal of International Law*, Vol.88, 1994.

Paik, Jin Hyun, "Development of Korea's Maritime Policy and Sea Power," in 21st *Century and Korea's Maritime Security*(conference proceedings), 1994.

Paik, Jin Hyun, "Asia-pacific Maritime Security Cooperation Challenge and Its Future," *International Area Studies*, Vol. 8, No. 3, 1999.

Paollilo, Felipe H., "The Future Legal Regime of Seabed Resources and the NIEO: Some Issues," Hossain, K. ed., *Legal Aspects of the New International Economic Order* (Nichols Publishing Company, 1980).

Pardo, Arvid, "Ocean, Space and Mankind," *Third World Quarterly*, Vol.6, 1984.

Pardo, Arvid & Christol, Carl Q., "The Common Interest: Tension Between the Whole and the Parts," MacDonald, R. St. J. & Johnston, Douglas M. eds., *The Structure and Process of International Law: Essays in Legal Philosophy, Doctrine and Theory* (Dordrecht: Martinus Nijhoff Publishers, 1986).

Park, Chan-Ho, Che-Hyung Kim, Hyun-Soo Kim, Seok-Yong Lee and Chang-Wee Lee, *Handbook to the UNCLOS I* (Ji-in Books, 2009).

Paulson, Stanley L., "Neumann's Rule of Law," *Diritto E Cultura*, Edizioni Scientifiche Italiane, 1/92.

Peters, Anne, "The Merits of Global Constitutionalism," *Indiana Journal of Global Legal Studies*, Vol.16, Issue 2, 2009.

Plunkett, Mark, "Reestablishing Law and Order in Peace-Maintenance," *Global Governance*, Vol.4, No.1, 1998.

Raz, Joseph, "The Rule of Law and its Virtue," Cunningham, Robert L. ed., *Liberty and the Rule of Law* (Texas A & M University Press, 1979).

Reydams, Luc, "Belgium Reneges on Universality: The 5 August 2003 Act on Grave Breaches of International Humanitarian Law," *Journal of Int'l Criminal Justice*, Vol.1, 2003.

Romano, "The Shift from the Consensual to the Compulsory Paradigm in International Adjudication," *New York University Journal of International Law & Politics*, Vol. 29, 2007.

Rose, Arnold, "Minorities," Sills, David L., ed., *International Encyclopedia of the Social Sciences*, Vol.10.

Sammons, Anthony, "The "Under Theorization" of Universal Jurisdiction: Implication for Legitimacy on Trials of War Criminals By National Courts," *Berkeley Journal of Int'l Law*, Vol.21, 2003.

Sato, K., "The Subjects of Basic Rights," Abe, T. ed., *Constitutional Theories and Precedents I*, 1976.

Schachte, Jr., William L. and J. Peter A. Bernhardt, "International Straits and Navigational Freedoms," Virginia, *Journal of International Law*, Vol. 33, 1993.

Schwebel, Stephen M., "Widening the Advisory Jurisdiction of the International Court of Justice without Amending its Statute," *Catholic University Law Review*, Vol.33, 1984.

Shim, Jae Seol, "Treasure Trove for Ocean Science: Ieodo," *in Ieodo: What Is It to Us Now?*, Proceedings for Policy Debate of Congressman Chang-Il Kang, 2007.

_____, Park Gwang-Soon, and Lee Dong-Yeong, "Construction Analysis of the Ieodo Ocean Research Station," *Ocean Policy Research*, Vol 11, 1996.

Slaughter, Anne-Marie, "The Real New World Order," *Foreign Affairs*, Vol.76, No.5, 1997.

Sloan, Blaine, "The United Nations Charter as a Constitution," *Pace Yearbook of International Law*, Vol.1, 1989.

So, Byung Chun, "Sone Thoughts on Discourse of Sovereignty in International Law," *The Korean Journal of International Law*, Vol.58, No.4, 2013.

Sohn, Louis B., "Settlement of Disputes Arising out of the Law of the Sea Convention," *San Diego Law Review*, Vol.12, 1975.

Steven, Lee A., "Genocide and the Duty to Extradite or Prosecute: Why the United States is in Breach of Its International Obligations," *Vanderbilt Journal of Int'l Law*, Vol.39, 1999.

Sucharitkul, Sompong, "Legal Developments in the First Half of the United Nations Decade of International Law," *ASIL Interest Group on the UN Decade of International Law Newsletter* (Issue No. 11), June 1996.

Suh, Po Geon, "Japanese Debate on Foreigners' Rights to Political Participation," *Journal of Public Law*, Vol.30, No.5, 2002.

Suh, Yong Dal & Kim, Yong Ki, "Ethnic Koreans' Rights of Participation in Local Politics," *Journal of Management And Economics*, Vol.33, No.1, 2000.

Summers, Mark A., "The International Court of Justice's Decision in Congo v. Belgium: How Has It Affected The Development of a Principle of Universal Jurisdiction That Would Obligate All States to Prosecute War Criminals," *Boston University Int'l Law Journal*, Vol.21, 2003.

The Federation of Korean Residents in Japan, "The Issue of Local Political Rights," Joseon Sinbo Publishing, 1996.

Thornburgh, Dick, "Today's United Nations in a Changing World," *American University Journal of International Law and Policy*, Vol.9, 1993.

To, Hoe Geun, "The Legal Status of Koreans in Japan," *Social Science Papers*, Vol.11, No.1, Ulsan University, 2001.

Tracy, Christopher, "The Growing Role of Non-Governmental Organization," *American Society of International Law Proceedings* (April, 1955).

Tyagi, Yogesh K., "The System of Settlement of Disputes under the Law of the Sea Convention: An Overview," *The Indian Journal of International Law*, Vol.25, No.2, 1985.

Tzevelekos, Vassilis P., "Revisiting the Humanization of International Law: Limits and Potential," *Erasmus Law Review*, June 2013.

UN Secretary-General, "The Secretary-General Statement to the Social Meetings of the General Assembly on Reform," New York, 16 July 1997 (http://www.un.org).

Urabe, N., "The Japanese Constitution and Foreigners' Right to Vote," Suh, Y. D. ed., *Permanent Residents' Right to Participate in Local Politics* (Nippon Hyoronsa, 1992).

Weiss, Thomas G. & Gordenker, Leon, "Pluralizing Global Governance: Analytical Approaches and Dimensions," Weiss, Thomas G. & Gordenker, Leon, eds., *NGOs, The UN, & Global Governance* (Lynne Rienner Publishers, 1996).

Wilner, Gabriel M., "The Role of the United Nations in the Maintenance of Peace before and after the Year Two Thousand: Introduction," *Georgia Journal of International and Comparative Law*, Vol.26, 1996.

Wolfrum, Rudiger, "Common Heritage of Mankind," in: R. Bernhardt (ed.), *Encyclopedia of Public International Law*, Installment 11, 1989.

Yun, Yong Taek, "The Legal Status of Ethnic Koreans in Japan," *Journal of Legal Studies*, Vol.22, Chonbuk National University, 2001.

Zoller, Elisabeth, "Institutional Aspects of International Governance," *Indiana Journal of Global Legal Studies*, Vol.3, 1995.

# Index

# Author

**Boo Chan Kim**, LL.B.(Seoul National University College of Law),
LL.M. and LL.D.(Pusan National University) is presently Professor of
International Law and Legal Philosophy at Jeju National
University(JNU) Law School. He researched as a Visiting Scholar
& Professor at Washington University in St. Louis Law School and
visited Cornell University Law School twice as a Visiting Scholar.
And he worked as a Visiting Professor at Soka University Law
School in Japan.

He served as the Dean of Planning Affairs, the Director of
Industrial–Academic Cooperation Foundation, and the Director of
the East Asian Institute at JNU. He served as the member of the
Policy Planning Committee of Jeju Free International City of
Government, the member of the International Law Advisory
Committee at the Ministry of Foreign Affairs(MOFA) and the
member of Legislative Support Committee of National Assembly
of Korea. And he served as the President of the Korean
International Law Review Association and the President of the
Korean Society of International Law(KSIL). He also served as the
President of the Youngnam Association of International Law and
the Director of the Dokdo Center at the KSIL. He is currently
serving as the member of the Committee of the Law of the Sea
at the Korean Coast Guard. He is currently member of the

American Society of International Law(ASIL), the Academic Council on the United Nations System(ACUNS), and the International Law Association(ILA).

He is the author of books; *Fundamentals of Legal Science*(1994), *New Lectures on International Law*(co-authorship, 2004), *The Strategy for Internationalization of Jeju*(2007), *Global Governance & International Law*(2011), *Special Lectures on International Law*(2014), *The Law of the Sea and Ieodo Problem*(2015), *Revised Edition of Special Lectures on International Law*(2018), *Dangerous Ideas in Law*(co-authorship, 2018) and *Law's Dilemmas* (co-authorship, 2020), and other scholarly books. In addition, he wrote many articles on International Law and Legal Philosophy.

Email: kimboo@jejunu.ac.kr

revised edition

## GLOBAL GOVERNANCE
## and INTERNATIONAL LAW

– Some Global and Regional Issues –


**Date of issue**   August 25, 2020

**Author**   Boo Chan Kim

**Publisher**   Heung Guk Kim

**Publishing Company**   Bogosabooks
337–15, Hoedong–gil, Paju–si, Kyeonggi–do
**TEL.**   82–2–922–2246
**E–MAIL**   kanapub3@naver.com

Price 30,000won

ISBN 979–11–6587–077–5   93360
ⓒ Boo Chan Kim, 2020 printed in Korea